CW00515738

CHINOOK ZD576

The Concealed Evidence

The final part of a trilogy

David Hill

The right of David Hill to be identified as author of this work has been asserted by him under the Copyright, Designs and Patents Act 1988.

The views expressed are those of the author alone and should not be taken to represent those of His Majesty's Government, the Ministry of Defence, HM Armed Forces or any Government agency, unless quoted. The events outlined are real.

Books by David Hill, in paperback and Kindle

Breaking the Military Covenant

Citadel of Waste

The Mull of Kintyre Trilogy:

Their Greatest Disgrace - The campaign to clear the Chinook ZD576 pilots

The Inconvenient Truth - Chinook ZD576: Cause & Culpability

Chinook ZD576 - The Concealed Evidence

The Red Arrows:

Red 5 - An investigation into the death of Flight Lieutenant Sean Cunningham

A Noble Anger - The manslaughter of Corporal Jonathan Bayliss

Citadel of Waste

All titles published by Nemesis Books

nemesisbooks@aol.com

The issues related in these books are ongoing, and they will be regularly updated. If you have purchased a previous edition, please contact the publisher for a free Kindle or pdf version.

https://sites.google.com/site/militaryairworthiness/home

All proceeds to St Richard's Hospice, Worcester

https://www.strichards.org.uk/raise-funds/

Acknowledgements

Air Commodore John Blakeley, engineer.

Squadron Leader Robert Burke, test pilot.

Tony Cable, Senior Engineering Inspector, Air Accidents Investigation Branch.

Captain Robin Cane, pilot.

Brian Dixon. BZ.

The late Captains Dick Hadlow and Ralph Kohn, and Captain Ron Macdonald, the '3 Fellows' of the Royal Aeronautical Society.

Dr Susan Phoenix, retired military nurse (Queen Alexandra's Royal Army Nursing Corps).

Contents

ADDENDA

Introduction (2024)

This reference book presents the main submission to Lord Philip Alexander's Mull of Kintyre Review. It is intended for those wishing to understand the detailed evidence that persuaded the Government to quash the findings of gross negligence against the Chinook ZD576 pilots. It is technical and procedural by nature, the essential point being the RAF investigation did not look at any of the matters discussed; and therefore the Fatal Accident Inquiry could not. It reveals what was actively concealed by MoD. The sole aim was to establish doubt, in a case where the legal test was *absolutely no doubt whatsoever*.

It is not a critique of the RAF's accident investigation. For that, may I point you to the Engineering Review of the Board of Inquiry, written by Air Commodore John Blakeley in 2003, and reproduced in full in 'The Inconvenient Truth' (2021) - the second part of this trilogy and which considers cause and culpability. We both looked at the airworthiness aspect, which the Board did not mention at all. John concentrated on continuing airworthiness of ZD57; while I studied attaining and maintaining airworthiness of the aircraft type (Chinook HC Mk2), offering a detailed analysis of the faults and defects found in what remained of ZD576. There is overlap, and I fully acknowledge and agree with John's work.

A general note on submitting to such Reviews. One can approach this in two ways. In 2007, with the Nimrod Review, I offered an Executive Summary of key issues (reproduced herein), inviting the Review to say what they wished me to expand on. I quickly realised this didn't work, not least because MoD had inveigled its way into the Review (e.g. providing the secretary) and it was unclear if submissions were reaching Mr Haddon-Cave. The factual errors in his report reinforce this suspicion. It was only when the father of one of the deceased hand-delivered a later submission that he acknowledged receipt.

When it came to submitting to the Mull of Kintyre Review, the public were given a 2-3 month deadline (beginning of November 2010); which is not long on such a complex subject. I contacted his secretary, this time provided by the Scottish Office, who advised me to send everything I wanted to. I did, and in the event Lord Philip asked for more, sought two extensions, and sat for around 10 months; completing his task in July 2011. In addition to the contents of this book, I submitted a CD-ROM containing 482MB of supporting evidence. That is not included here for obvious reasons, but it is important to understand that every statement made herein is supported within that evidence; and Lord Philip accepted this. I invite you to compare and contrast my submission with the official MoD and Government position.

My motivation in publishing so many years after the event is two-fold.

First, it complements my two books on the accident: 'Their Greatest Disgrace', about the campaign to clear the pilots, and 'The Inconvenient Truth'. Second, despite the Government and Defence Council accepting Lord Philip's recommendation to overturn the findings against Flight Lieutenants Jon Tapper and Rick Cook, neither they nor MoD have accepted his full report. Nor have they made public or acted upon the facts revealed; a failure of duty of care that resulted in more deaths by the same root causes. Moreover, a small number of very senior RAF officers, both serving and retired, continue to vent in the media about the pilots' guilt. It is never explained that this cabal have personal liability; or that the system allows them to act as judge, jury and executioner, blaming the innocent while marking their own homework.

The families and their technical and legal advisors are seldom given the opportunity to present the truth; and on the odd occasion they have, MoD has refused to debate the issue. Their voice must be heard, especially in the face of the RAF's formal stance. Lord Philip:

'(Air Chief Marshal) Sir John Day's approach places the onus of disproving negligence on the deceased, which is also wrong'.[1]

This position is so venal, those who proposed it and still support it must be named and shamed. Also, the notion that these very senior officers are above the law, and cannot be wrong by virtue of their rank, must be aired and challenged.

For 17 years MoD and Government called for 'new' evidence before they would consider reviewing the case. This submission proves new evidence was not required - sufficient was available but they chose to ignore it because the truth was too inconvenient. Nevertheless it provides it, revealing that the offences committed by these senior officers were so serious as to be imprisonable.

---

1 Mull of Kintyre Review, paragraph 6.2.9.

Lord Philip's report is 112 pages, but the key passage is in paragraph 2.2.8:

'Having considered all the advice available the Controller Aircraft, Sir Donald Spiers, issued an INTERIM Controller Aircraft Release for the HC-2 on 9 November 1993 which contained (and therefore mandated) these recommendations. This was followed shortly after by Assistant Chief of the Air Staff, Air Chief Marshal (ret) Sir Anthony Bagnall, issuing the HC-2 Release To Service. The two documents were essentially identical carrying forward the mandated restrictions of the Interim Controller Aircraft Release.'

I explain this in full; but briefly the Controller Aircraft Release is the statement by MoD's Controller Aircraft to the Assistant Chief of the Air Staff (ACAS) that the aircraft is airworthy at a given build standard, subject to stated Limitations. It is not authority to fly the aircraft. That is provided by ACAS. The key word is *'mandated'*. What Lord Philip omitted, perhaps for political expediency, was an explanation of the significance of 'INTERIM', and *what* was mandated...

INTERIM is not a temporal term, but a type of clearance providing 'Switch-On Only' clearance. It means the aircraft or equipment in not to be relied upon in any way whatsoever. What did mandate apply to? Among other things, the Navigation System, in its entirety. The Fuel Computers, and hence the Engines. This prohibited engine start-up, never mind flight, but aircrew were not told this.

The precise reasons were set out in a series of reports by MoD's experts, including RAF pilots and engineers, at the Aeroplane and Armament Experimental Establishment, Boscombe Down. I dissect them in detail, revealing it was mandated upon ACAS that they be read in conjunction with a document issued *'in the form of INTERIM Controller Aircraft Release Recommendations'*. It was not a 'release' of any kind, but a progress report reporting little progress. One reason was Boscombe had yet to receive a representative Chinook HC Mk2, which is a significant hindrance when tasked with testing one. What they had, they termed a *'prototype'*.

On 2 June 1994 the Chinook HC Mk2 was not to be relied upon in any way, and the RAF were not permitted to fly it. To withhold that key information must have been deliberate, and one must ask *Who benefitted?* This was the only 'new' evidence contained in the Review's report, so there can be no doubt it is what prompted the quashing of the findings.

The Board of Inquiry consisted a Wing Commander (pilot) and two Squadron Leaders (pilot and engineer). In RAF terms, these are senior officers. Their narrative report did not say the pilots were negligent to any degree. That was a decision taken by the two Senior Reviewing Officers and the Chief of the Air Staff.

The Board President, who in 2013 himself became Chief of the Air Staff, later voiced regret at his choice of words when proposing that the aircraft Captain made an error of judgment. Moreover, the hitherto concealed evidence proves his report wrong in crucial areas. The Board must be reconvened, by order of the Defence Council, and re-issue its report based on the known facts; especially the central point of the Review, that the Mk2 was unairworthy. In saying this, I accept that the members were grossly misled and lied to.

As the Senior Reviewing Officers' remarks, finding gross negligence, are now seen to be set aside, they must be replaced. When ordering the Board be reconvened the Council must appoint new Reviewing Officers, or perhaps simply annotate the new report that no blame is attached to the deceased pilots.

Similarly, the Fatal Accident Inquiry must be re-opened. I have proposed elsewhere that this could be a brief affair; the Sheriff, Sir Stephen Young, now 3rd Baronet of Partick, issuing a statement that he, too, accepts the 'new' evidence; and reflects this in a revised determination.

Significantly, there is also the evidence we know of, but have not seen. This, too, must be made public. For example, eye-witness testimony from fishermen, a yachtsman, and potentially US servicemen on the Mull. Also, the priests at Garron Tower who were the last to see ZD576 head out from the Northern Ireland coast across the North Channel. Meaningfully, their evidence, referred to briefly just once in the House of Lords, wholly contradicts that of the Chief of the Air Staff; who was not there but remains insistent they were *some miles off course*. Unfortunately for Air Chief Marshal Graydon, the priests saw the aircraft heading slightly left of the Mull headland, precisely on course. A neutral observer might think it convenient to MoD that this was not revealed by its investigation. Crucially, it has emerged that physical evidence in the form of personal electronic devices were removed from the scene by security services, and withheld from accident investigators; and personal possessions, such as wrist watches, have not been returned. In an accident where MoD's claims as to excessive speed relied on precise timing of take-off and impact, this is dubious and untrustworthy behaviour. It is more than that. It defeated the ends of justice. It was criminal.

Any or all of this would have a profound knock-on effect. Police Scotland's current position is the same as the London Government's. *The case is closed, as the guilty are known. They are dead, so no further action is necessary.* But the guilty are not dead. Lord Philip's report, and the quashing of the findings, demand that the police inquiry into 29 deaths re-open. (If there ever was one to begin with, of which there is no evidence and about which Police Scotland refuses to comment).

The disposition of the case rests with the Lord Advocate in Edinburgh, the senior law officer in Scotland and a Government Minister. Successive incumbents have refused to re-open the Fatal Accident Inquiry, or instruct the police. That is bad enough; but they have in the process wilfully ignored the known facts, content in the certain knowledge their 1996 Inquiry was lied to. However, the Crown Office and Procurator Fiscal's Service, who act on behalf of the Lord Advocate, *have* considered the 'new' facts; albeit briefly. (They have everything in this Submission). Their decision was that, despite the accident and deaths occurring in Scotland, this was a matter for the Metropolitan Police in London, as that is where the offences took place.[2] (Primarily, the decision to issue the illegal airworthiness certification, a known fact it does not challenge). Unsurprisingly, the Met have not replied to formal complaints. This impasse needs resolving at a political level.

Meanwhile, the bereaved families, all 29 of them, are in limbo. Who caused the death of their loved ones? It is clear some have accepted the findings against the pilots, and moved on as best they can. A small few have always taken a keen interest in the facts and sought to understand them, remaining consumed by grief and the deceits perpetrated upon them. The parents of the two pilots have passed away. Only one lived to see his son cleared. But the pilots' children deserve the truth.

As matters stand, if one asks MoD for the official record it will provide a report saying the pilots are guilty. At the very least the 'new' evidence must be placed in the official record. Until then, this book will have to suffice.

This case is not over. Not by a long way.

David Hill, January 2024

---

2 Crown Office & Procurator Fiscal Service, Scottish Fatalities Unit, letter LP-4, 8 November 2016.

SUBMISSION FOR CONSIDERATION BY THE MULL OF KINTYRE REVIEW

A report discussing systemic airworthiness failings in the Ministry of Defence, and how this affected the Chinook HC Mk2 in 1993/94

Prepared by David Hill

Issue 4 - June 2011

Submitted to: Mr Alex Passa, Secretary, The Mull of Kintyre Review, 1 Melville Crescent, Edinburgh EH3 7HW (For the attention of The Right Honourable Lord Alexander Philip)

Issue Record

Issue 1   10.11.10 Initial Submission to Mull of Kintyre Review.

Issue 2   25.1.11   Addition of Addenda A, B & C. Updated Bibliography supplied separately to the Review on CD-ROM.

Issue 3   31.5.11   Major update following receipt of CHART report. Addition of Appendix 12. Updated Bibliography supplied separately to the Review on CD-ROM.

Issue 4   26.6.11   Minor update including CHART analysis.

In this published version all tables have been converted to narrative to cater for e-books, and minor typographical errors corrected.

Executive Summary

This submission presents evidence that the systemic failure to implement MoD's airworthiness regulations and procedures, confirmed by Mr Haddon-Cave QC in his Nimrod Review of 2007-09 [B1], applied equally to the Chinook HC Mk1 and Mk2.[3] Consequently, an immature Chinook HC Mk2 was released to service in November 1993. The attendant risks and hazards were not advised to aircrew.

The aim is to demonstrate that, far from being negligent to a gross degree, the pilots were themselves victims of an abrogation of duty of care and maladministration amounting to gross negligence; which knowingly placed them, their fellow aircrew, and passengers, at grave risk. And that this introduces overwhelming doubt as to the safety of the findings. Evidence is offered demonstrating:

- MoD policies and practices of the day compromised the ability of staff holding airworthiness delegation to carry out their duties in accordance with the Secretary of State for Defence's regulations and Controller Aircraft Instructions.

- The effect of these policies and practices was ignored at the highest level, despite a series of official reports, audits and warnings.

- Airworthiness regulations were not implemented properly and the Chinook HC Mk2 was non-compliant on numerous counts.

- Previous Chinook accidents had been directly attributed to these systemic failings.

Also discussed is evidence not assessed by the Board of Inquiry, the Fatal Accident Inquiry, or the Houses of Commons and Lords. In the context of maturity of design, understanding of the aircraft, and airworthiness, this includes evidence that:

- The implementation of safety critical software was condemned as *'positively dangerous'* by MoD's Independent Safety Auditor.

- The INTERIM Controller Aircraft Release, mandated upon the Assistant Chief of the Air Staff, granted Switch-On Only clearance only, meaning the RAF was prohibited from relying on the aircraft in any way whatsoever.

- The Release to Service (the Master Airworthiness Reference) issued by the Assistant Chief of the Air Staff on 22 November 1993 ignored

---

3 https://www.gov.uk/government/publications/the-nimrod-review

this mandate, falsely stating the aircraft was airworthy. This misled aircrew into believing the airworthiness regulations had been implemented properly.

This submission recommends the Review establishes, through interview, why senior RAF staff in the airworthiness chain of command chose to disregard the regulations they were bound by. Moreover, given the influence in such matters attributed to him by Mr Haddon-Cave, the RAF Chief Engineer of the day (Air Chief Marshal Sir Michael Alcock) should be asked what part he, his staff, or his superiors played in the decision to disregard orders. Also, what action he took following the publication of (a) the Chinook Airworthiness Review Team report of 1992, and (b) the ZD576 Board of Inquiry report. Both reported evidence of systemic airworthiness failings. When considering these issues, the Review is invited to reflect on whether any degree of negligence, maladministration, failure of Duty of Care, or misleading by omission or commission, occurred before or after the accident.

Mr Haddon-Cave noted *'the episode of cuts, change, dilution and distraction'* that adversely affected airworthiness, but erroneously baselined this at 1998. In doing so, he named and blamed the wrong senior officers.[4] These factors were evident on Chinook from 1985, and systemically from 1988. While I am generally supportive of the Nimrod Review, the errors of fact contained therein had the effect of diverting attention from longer standing systemic failings and those responsible; notably in the Mull of Kintyre case.

This submission is in many ways an Addendum to the Nimrod Review. It includes a comprehensive audit trail, from initial notification of the failings in 1985 to the Review's 2009 report; encompassing the development, conversion, and release to service of the Chinook HC Mk2. In doing so, it explains direct linkages to Nimrod XV230 and other accidents. This, then, is the detailed background to Mr Haddon-Cave's confirmation that:

'There was a shift in culture and priorities in the MoD toward business and financial targets, at the expense of functional values such as safety and airworthiness.'[5]

---

4 Nimrod Review, chapter 1, paragraph 22.
5 Nimrod Review, chapter 1, paragraph 21.

Section 1 - Introduction

Background

On 2 June 1994 RAF Chinook HC Mk2 ZD576 crashed on the southern tip of the Kintyre Peninsula (the Mull of Kintyre), Argyll, Scotland, killing all four crew and 25 passengers.

RAF regulations stated:

'Only in cases in which there is <u>absolutely no doubt whatsoever</u> should deceased aircrew be found negligent'.[6]

The RAF Board of Inquiry reported:

'There were many potential causes of the accident and despite detailed and in-depth analysis, the Board was unable to determine a definite cause'.[7]

The Senior Reviewing Officers, Air Chief Marshal Sir William Wratten and Air Vice Marshal John Day, disagreed. Based on the same evidence, they found the pilots negligent to a gross degree.

Source Material

This submission draws on various MoD policies, regulations, procedures and guidelines issued to staff having airworthiness delegation, or who contribute toward airworthiness/safety and financial probity. These staff are advised to retain full records of decisions and recommendations they make, especially when they are overruled. This, because a decision may have to be defended, so the decision making process must be documented and all judgments and assumptions validated. Especially so following repeal of Section 10 of the Crown Proceedings Act (1947), which effectively removed Crown Immunity for individuals. Therefore, this submission also draws on contemporaneous notes and diaries.

A detailed Bibliography (contents annotated as [B#]) is included, but the nature of many documents means maintained copies must be obtained from MoD. (The ability, or otherwise, of MoD to supply these documents is itself an excellent test of the airworthiness system, due to the requirement to retain a full audit trail). Primary sources are:

- The INTERIM Controller Aircraft Release, at Amendment 1. [B2]

- The INTERIM Release to Service, at Amendment 1. [B3]

---

6 AP3207, Annex G, paragraph 9.
7 RAF Board of Inquiry report, paragraph 2.37.

- The Board of Inquiry report. [B4]
- A&AEE Boscombe Down Letter reports (various).
- The Macdonald Report (2000) (aka 'The 3 Fellows' report). [B5]
- First-hand experience of various serving and retired aircrew, groundcrew, and former MoD(PE), Air Member Supply and Organisation (AMSO) and Air Member Logistics (AML) staff.

And by reference to the following MoD material:

- Controller Aircraft Instructions - Replaced AvP88 Handbook of Controller Aircraft Instructions in 1991. Their purpose was to ensure procurement policy was implemented consistently, and were mandated upon all staff and in all aircraft related contracts. [B6]
- Joint Service Publication 553 - Military Airworthiness Regulations. [B7]
- Compendium of Guidelines for Project Managers - first published in 1977 to supplement AvP88. Final amendment was by Amendment List 22 in 1991, pending replacement by Chief of Defence Procurement Instructions (never fully promulgated and later abandoned). [B8]
- Defence Standard 05-123 - Technical Procedures for the Procurement of Aircraft, Weapons and Electronic Systems (formerly AvP123, but not a direct replacement). [B9]
- Defence Standard 05-124 - Technical Procedures for the Procurement of Aircraft Engines and their Accessories. [B10]
- Defence Standard 05-125/2 - Technical Procedures for Post Design Services (Electronic Equipment), incorporating (as book 2) Post Design Services Specifications 1-20. (Formerly AvP45, but not a direct replacement, and mandated in all aviation contracts). [B11]
- Defence Standard 00-970 - Design and Airworthiness Requirements for Service Aircraft. [B12]
- Defence Council Instruction GEN 89/1993 - Airworthiness Responsibility for UK Military Aircraft. [B13/B6]
- DUS(D)/924/11/2/9 dated 14 December 1989 - Joint MoD(PE) / Industry Computing Policy for Military Operational Systems. [B14]
- D/MAP/12/20B-38 Issue 3 dated November 1993 - Application of Technical Procedures. [B15/B6]

Terminology constantly changes in MoD, as does the legislation it is bound by. When discussing regulations, requirements, procedures and practices, those extant *at the time* are used. It is a feature of MoD responses that it speaks in the present tense. For example, a common statement is *'the Chinook Integrated Project Team (IPT) has no record'* (of an event) - disingenuous when discussing events of 1993/4, as the IPT was only formed in 1999. [B17] Also, the implication is that only the Chinook IPT would know the answer, when in fact the structure of the MoD means they may not, but many others do. MoD's airworthiness regulations require retention of this corporate knowledge and audit trail. Numerous examples of failure to comply are cited.

The Safety Case, Controller Aircraft Release and the Release to Service

Detailed MoD airworthiness procedures are discussed, using terminology often unique to MoD. Please refer to the Glossary of Terms and Abbreviations. But the three most important terms, Safety Case, Controller Aircraft Release, and the Release to Service need explaining now. An early 1990s timeframe is being discussed.

The Safety Case

Before being made compulsory in MoD the Safety Case was often referred to as the Safety Argument. A Safety Case is the:

'Study of an aircraft or item of aircraft equipment to identify and show acceptability (or otherwise) of the potential hazards associated with it. It provides a reasoned argument, supported by evidence, establishing why the Design Authority is satisfied that the aircraft is safe to use and fit for its intended purpose'.

(From the Westland Helicopters Limited Safety Case Policy, WER-01006-20-128, dated March 1993 - the policy during Chinook HC Mk2 development and at the time of Release to Service. This reflected the definition used by the Aeroplane and Armament Experimental Establishment (A&AEE) at Boscombe Down, Wiltshire when making airworthiness recommendations).

Unlike most areas of the law, the activity is not presumed to be safe (innocent) until proven unsafe (guilty). The Safety Case/Argument must prove the system or aircraft is safe, so there is a different legal starting point. As Chinook HC Mk2 was in Service (obviously) at the time of the accident, there should have been three levels of Safety Case.

1. The Designer's (Boeing Helicopters), addressing the whole aircraft configuration identified in the Master Record Index.

2. The MoD Project Director's, comprising the Designer's Safety Case plus the safety justifications used by the Project Director to underpin

17

his own certification. This addresses the aircraft configuration as presented for Controller Aircraft Release trials. As such, there are occasions when (1) and (2) are the same. This utilises independent assessments (e.g. from Boscombe), Safety Cases for Government Furnished Equipment, and other, non-standard equipment. This Safety Case must reconcile any differences between the various sources of evidence.

3. The Release to Service Authority's, subsuming the first two plus the safety justifications used to underpin the Release to Service. This evolves to include, for example, Service Engineered Modifications, Service Deviations, and Special Trials Fits. Again, but less likely, this can be the same as the Project Director's Safety Case.

Safety Cases are referenced to a defined build standard, and in turn to a Statement of Operating Intent and Usage. Therefore, by definition, these must be valid and maintained. The process by which this is achieved is governed by Defence Standard 05-125/2 (above); hence why it is mandated in all aviation contracts.

The Controller Aircraft Release (CAR)

The CAR is:

'The statement of the operating envelope, conditions, Limitations and build standard for a particular aircraft type, within which the airworthiness has been established as meeting the required level of safety.'[8]

It is the notification by Controller Aircraft to the Service - here the RAF - that a new type or mark of aircraft, or aircraft weapon system, has been developed to the stage where it is suitable for use by Service aircrew. It defines the formal build standard and operational Limitations which MoD(PE) is prepared to underwrite, and is <u>mandated</u> upon the Service.

Having developed the aircraft to the point where he deems it airworthy, perhaps with certain Limitations (which can be worked around, and distinct from Constraints which cannot), Controller Aircraft asks the Service Sponsor, the Assistant Chief of the Air Staff (ACAS), to state he concurs. He <u>must</u> do so in writing, providing an audit trail demonstrating he agrees with its content, in particular the Limitations it contains. This ensures nothing comes as a surprise.

There is no evidence this occurred on Chinook HC Mk2, and MoD has stated it cannot find this part of the audit trail, which the Secretary of

---

8 Controller Aircraft Instructions.

State requires to be retained through-life.[9] [B16] However, this is in part contradicted in a Defence Equipment & Support letter of 11 May 2011 in which, for the first time, MoD was able to state a precise date of 22 November 1993 for the Release to Service.[10] (The actual Release merely says *'November 1993'*). This indicates MoD has access to further information it will not release. See also Appendix 6, discussing a further contradiction whereby MoD denies the existence of Releases to Service altogether.

Upon ACAS concurring, Controller Aircraft signs his CAR and issues it.

In other words, Boscombe provides Controller Aircraft with recommendations, and if he accepts them he issues them as a statement.

For all practical purposes, Controller Aircraft's role then becomes one of support to an In-Service aircraft. In regulatory terms, he moves from complying with JSP553 (Military Airworthiness Regulations) Chapter 4 (attaining airworthiness), to Chapter 5 (maintaining airworthiness).

The central point of this submission is that there was no CAR for the Chinook HC Mk2 on 2 June 1994. There was an INTERIM CAR; the term 'INTERIM' having a specific meaning - aircrew were not permitted to rely *in any way whatsoever* on the subject of the INTERIM caveat, be that an individual equipment or the whole aircraft. It is not a temporal term. It describes the type of release. In this case, INTERIM applied to the entire Chinook HC Mk2. Ergo, the aircraft was not airworthy.

The Release to Service (RTS)

The CAR, at Initial Issue (not INTERIM), is passed to ACAS, who creates an RTS. The CAR, as issued, forms Part 1. Having agreed its content, ACAS is not permitted to amend it. He may add a Part 2, a list of Service Deviations. (Typically, a Deviation may arise because the RAF has changed the build standard or use from that assessed for the CAR). ACAS then issues his RTS with a letter of promulgation. This letter, not the RTS, is the authority to commence Service regulated flying. The first such letter on Chinook HC Mk2 is dated 10 January 1996.[11]

The RTS is the Master Airworthiness Reference in the Aircraft Document Set. ACAS appoints a subordinate responsible for its subsequent upkeep;

9 Letter RTSA RW/11/5/3, 8 March 2010.
10 Defence Equipment & Support letter 16-03-2011-103347-004, 11 May 2011.
11 Assistant Chief of the Air Staff letter D/DD Mar & Hels 270/2/1, 10 January 1996.

including the In-Use Safety Case and the Statement of Operating Intent and Usage which underpin it. (The practical application of this is discussed later).

The build standard reflects the intended uses/roles of the aircraft, and the Safety Case is a reasoned argument that it is safe in those uses/roles. If any of these components (build standard, role and use) change, at any time, then the others must be re-validated and re-verified. This is a fundamental principle of Safety Management.

JSP553 (Military Airworthiness Regulations) and (any) Safety Management System mandate continuous feedback and review, intended to ensure that, as far as possible, the CAR, RTS, Safety Case (all levels), Statement of Operating Intent and Usage, and build standards, can be reconciled.

General

While the evidence presented here demonstrates the Chinook HC Mk2 was released to service prematurely, that does not mean it remained sub-airworthy. As many witnesses testified, in time some of the shortcomings and their underlying causes became better understood. Also, it is assumed (but should be confirmed) that a stable baseline build standard emerged, aircraft equipment was trialled against this baseline, its installed performance established, and a recommendation issued by Boscombe Down that the aircraft was airworthy. But, on 2 June 1994 none of these milestones had been achieved.

The purpose of Controller Aircraft Release trials is to gain this understanding so that the Aircraft Document Set (see Appendix 1) can give accurate and adequate information to users and maintainers. Evidence taken by the Board of Inquiry and subsequent Inquiries confirmed this understanding had not been adequately achieved by 2 June 1994, and the Aircraft Document Set was deficient - witness Boscombe's decision to cease flying their trials aircraft on airworthiness grounds immediately before the accident. (Boscombe aircraft are part of the Procurement Executive Fleet, not Service aircraft. They fly under MoD(PE)'s Director Flying rules, necessary for flying aircraft that only have Experimental Flight Approval).

The Nimrod Review

In 2009 an event occurred that cannot be ignored in the context of ZD576 - Mr Charles Haddon-Cave QC issued 'The Nimrod Review'. In

December 2007 Secretary of State for Defence, The Right Honourable Des Browne MP, had ordered the Review based on (a) pre-Inquest evidence to the Oxford Coroner, and (b) this assertion by Air Chief Marshal Sir Clive Loader in the Nimrod XV230 Board of Inquiry report:

'I conclude that the loss of XV230 and, far more importantly, of the 14 Service personnel who were aboard, resulted in shortcomings in the application of the processes for assuring airworthiness and safe operation of the Nimrod. I am clear that further activity must be undertaken for our other aircraft types to check whether there is any read-across of lessons we have learned from this accident at such enormous (and immensely sad) cost.'

It is a feature of the Review that it incorrectly baselined systemic failings to implement the regulations at 1998. Evidence had been submitted that these failings extended back to, at least, 1990. (See Appendix 1). This was supported by, for example, the Coroner's Inquest into the loss of Hercules XV179, where evidence revealed similar failings going back to 1980. In fact, Coroner Andrew Walker stated Nimrod had not been airworthy since 1969.

MoD accepted all these findings. But the effect of the 1998 baseline, intended or otherwise, was to divert attention from other, older accidents and aircraft affected by the same failings. This submission presents and explains detailed evidence showing systemic, as opposed to isolated, failings can be traced to 1988 (see Appendices 4 & 5).

Therefore, Air Chief Marshal Loader's second recommendation, that other aircraft types be checked, becomes relevant to the period leading to the release to service of the Chinook HC Mk2. It is unclear if he knew of previous recommendations that, if implemented, may have prevented other accidents. The point is, MoD's failure to implement regulations has been well known since at least 1988, and the subject of many adverse reports and direct warnings. Perhaps the key event following the Nimrod Review was the establishment of the Military Aviation Authority in 2010. It is not just a Nimrod Authority, but a pan-MoD Authority - a clear admission of systemic failings.

This submission demonstrates the failure to implement airworthiness regulations was advised to senior staff in the six years preceding release to service of the Chinook HC Mk2.

Aim

MoD's stated position is that the pilots were to blame beyond any doubt whatsoever. Its case is they were grossly negligent at or before a certain point in the flight - the point in time at which they made a waypoint change to the Tactical Navigation System (SuperTANS), to provide guidance to the next waypoint. MoD asserts that anything that happened before this event (for example, an organisational fault) is irrelevant. The Nimrod Review makes much of such organisational faults, and this submission provides evidence the same applied to Chinook.

(Note: SuperTANS is not an auto pilot, nor is it a data recorder. It provides steering guidance, requiring pilot input to follow that guidance. 'Super' indicates a newer version integrated with a separate GPS unit).

In focusing on this narrow timeframe, MoD deemed irrelevant any latent fault or defect. For example, one that would only become apparent when the handling pilot tried to execute a turn after a straight run. This, despite the RAF's most experienced Chinook test pilot having encountered such failures, in flight and on the Chinook HC Mk2. (See Appendix 11). This setting of restrictive boundaries served to conceal evidence demonstrating, beyond any doubt, the pilots had been failed by those who owed them a duty of care.

MoD's argument is not discussed in detail. That has been done by the Fatal Accident Inquiry, the House of Lords, and House of Commons. All rejected MoD's position. Rather, the following argument is pursued... The regulations, especially those governing the conduct of Boards of Inquiry, require the timescale under investigation to extend back to encompass the possibility of organisational fault. There can be no greater organisational fault than a conscious failure to implement airworthiness regulations, and falsely stating they have been. If others failed in their duty, then it is unreasonable to blame only the pilots, even if it could be proven they erred.

As Mr Malcolm Perks, MoD's own expert witness on the Full Authority Digital Engine Control system, wrote on 10 November 1997:

'The key issue as far as I am concerned is that if there is any doubt as to whether the foundations were laid properly...the whole structure is suspect. It is impossible to say what might eventually go wrong, but the chances are something will break, sometime'.

The implementation of robust airworthiness regulations is, in this case, the 'foundations'. The Chinook's foundations were made of sand.

In presenting this argument, the process of attaining and maintaining airworthiness in the period to June 1994 is discussed, concentrating on two activities:

1. Mapping the content of the Release to Service to MoD regulations

and procedures, noting where the documents are Compliant, Non-Compliant, or Partly Compliant. See Section 2.

2. Examining evidence of airworthiness failings in the months preceding release to service, primarily through assessment of Boscombe Down reports. See Section 4.

The aim therefore is to demonstrate the Nimrod Review baseline extends back to, at least, 1988. The resultant systemic failings in the implementation of the MoD's airworthiness regulations and procedures create (more) doubt as to whether the criteria for gross negligence was met. Evidence is presented illustrating others were negligent by virtue of failing in their duty of care obligation to the aircrew and passengers. And because that failure, and the predictable outcome, was known in advance, this amounted to gross negligence.

In pursuing this aim, it will be shown that the Chinook HC Mk2 did not meet the MoD's own maturity criteria, was not airworthy, and Release to Service should not have been granted.

Section 2 - Chinook HC Mk2 Release to Service Compliance Matrix

Executive Summary

This section assesses the Chinook HC Mk2 Release to Service against the regulations of the day. The primary references include Joint Service Publications 553 and 318B (Military Airworthiness Regulations and MoD Aircraft Operating Policy), Controller Aircraft Instructions (CAI) and Defence Standard 05-125/2. During the period under discussion MoD conducted courses to provide refresher training and up-to-date official guidance on new legal requirements and their implementation. This training was based, primarily, on D/MAP/12/20B-38, Issue 3, November 1993 (Application of Technical Procedures) [B6] - precisely the period in which the Chinook HC Mk2 Release to Service was issued.

Note: The original tabular format has been converted to narrative form to cater for e-books. It lists mandated requirements in *italics*, along with comments on the non-compliances. Unless otherwise stated, the Release to Service was non-compliant on 2 June 1994.

Compliance Matrix

General

(Information only). *Operations that can reasonably be construed as to be within the cleared envelope described in the Aircraft Document Set and within the Limitations in the Release are permitted, unless expressly prohibited.*

Implicit in this policy statement is that the Aircraft Document Set and Limitations in the Controller Aircraft Release (CAR) and Release to Service (RTS) must be properly constructed, validated, verified and promulgated.

Correct and meticulous registry procedures are essential.

The concept of dedicated Registries was shelved in successive cutbacks throughout the 1990s.

The Audit Trail

The Release to Service contains vital safety information, and procedures should be in place to ensure that they are tracked and preserved.

MoD cannot supply the correspondence between Controller Aircraft and the Assistant Chief of the Air Staff (ACAS) leading to the signing of the INTERIM CAR, or a Letter of Promulgation signed by ACAS.

The special handling caveat 'Airworthiness/Safety Information' should be applied to the Release to Service. This caveat should dictate that such documents must be subject to permanent retention.

Neither the INTERIM CAR nor Release to Service has such a caveat, and MoD cannot supply key documents.

Trials (must be) conducted in which the operating envelope and performance of the aircraft and its systems are fully investigated.

Installed performance must be established to satisfy the MoD UK policy of a Limitations-based airworthiness system. That is, without establishing performance one cannot advise Limitations to the aircrew. This work had been suspended on 2 June 1994.

Controller Aircraft Release (General)

Boscombe (must be) properly tasked, on time, to fulfil the requirement to provide the Aircraft Project Director with CAR recommendations.

Boscombe were given too little time. They did not have a representative Mk2 at the time of the Release to Service in November 1993. On 2 June 1994 the status of the Mk2 remained *'not airworthy'*, primarily due to *'positively dangerous'* Full Authority Digital Engine Control software implementation.

Conduct a Training and Familiarisation Phase following CAR and Release to Service.

A Training and Familiarisation Phase was planned, as the RAF had requested INTERIM (Switch-On) clearance to do so. On 2 June 1994 the Mk2 was still in this phase, which was restricted to ground training only. (Partially compliant).

Controller Aircraft shall only sign the CAR when the Service Operational Requirements Branch formally signifies their willingness to accept delivery of the aircraft to the agreed standard.

MoD has declined to provide this evidence, saying it cannot be found. Yet, it has been able to supply the documents immediately before and after from the same file.

It is essential that the layout and structure of the CAR is in a form which is mutually agreed between the Aircraft Project Director and the RAF Operational Requirements Branch.

The format and structure are generally compliant, but the content is not. (It could not be, due to the general immaturity of the design).

Content of the Controller Aircraft Release & Release to Service (Part 1)

The minimum content of the CAR is defined in Annex A to CAI 2:3:5: It is fundamental that all equipment that is authorised for carriage in, of fitment to, the aircraft is included in the Release.

There are crucial omissions. Instead of a proper build standard section there is a simple list of modifications, which is not the same thing. It is considered this is related to there being no proper contracts to maintain the build standard (see Addendum C), and the design was not under proper configuration control (later admitted by the Chief of Defence Procurement to the Public Accounts Committee).

Of greater import is the failure to list all aircraft equipment. Consequently, there is no authority to fit or use said equipment. This is linked to Boscombe's recommendation that the entire Navigation and Communications Systems have Switch-On Only clearance.

MoD(PE) Letter of Controller Aircraft Release (promulgation).

Signed by Sir Donald Spiers on 9 November 1993. However, it does not reflect the fact Boscombe had declined to issue CAR recommendations, stating CAR should not be granted. Nor does it refer to associated reports that Boscombe had stated must be read in conjunction with the CAR, and each other. While annotated *'INTERIM'*, it does not spell out the meaning. Nevertheless, it would be clear to ACAS, given the requirement for him to agree the content beforehand.

Distribution List.

Aircraft Performance and Requirements Section (at Boscombe) and DRA Farnborough Modelling and Simulation Division omitted. (Partially compliant).

Content and List of Effective Pages.

See above. Build standard and Air Publications incomplete.

Definitions of the various terms used in the CAR are to be given.

No definition is provided for 'INTERIM Recommendations', despite each page being so annotated. Given the meaning (Switch-On Only clearance, not to be relied upon in any way), this is a crucial omission.

Release Statement, Definitions and Airframe Limitations.

The Release Statement says the aircraft is cleared for operation, but omits Boscombe's statement that the aircraft is not airworthy. The clearance relates to ground use only.

Engine and Auxiliary Power Unit Limitations.

The major failing relates to the Digital Electronic Control Unit connectors and SI/Chinook/57. See Appendix 10. (Partially compliant).

Avionic Equipment - To list all equipment fitted (e.g. communications, navigation, etc.), with associated Limitations, Airborne Radio Installation numbers and the level of clearance. Any Warnings and Operating Notes associated with each equipment are to be included. That is, there must be a positive statement of clearance, not an implied clearance through not noting any Limitation or warning.

There are multiple failures on each point, so much so it is easier to list the few areas of compliance. The most serious is the failure is to state, anywhere, that a system is cleared to a given level.

There is insufficient clearance to conduct operations in Instrument Meteorological Conditions, immediately rendering unsafe any criticism of aircrew. Along with the FADEC software implementation being *'positively dangerous'*, this is the most obvious reason why Boscombe refused to recommend CAR. (See Appendices 6 & 7).

Build standard and modifications - The aircraft basic build standard is to be defined, together with a list of all modifications which affect CAR.

On such a conversion programme (Mk1 to Mk2) it is not enough to say *'Modification 200 Basic Conversion'*. The content of this section is more applicable to a brand-new aircraft type. The most obvious omission is the

Issue status of the FADEC safety critical software.

There is no indication what action was taken against the many Service Engineered Modifications (SEM), Servicing Instructions (SI), etc. that pre-existed in the Mk1. On one hand, the implication is Mod 200 'covered' them all, incorporating them into the Design Authority build standard. However, this is contradicted by the failure to mention any of these SEMs (primarily avionic equipment) in the body of the INTERIM CAR or RTS. Crucially, the Board of Inquiry and Inquiries heard that much of this equipment was (unavoidably) used by the crew of ZD576, but no deeper investigation was carried out to ask if this use was cleared. See Annex 2 to Addendum A.

This introduced a serious Human Factors Hazard as the crew would be left confused and uncertain as to the clearance and performance of critical equipment.

Air Publications (AP) - A full list of APs applicable to the basic aircraft is to be given. The AP reference for the Aircrew Equipment Assemblies cleared for use and the current amendment state for the Operating Data Manual are to be included. A statement should be made to the effect that the Publication Authority for each AP is responsible for ensuring that the information and data contained therein conforms in full with the conditions and Limitations laid down in the CAR.

Non-compliant on every count. The failure to maintain the build standard explains this. If APs are not routinely maintained, then the requirement cannot be met. Notably, in Annex C to the CHART report of August 1992 (see Addendum C), the Inspectorate of Flight Safety recorded that Chinooks were being maintained using captured Argentinian APs.

'APs' includes three principal prerequisite airworthiness documents:

- Flight Reference Cards (FRC) - AP Topic 14 (issued by RAF Handling Squadron, Boscombe Down)
- Aircrew Manual (AM) - AP Topics 15A & B (ditto)
- Operating Data Manual (ODM) - AP Topic 16) (Issued by Aircraft Performance and Requirements Section, Boscombe Down)

At the time, it was common practice for MoD's Air Technical Publications (ATP) department to manage APs by contracting the respective Design Authorities to prepare them. ATP would validate and verify them. However, for the ODM, AM and FRCs it was common for RAF Handling Squadron (RAFHS) and Aircraft Performance and Requirements Section to do the entire job themselves. (This was the case for the Mk2). Many disagreed with this, not least some RAFHS staff, as they very often did not have the resources; so these APs were seldom up-to-date, often incomplete, and did not reflect the RTS. This applied to the Mk2. Today, RAFHS usually confine themselves to validation - that is, the process is the same for all APs.

The legacy Mk1 APs formed the basis of the Mk2 suite. As MoD had stopped funding their routine upkeep in 1991, the Mk1 suite was not up-to-date (see Addendum C). Therefore, the Publications Management Plan for the Mk1 to Mk2 programme should have a significant section dealing with resurrection and stabilisation of this part of the build standard. If it did, it was not implemented properly or on time.

Finally, the Air Accidents Investigation Branch (AAIB) Inspector, Mr Tony Cable, stated in his report (paragraph 7): *'The examination was hampered in some areas by lack of complete manuals and test facilities for the HC Mk2'.* It is a fundamental principle that if a repair cannot be verified, then the repair is incomplete. If the AAIB could not gain access to Chinook HC Mk2 manuals and test facilities, how did the RAF verify any attempted repairs?

Release to Service (General)

Part 1 shall be a direct copy of the CAR.

As the INTERIM CAR is non-compliant, ultimately so too is the Release to Service.

Part 2 shall contain any Service Deviations (SD)

Part 2 was not promulgated at Initial Issue. MoD states this was because there were no SDs. However this reasoning is flawed, because the status of the large number of Mk1 SDs should have been advised. That is, were they still applicable to the Mk2 (and hence to be reissued as separate Mk2 SDs), or were they cancelled or superseded? This is a major failing which could only result in aircrew confusion, especially relevant to ZD576 as the crew had been flying under Mk1 release conditions (and SDs) for some months before the accident. This constitutes a significant Human Factors Hazard. (See Annex 2 to Addendum A).

There shall be a cover page bearing the Release to Service title, substituted for the equivalent CAR page.

Provided by MoD under Freedom of Information, but not as part of a structured Release to Service document. It is a stand-alone single sheet. (Partially compliant).

There shall be a Letter of Promulgation signed by ACAS, substituted for the equivalent CAR page.

The first such letter is dated 10 January 1996.

There shall be a Distribution List, substituted for the equivalent CAR page.

Not included.

Content of Release to Service

Classified Section - If classified equipment is fitted to the aircraft, a separate Classified Section is required in the Release to Service. The existence of this section must be noted in the 'Contents' but is not promulgated in normal distribution.

There is no Classified Section in any version of the Release to Service, to 1998. (Nor in the Mk1). Yet in his evidence to the Board of Inquiry, Squadron Leader Stephen Brough stated:

'I hereby present to the Board for their perusal all the associated engineering documents for Chinook HC2 ZD576. The only classified item in the Chinook HC2 standard Northern Ireland role fit is the (redacted)'.

There is no need to speculate here what that equipment was. The issue is that it was not recorded in the Release to Service, and did not form part of the build standard. It follows that it was not considered in any Safety Case, and there is no evidence to show its installed performance has been assessed or that it had no adverse effect on other systems, such as an Electro-Magnetic Compatibility failure. There is no evidence to prove it was assessed as safe to install or use.

Recording of Modifications - It must be assumed by all those who use the Aircraft Document Set that unless a modification is identified in the Release to Service, or is fully addressed in a temporary change to the Release, the modification is not authorised for use or embodiment. (As users of the Release need to know the effect that authorised modifications have on the Release and/or Aircraft Document Set).

It is a feature of the Mk1 and Mk2 RTSs that the former identifies many Service Engineered Modifications associated Service Deviations, and basic equipments, that are not mentioned in the Mk2 Release. As such, none of the following were authorised for use in the Mk2:

- Racal CCS (Intercom) (rendering any radios or homing equipment irrelevant).
- Sky Guardian Radar Warning Receiver
- Decca Automatic Chart Display
- Decca Navigator Mk19
- Marconi AD380 Radio Compass
- Decca 671 VOR/ILS
- Cossor 1520 IFF/SSR
- Marconi ARC340 VHF(AM) Homing
- Chelton 7 VHF (AM) Homing
- M130 Chaff & Flare Dispenser
- AN/AAR 47 Loral Missile Approach Warner
- BOH300 Countermeasures Dispenser
- PRT1751 WWH HaveQuick II UHF radio
- Avionics Crate at Station 190 (and all that it hosts)
- Twin Filter Modification to UHF Radios
- NVG Anti-Collision Lights
- OMEGA Grid Mode Selector
- NVG modification for PTR 1750 UHF Radio Control Units
- Keystone/Cougarnet Secure Communications
- Delco Carousel Inertial Navigation System
- UHF Secure SATCOM

This deficiency is reflected in Boscombe's Switch-On Only clearance recommendation.

All contractually agreed modifications need to be identifiable as one of the following:

- *Not Authorised*
- *Essential*
- *Affects Release*
- *Affects Aircraft Document Set*
- *No Effect on Release*

See above. The RTS does not note *any* of these categories against *any* modification. It does however have an 'Essential Modifications' section, with NONE listed. (Noting Boscombe's concern that an Essential modification relating to Differential Airspeed Hold runaways had not been developed, despite being recommended following the February 1987 fatal Chinook crash in the Falkland Islands).

Aircraft Document Set

AP Topics 14, 15A/15B and 16 should be validated, verified, issued and maintained. (Flight Reference Cards, Aircrew Manual and Operating Data Manual).

These principal documents were issued, but evidence to all Inquiries characterised them as immature, incomplete, misleading and unfit for purpose.

The CAR shall be re-issued to cater for changes to the basic aircraft Limitations, build standard, modifications, etc. The Aircraft Project Manager (APM) will initiate immediate action.

The ability to fulfil this requirement was wholly compromised by the failure to maintain the build standard, of both aircraft and equipments.

Upon issue of a CAR amendment, the APM shall formally action RAF Handling Squadron to amend the AM and FRCs, and Aircraft Performance and Requirements Section to amend the ODM.

There is no evidence any publication was amended to reflect changes between INTERIM CAR (November 1993) and time of accident.

Airworthiness Regulations - Delegation of Authority

'In discharging your airworthiness responsibility, you are to ensure compliance with...' (inter alia):

- *JSP553*
- *Defence Standard 00-970*
- *Defence Standards 05-123, 05-125/2*
- *AvP 67 Flying Orders for contractors*

The ability to comply was compromised by the decisions to disband the HQ Modification Committees in June 1991, and the specialist Technical Agency posts whose sole job was to maintain build standards. Having achieved this, from 1991-94 direct airworthiness funding was cut by ~28%

each year. (The CHART report notes the 1992 cut).

You are to ensure that any of the aircraft flown before issue of an appropriate Release is airworthy and safely operated.

ACAS issued his RTS in the face of Controller Aircraft's mandate that the aircraft was not to be relied upon in any way. Also, by failing to ensure the Aircraft Document Set was of the required standard, he denied aircrew the opportunity to fly the aircraft to the required standards.

As part of your airworthiness responsibilities you are to review periodically the safety and airworthiness arrangements for the aircraft and its associated equipment including software.

The CHART report of August 1992 exposed systemic failure to implement this. Any review from September 1993-on would have immediately revealed Boscombe's statement that the Mk2 was not airworthy and safety critical software *'positively dangerous'.*

If you believe that there is any lack of clarity of responsibilities, or become aware of any practice or procedure being followed which may compromise airworthiness standards, you are to take immediate steps to correct the situation. If it lies outside your control, you are to inform (ACAS) and (the RAF User).

The CHART report was submitted to the RAF Chief Engineer (Air Chief Marshal Michael Alcock) on 15 August 1992 and ACAS (Air Vice Marshal Anthony Bagnall). As of 18 May 2011, MoD has declined to provide evidence of any action plan to implement the 48 recommendations.

Boscombe fulfilled their duty by informing the Aircraft Project Director of the above airworthiness concerns. Despite knowing of these concerns ACAS signed the RTS.

MoD(PE) and DD/Avionics (RAF) staff formally notified their line management of concerns between 1988 and 1993, when funding was being cut and safety knowingly compromised. Ultimately, this was escalated to the Permanent Under-Secretary of State (PUS) and Ministers, with no action taken.

The Aircraft Project Manager/Director is to ensure the airworthiness by making arrangements for the implementation of the Safety Management Systems, including the management of configuration of the design throughout the life cycle, and custody of design records.

Given the evidence to the Board regarding poor documentation, etc., and repeated in the AAIB report, the conclusion must be that Ministers were misled. Previous Ministers have not corrected their statements when presented with the facts, and the current Minister for the Armed Forces (Mr Nick Harvey) has so far declined to take action (Letter D/Min(AF)/NH MC03367/2010 dated 24 August 2010), although was sufficiently concerned to call a meeting on 17 January 2011, attended by a former Chinook IPT Leader, at which he (Mr Harvey) tabled the CHART report. (I attended this meeting, via conference call).

The aircraft Release shall be derived from the platform, equipment and integration Safety Cases (or arguments).

The ability to comply was compromised by (e.g.) (a) disbanding HQ Modification Committees, (b) funding cuts, and (c) Safety Cases not being updated as a result of Service Engineered Modifications.

An Integrated Test, Evaluation and Acceptance Plan shall be drawn up and implemented.

If a plan was drawn up, implementation was immature, witness the failure to complete basic performance testing prior to Release, a situation which remained static on 2 June 1994.

Ensuring that a suitable process is in place for all modification proposals.

In 1993/4 this process was mandated, to be managed by Local Technical Committees and overseen by HQ Modification Committees. But these committees had been disbanded in June 1991, as were the specialist sections containing the Technical Agencies (the named individuals who managed the build standards, the most senior chairing the committees).

Modifications, SEMs, SIs and STIs

All associated MoD departments shall comply with the requirement to maintain the build standard of equipment and aircraft.

(Rather than list all requirements, a few relevant examples are given below. Additionally, Addendum C provides a Cross Reference Index mapping CHART failures to Defence Standard 05-125/2).

Following the transfer of specialist staff from MoD(PE) to AMSO (Air Member Supply and Organisation), funding for Post Design Services (which controls the conduct of the Local Technical Committees - see above) was cut by approximately 28% for the three years to 1993/94. In June 1991 the Radio Modification Committee was disbanded, thus removing the ability to comply with JSP553 and various mandated procedural Defence Standards, such as 123 and 125/2.

A modification proposal shall be considered by the Local Technical Committee and, subsequently, the relevant HQ Modification Committee.

See above, structure dismantled in 1991, with resource and funding requests refused thereafter.

Service Engineered Modifications (SEM) - The Service Support Authority shall consult the Aircraft Project Manager for the possible effects of each SEM on the CAR, prior to the issue of that SEM.

The general issue here is that there is no record in the Mk2 INTERIM CAR or RTS of the status of various SEMs that pre-existed in the HC Mk1. It is not stated if they have been subsumed into the Mk2 build standard, and Cover Modification action taken. Nor is there evidence that their installed performance has been re-established at the new aircraft build standard. It is this basic failure that gave rise to the INTERIM CAR.

Servicing Instructions (SI) and Special Technical Instructions (STI) - The Resident Project Officer (RPO) must refer draft SIs, before issue, to the APM for consideration of possible effects on the CAR. (And, implicitly, the Aircraft Project Manager must assess the SI/STI for safety).

The most obvious example is SI/Chinook/57, as amended by RAF Odiham, whereby aircrews were instructed to carry out in-flight servicing by checking the security of Digital Electronic Control Unit (DECU) connectors. The regulations require the design problem to be solved. Had they been implemented, the DECU and connectors would not have been cleared for flight. (And in any case the DECU hosts the safety critical software, the implementation of which was *'positively dangerous'*). As the DECU is an electronic unit, it was covered by (at least) Defence Standard 05-125/2, and should have been under the remit of the Radio Modifications Committee. It was not.

Operations

Operations outside the scope and Limitations of the CAR are not permitted; any extension or easement to the scope and Limitations is to be sought by formal amendment action.

The scope of the INTERIM CAR and Release to Service is wholly compromised by both being non-compliant in the first place. Ergo, this regulation was ignored.

There are only two special cases where operations outside the scope and Limitations are authorised - Contractor or Experimental Flight Trials, and under Service Deviation to the RTS. The final flight of ZD576 was not for contractor or experimental purposes. There is no Service Deviation authorising use of the aircraft outside the Limitations; for example, in Instrument Meteorological Conditions, under Instrument Flying Rules, or in excess of Icing Limitations. Nor is there a Service Deviation authorising use of the avionic equipments not listed in the INTERIM CAR/RTS; or even those listed but subject to Switch-On Only clearance.

Software

General MoD Software Policy (information only).

DUS(DP) letters 924/11/2/9 dated 31 December 1987 and 14 December 1989 refer. On these dates the respective Deputy Under Secretaries of State for Defence Procurement issued a MoD(PE) / Industry Joint Policy Statement outlining the approach to be adopted in the procurement of computer-based military operational systems. These were the authoritative policy requirements during the development and production of FADEC. This joint effort was agreed by MoD, the Electronic Engineering Association, the Society of British Aerospace Companies, and the Computing Services Association.

'Project offices are required to incorporate the provisions (of this policy) into specifications, Invitations to Tender and other project documents'.

MoD has denied the existence of this policy. It is included as [B14].

MoD should consult both the Operational Requirements Branch and technical advisors (Boscombe) *before departing from this policy.*

In general terms DHP did consult with Boscombe, in that the latter were tasked to conduct software validation and verification. However, their advice was that the software implementation was *'positively dangerous'*, it should be re-written, and the aircraft was not airworthy. Controller Aircraft accepted this, mandating it upon ACAS.

A compliancy matrix shall be provided in every Invitation to Tender detailing the degree of compliance required for every aspect.

If a matrix was requested, then it was non-compliant or otherwise inaccurate, given the numerous non-compliances notified by Boscombe and its cessation of flying.

It is essential that MoD should have all the rights it needs for in-service support of the software and for critical analysis if this should be needed.

Boscombe were unable to conduct the level of analysis required on this safety critical software, as they lacked information and encountered too many anomalies.

A key question is what advice was sought from, and provided by, the Principal Director of Patents, MoD; as required by paragraph 3.1.

The use of non-structured, local or idiosyncratic analysis and development methods is strongly deprecated.

Boscombe's approach was structured, but ultimately compromised by MoD's failure to comply with associated regulations.

Any analytical tools must conform to the interface standard.

Boscombe used appropriate tools supplied by MoD, and acted within the regulations; but were unable to complete the task due to MoD failings.

All software documentation must comply with JSP188 (preceding Defence Standard 00-55).

See evidence to the Board regarding lack of information on FADEC.

Safety critical software must be subjected to formal mathematical analysis.

Boscombe conducted, as far as they could, such analysis, based on the fact (agreed by MoD and Boeing) that the software was safety critical. MoD rejected the results and recommendations, and post-accident claimed the software was not safety critical.

It is essential that every project should carry out analyses of both threats and risk (vulnerability) at an early stage to identify critical areas and to determine which of the range available analysis, validation and, where possible, verification techniques should be applied.

DUS(DP)'s policy was to define safety critical software as *'whose failure could result in loss of life or serious damage to the environment in circumstances where there is no possibility of reversion to manual control'*. MoD later lied to the Public Accounts Committee, saying the reason why FADEC software was <u>not</u> Safety Critical was because of the use of the word 'would' in UK policy; when it actually said 'could'. In any case, as FADEC was Full Authority, with no manual Reversionary mode, its software was Safety Critical.

If it is a condition of contract that validation procedures be carried out by an independent agency, it is more than ever important that MoD should secure adequate rights of access and use of design information and code for itself and its agents.

It *was* such a condition (as Boscombe were tasked to conduct validation and verification), but MoD did not acquire the necessary rights, meaning Boscombe did not have the necessary information.

A hazard analysis shall be carried out during Project Definition to identify Safety Critical components

See above. If conducted it was later ignored when MoD and the RAF lied to Ministers.

Product acceptance procedures need to be decided at an early stage and incorporated in the system development specification so that they can be included in the contract.

This process broke down, evidenced by Boscombe's inability to conduct validation and verification. Despite this, DHP paid off the FADEC contract. This transferred all risk to MoD, and <u>must</u> have involved (a) a false declaration, or (b) a waiver.

The situation in methodology, especially in formal methods, is to be kept under constant review.

See above. Had this been implemented Boscombe's concerns over *'positively dangerous'* implementation would have been dealt with before issuing the RTS. (See Appendix 10).

Safety critical software must be subjected to additional validation and verification to establish the safety of the system.

While Boscombe sought to comply, they were undermined by having insufficient information.

Pending issue of Defence Standards 00-55 and 00-56, D/CSSE/4/22 of 14/12/87 is the preferred standard for safety critical software.

This policy guidance notes Defence Standard 00-31 and DO178A are less rigorous in their procedures and do not include Static Code Analysis. Paragraph A3.8.1 notes the tools MALPAS (Malvern Program Analysis Suite) and SPADE (Southampton Program Analysis and Development Environment) are available for Static Code Analysis, and RSRE Malvern should be consulted on their use. They were used by Boscombe.

(Information only) *Particularly stringent standards may be applied to processor architectures for Safety Critical applications.*

The processor was the subject of the *'positively dangerous'* statement, and only replaced in 2010. It is important to ascertain precisely what changes were made to the DECU and its software, due to the requirement to record Software Issues in the RTS.

General Engineering

Where transmissions may adversely affect the operation of a working receiver, the crew shall be provided with a label or warning indication that the system is temporarily degraded during the period of transmission.

Electro-Magnetic Compatibility (EMC) issues existed between Electronic Warfare, Radio and Navigation equipment. MoD has been unable to supply details of EMC testing conducted prior to the crash.

Engineering Investigations (examples)

Example 1 - SuperTANS

Regarding the post-accident SuperTANS 'testing', MoD continues to claim this as evidence that the entire navigation system was both serviceable and accurate. This has no engineering basis.

The Racal testing was not carried out in a representative environment, especially regarding EMC/EMI. Its report is barely useful background information, and cannot be used to verify or even hypothesise what happened during the flight.

Of equal import is the Human Factors effect on the pilots. They had no confidence whatsoever in the SuperTANS. They would be only too aware that their documentation told them that the GPS had no declared Initial Operating Capability in the United States, could not be relied upon, and that error codes in the TANS were now to be regarded as *'meaningless'*.

These are serious failings, with no indication of when installed performance will be measured.

Example 2 - Radar Altimeter

The evidence shows that the Transmitter/Receiver (the 'black box') was carrying defects, as well as faults. Most notably, the Sensitivity Range Control was set wrongly, an electronic component was unserviceable which compromised indications, and another component was installed the wrong way round. This would cause spurious or wrong indications, but was dismissed by MoD as irrelevant.

Organisational and Administrative

Compliance with the Civil Service Code and Queen's Regulations; Integrity, Honesty, Objectivity and Impartiality

Multiple failures noted in this submission.

(Examples)

If any party has been informed of a truth relevant to the accident, but not mentioned it, that it is misleading by commission or by omission.

Both the INTERIM CAR and RTS are examples of misleading by commission and omission, in that they falsely misrepresent the facts by purporting to be Boscombe's CAR Recommendations.

A practice is misleading by commission if it gives false information or deceives or is likely to deceive the average consumer, even though the information given may be correct.

As above.

Actions or practices may also be misleading by omission, for instance by leaving out important information, giving unclear or ambiguous information or failing to indicate prices/costs.

An example is articulated in Appendices 4 & 5, whereby AMSO staff knowingly wasted airworthiness funding, in doing so making false declarations that 'requirements' passed scrutiny, when they did not. Also, both Controller Aircraft and ACAS omitted that the aircraft was not airworthy.

Requirement to exercise a duty of care.

In a regulatory sense, the Secretary of State 'asks' Controller Aircraft and ACAS if the aircraft is airworthy. Both he and aircrew were lied to.

'Professional diligence' means the standard of special skill and care that may reasonably be expected to exercise towards (users).

RAF personnel relied entirely on the professional diligence of, for example, Boscombe, Controller Aircraft and ACAS. Demonstrably, Boscombe satisfied that requirement when declaring the aircraft unairworthy. The others did not.

Section 3 - General airworthiness discussion

Executive Summary

This section explains and discusses:

1. Airworthiness
2. Fitness for Purpose
3. Responsibilities

It complements the Nimrod Review, which took a 'top-down' approach but did not address practical implementation. In practice, senior officers and officials have little or no knowledge of everyday problems faced by the majority of those with airworthiness delegation, due largely to the reluctance of junior and middle-ranking subordinates to inform them for fear of disciplinary action. For example - Ministerial Correspondence (MoD briefing to Minister for the Armed Forces) - Ref 2214/2003 dated 23 April 2003, stated (at paragraph 6) that only one person in MoD thought it right to implement mandated airworthiness and financial probity regulations; and that he was wrong. [B18]

Airworthiness

Airworthiness is defined as:

'The ability of an aircraft or other airborne equipment or system to operate without significant hazard to aircrew, ground crew, passengers (where relevant) or to the general public over which the airborne systems are flown.'[12]

Airworthiness is governed by JSP553 (Military Airworthiness Regulations), which articulates the requirement to, *inter alia*, attain and maintain airworthiness. While not all Defence Standards are mandatory, they become mandatory when invoked in a contract. But Controller Aircraft Instructions mandated, for example, the 05-series of procedural Defence Standards in every contract. Implementation relies on various airworthiness components, such as experience, competence, training, corporate knowledge and resources.

The legal obligation to attain and maintain airworthiness by implementing these regulations is placed upon MoD employees through letters of delegation.

---

12 Joint Service Publication 318 (Military Flying Regulations).

Fitness for Purpose

Fitness for Purpose is a widely used but little understood phrase. To an engineer (and this submission is all about the failure to implement basic engineering protocols), fitness for purpose is the definition of Quality. In the context of operating Military Aircraft, it is an Operational term. Yet, there is a lack of information as to how it is to be achieved and who is responsible for attaining and maintaining it. Indeed, MoD has been unable to answer this question in court (Hercules XV179 Coroner's Inquest). Nevertheless, it is generally held to refer to three main scenarios (and variations thereof):

- When the aircraft does not comply with its specification. For example, it is carrying faults or is not up to modification state.

- When the operational imperative requires it to be flown beyond the boundaries of the Release to Service.

- When, given new threats, its configuration must be enhanced to maintain its safety.

This last is important, because Fitness for Purpose is usually seen as a temporary lowering of standards to meet the operational imperative, often because resources are not available. But it also refers to the need to raise those standards, requiring extra resources, and most commonly seen in the Theatre Entry Standard concept. As this addresses Fitness to Fight, that can be seen as a subset of Fitness for Purpose.

At this Operational level, through the system of delegation, down to squadron engineers, and within defined limits, temporary lowering of standards is acceptable; although more normally applied to the serviceability of an aircraft (which is not mentioned in JSP553). Airworthiness and serviceability are often used as interchangeable terms, but the former facilitates the latter. In assessing both, the overriding factor is engineering judgment. However, the ability to apply this may become compromised if the basis for the judgment, for example, the Safety Case, Release to Service or supporting documentation, is flawed. And the entire process is compromised if, as occurred from 1990, engineering judgment itself can be overruled on cost grounds; forsaking safety at the expense of (often false) savings. This was reiterated by Mr Haddon-Cave.

A topical example is Explosion Suppressant Foam (ESF) in RAF Hercules C-130. At MoD's request, the basic aircraft, as built for the RAF, did not have ESF. Based on the original Staff Requirement and Statement of Operating Intent and Usage, a Vulnerability Analysis would be conducted to determine if inert projectiles posed a risk (penetration of fuel tanks, leading to fire or explosion). If so, and the aircraft had to be put to the use that exposed it to this risk, then the <u>required</u> mitigation was ESF (see Defence Standard 00-970 and JSP553). Otherwise, the aircraft was neither airworthy nor fit for purpose.

Fitness for Purpose refers to short term operational aspects. This does not apply to the final flight of ZD576. It was a passenger transit and by no stretch of the imagination operationally imperative. Thus, by eliminating Fitness for Purpose as a consideration, the remaining question is: *Was the Chinook HC Mk2, and ZD576 in particular, compliant with the airworthiness regulations?*

Responsibilities

So, within MoD(PE) and Air Staff, the regulations are clear cut and must be implemented. This is a fixed, non-negotiable obligation.

The operational application is, effectively, delegated to forward commanders, responsible for day to day use. This is where variables arise. They rely entirely on MoD(PE) and, especially, the Air Staff, providing a stable airworthiness baseline against which they can make a fit for purpose judgment when the aircraft deviates from that baseline. However, flexibility is limited by many constraints. For example, the C-130 Operational Commander was in no position to fit ESF. And MoD(PE) cannot readily procure it if the Service has not made adequate provision, or erred by not specifying it. The Commander must be given the basic tools for the job - an airworthy aircraft that is fit for the purpose he has been set. The same applies to aircrew.

Each echelon cannot be expected to constantly monitor, far less control, what the others are doing. They place total reliance on each doing their job properly. If others fail in this duty, it defies natural justice to place sole blame on the aircrew. In the case of Chinook HC Mk2, the Compliance Matrix at Section 2 amply demonstrates others failed.

However, this is not to say Operational Commanders and aircrew have no say or role. They have a duty to provide constant feedback on safety matters. Here, the pilots demonstrably met this obligation as they expressed concern over the status of the Mk2 and requested they be allotted a Mk1. This was refused, but it is unclear if their superiors met *their* obligation by passing these concerns up the chain of command, or if they were investigated. This should be established.

Section 4 - Events from July to October 1993, immediately prior to INTERIM Controller Aircraft Release

Executive Summary

This section explores Boscombe Down's work and recommendations, concluding that the regulations requiring certification of the Full Authority Digital Engine Control (FADEC) design, and in particular its safety critical software, were not implemented properly. Thus, the Chinook HC Mk2 was not of sufficiently mature design at release to service or on 2 June 1994.

On 30 September 1993, Boscombe advised MoD:

- *'Controller Aircraft Release with this version of software for FADEC cannot be recommended'*. This status remained on 2 June 1994.

- The FADEC software implementation was *'positively dangerous'*.

- *'Essential modifications'* were still outstanding, and other modifications were recommended.

- The Chinook HC Mk2 should <u>not</u> be released to service.

On 26 October 1993, two weeks before the INTERIM Controller Aircraft Release was signed by Controller Aircraft, Engineering Systems Division Report E1109 reiterated:

'ESD is unable to recommend Controller Aircraft Release for the operation of the Chinook HC Mk2 due to the inadequate standard of safety critical software used in the FADEC system. A software rewrite to RTCA/DO-178 Level 1 standard, which can be independently verified, is considered essential'.

Background

What is FADEC? In simple terms it is an electro-mechanical system with a computer that manages fuel flow to the engines. It has Full Authority, as opposed to Partial Authority, because it provides fuel control over the entire range. It is also 'Full' in the sense there is no manual reversionary mode; whereas the Chinook HC Mk1 had. This difference assumes vital importance in the context of the controlling software. Because there is no manual backup, the software is deemed safety critical, and subject to more stringent standards of design, validation and verification. MoD serially misled Inquiries over this issue, claiming it was not safety critical.

The earliest relevant reference to be found is D/DHP/28/6/11 dated 9

November 1984, tasking Boscombe to carry out an assessment of FADEC fitted to the Avco Lycoming T55-L-712 engines on the Chinook HC Mk1. The Mk2 programme was not approved until 1988, and the delay to the FADEC programme meant it was prudent to embody it with the Mid-Life Upgrade. (MoD, incorrectly, termed it an Update).

In 1990 MoD placed a contract on Boeing Helicopters to upgrade 32 Chinook HC Mk1 helicopters to Mk2. The conversion involved the replacement of transmission, hydraulic and electrical systems, and various structural modifications. Configuration control considerations and procedures meant the extent of this upgrade required re-designation to Mk2. Configuration control is defined by Defence Standard 00-55 as:

'Activity to ensure that any change, modification, addition or amendment is prepared, accepted and controlled by set procedures'.

In turn, this meant a new Controller Aircraft Release, Release to Service and Safety Case were required, as opposed to amendments to the Mk1 documents.

For practical reasons, several proposed updates were included in the upgrade. This is normal practice. But there would seem to have been less than robust project management, witness the failure to re-schedule the programme when it became clear FADEC was not only delayed, but was the critical path. The timescales placed on Boscombe were unrealistic, exacerbated by an inability to provide them with the necessary information. Evidence of this can be seen in the fact they were still trying to validate and verify safety critical software *after* the accident, having ceased flying their trials aircraft on airworthiness grounds immediately beforehand.[13]

MoD policy and practice was to task Boscombe to conduct ground testing and flight trials (termed Controller Aircraft Release Trials), the intended output being Controller Aircraft Release Recommendations to the Project Director in MoD(PE). (Set out earlier).

The same policy required full Aircraft Design Authority (Boeing) involvement in a joint trials process. There is no evidence of this, which would prolong the process by duplicating effort and transferring major risks to MoD. Exacerbated by FADEC not being contracted to Boeing, and

---

13 Validation is the process of evaluating a product at the end of the development process to ensure compliance with contracted requirements. Verification is the process of determining whether or not the products of a given phase of development fulfil the requirements established during the previous phase.

in any case the company not being regarded as a suitable Design Authority. (See CHART report). Thus, it was an MoD liability to deliver a fully cleared engine using FADEC. It failed to do so.

This CAR trials process is progressive, and a number of reports indicating (lack of) progress were issued in the months before November 1993. These were collated by the RAF Support Authority and a consolidated list was issued in May 1994.[14]

As the main technical and programme risk was FADEC, much of the correspondence and reports reflect the activity being undertaken to validate and verify FADEC software. Without finishing this task, Boscombe could not establish the installed performance of many aircraft systems (especially avionics), in turn preventing any Limitations being determined. That is, while FADEC software remained unvalidated and unverified it was impossible to issue any meaningful CAR recommendations. This immaturity of process and design is why Chinook HC Mk2 had Switch-On Only status on 2 June 1994.

As one would expect, the two main assessments conducted by Boscombe, Engineering and Performance, offered a varying and confusing picture. Plainly, there were unchanged elements from the Mk1 that remained wholly satisfactory. But long-term unsatisfactory elements remained. However, and taking FADEC as an example, the achieved performance is only representative and valid if undertaken with a validated and verified software version embodied. This was never the case.

Measured maturity of a system of systems (the aircraft) must default to the lowest maturity level of an individual system (in this case, FADEC). So, despite there being some good parts to the Mk2, overall it had to be assessed as grossly immature and unairworthy. This is a non-negotiable mandate placed upon the Aircraft Project Director, Boscombe and the Services. (See Appendix 2).

The Certificate of Design

It is worth discussing the regulations governing the Certificate of Design concept and process, because a valid Certificate did not exist for FADEC on 2 June 1994.

Controller Aircraft's Instructions (CAI), Chapter 2.3.2, state:

'The Project Director, or a Project Manager acting on his behalf, is responsible for accepting the certification given by the Design Authority as to the compliance of the

---

14 D/PM RAF Hels 270/2/1, May 1994.

design with the specification requirements'.

The mandated procedural Defence Standard outlining how to implement this policy is 05-123 (Chapter 104).

Why is Certification needed? The Design Authority <u>must</u> demonstrate to MoD that materiel meets the contracted specification, *in toto* or with declared Limitations and/or exceptions. Until Limitations are cleared, or a Concession or Production Permit agreed by MoD, only an INTERIM Certificate of Design may exist.[15]

When MoD takes delivery of an equipment, either of development or production standard and for whatever purpose, it needs to know the build standard at delivery - the Certificate fulfils this need. This is directly linked to the Safety Case, which must reflect the current build standard, in turn reflected in the Controller Aircraft Release and Release to Service.

It follows that, if there is no valid Certificate of Design, the equipment cannot be fitted to Service aircraft. (Boscombe aircraft are operated under different rules, which recognise the need to test fly immature designs. If Boscombe deem their aircraft unsafe to fly, this affects any Service aircraft authorisation at the same build standard).

What constitutes a Certificate of Design? The certification is provided, for aircraft, on a CA(PE) Form 100. For a component, equipment or system (such as FADEC), on a CA(PE) Form 100A. The Certificate <u>must</u> be supported by:

- A Master Record Index or equivalent.
- A list of reports on all tests conducted to show compliance with the specifications.
- A list of subsidiary Certificates of Design agreed by the Design Authority for materiel designed and developed by other Design Authorities or sub-contractors and incorporated in the design.
- Specific evidence of structural integrity.

The above regulations have a general application. But for safety critical software, such as that in FADEC, a further process must be undertaken - the Certification and Acceptance into Service of Safety Critical Software, as laid down in Defence Standard 00-55 (Part 1). This is discussed in deeper detail in Appendix 3, but it is worth listing the basic requirements:

- Certification <u>shall</u> be a <u>pre-condition</u> for delivery of safety critical

---

15 Defence Standard 05-61 - Quality Assurance Procedural Requirements. Part 1 - Deviation/Production Permits and Waivers/Concessions.

software.

- The software Design Authority <u>shall</u> submit a Safety Critical Software Certificate to the MoD(PE) project manager <u>prior to delivery</u>. The certificate shall be an unambiguous, clear and binding statement by accountable signatories from the Design Authority, countersigned by the Independent Safety Auditor (Boscombe Down) and Royal Signals and Radar Establishment at Malvern, that the safety critical software is suitable for service in its intended system and conforms to the requirements of (Defence Standard 00-55). Certification shall be supported by the evidence in the Safety Records Log and supporting documentation.

- The Design Authority <u>shall</u> prepare an Acceptance Test Schedule for approval by the MoD(PE) project manager (noting the Aircraft Design Authority must clear safety critical software).

- Acceptance into service <u>shall</u> be based on acceptance tests and trials, <u>plus</u> the Safety Critical Software Certificate.

- Shortfalls against the agreed requirement that are not apparent at acceptance <u>shall</u> be rectified promptly, without additional cost to MoD.

- In addition to normal statements of conformity, the Certificate <u>shall</u> contain:

  a. Certification of conformance to the standards stated in the contract.

  b. Reference to any Limitations recommended by the Safety Assurance Authority (Boscombe Down).

Did FADEC development comply with these regulations?

Unequivocally, the answer is no. The most obvious reason is that not all the required signatories signed the Safety Critical Software Certificate or Certificate of Design (if, indeed, they exist at all). As both are required before delivery, then it follows the audit trail from software specification, to use in ZD576 on 2 June 1994, is largely incomplete.

Boscombe then declared the safety critical software implementation *'positively dangerous'*, and the validation and verification activity was stagnant on the day of the accident. By no stretch of the imagination could the regulations be said to have been met for in-service aircraft. The requirement for a certification *'prior to the delivery of the first production equipment'* was not met.

Assessment of Boscombe Down reports from July-October 1993

The following is an assessment of various reports and correspondence issued by Boscombe in the months immediately preceding INTERIM Controller Aircraft Release and Release to Service. The problems with FADEC did not come as a surprise to MoD(PE)'s Directorate of Helicopter Projects. In the context of MoD(PE) issuing an INTERIM CAR for the Mk2 in early November 1993, the following extracts are critical. They are placed in chronological order so the reader can gain an appreciation of Boscombe's increasing frustration at being ignored, and the short timescales involved for such a major work package.

1. Reference PE/Chinook/40 APF/246/011/1 dated July 1993 (Chinook HC Mk1 - Assessment of T55-L-712F FADEC) [B19]

This is an assessment of the T55-L-712F engine FADEC for Chinook HC Mk1 by Boscombe's Rotary Wing Performance section, referencing the original FADEC tasking and various reports dating from November 1984. In parallel, the Rotary Wing Engineering section would produce a separate report, and both would be submitted to D/Flying, a separate MoD(PE) department located at Boscombe. Both would report to Assistant Director Helicopter Projects 1 (AD/HP1), the Aircraft Project Director in MoD(PE). In practice, safety related concerns would be widely distributed as soon as they became evident. Boscombe's formal position on safety/airworthiness of the trials aircraft would be stated by Superintendent of Engineering Systems. Various points arise from this report, including:

- The final manufacturer's trials report was unavailable to Boscombe - confirming a separate MoD and contractor trials process, whereas a joint process was required by Controller Aircraft.[16]

- The testing methodology developed by Boeing was considered *'inappropriate'* by Boscombe, so direct comparison with earlier engine types was not possible. This lack of a baseline would concern any tester. Other tests developed by Boeing were found to *'introduce large transient stresses into the drive train, or to require calculation and/or extrapolation to come up with an acceleration indicator'*. Given the Safety Critical status of the software, Boscombe followed extant MoD policy, using a different methodology.

- Autorotation was not possible at lighter masses (the range tested was

---

16 Compendium of Project Management Guidelines - chapter 0766.

14700 to 22700kg).

- In-Flight starting was less than ideal in Reversionary mode due to *'poor fuel scheduling'*. Reference is made to a 1990 Boeing report discussing the phenomenon, implying nothing has been done.

Boscombe note the following recommendations had been made in 1990, but had not been incorporated in the aircraft under test. All these issues indicate a lack of Boscombe involvement in Design Reviews:

- **Essential** - a modification to inhibit selection of FADEC 'OFF' during flight. They had expressed uncertainty over how the system worked, even after discussions with Boeing.[17]

- **Highly Desirable** - a modification to a FADEC control panel to prevent unintentional reselect of Primary mode, caused by a poor switch guard design.

- **Highly Desirable** - a modification to move Reversionary mode beep trim switches from the overhead console to the Collective levers, similar to those on the pre-FADEC Mk1.

- **Highly Desirable** - a modification to relocate the load share select switch to the cockpit.

- **Highly Desirable** - a modification to relocate the overspeed test switch to the cockpit.

Boscombe further state that the Aircrew Manual and training should contain information advising aircrew of the likelihood of significant torque splits when operating FADEC in Mixed Mode, and degraded rotor speed control when operating in dual Reversionary mode. Finally, they assert that confirmatory testing should be conducted during Chinook HC Mk2 CAR trials. None of this took place.

What is beginning to emerge at this point, a mere four months before the Assistant Chief of the Air Staff signed the Release to Service, is that for some years Boscombe had been making safety-related recommendations which had been ignored or rejected. It is considered impossible that, in the following four months, these modifications could be schemed, embodied and trialled. Notwithstanding this opinion, it is a mandated requirement of the Safety Management System to record the decisions and reasoning arising from the refusal to implement these

---

17 When the RAF Training & Development Group tasked with preparing training schedules to 'train the trainers' visited Boeing in 1992 to establish how FADEC worked, Boeing expressed ignorance due to being excluded from the contract. This event should have been a major red flag.

recommendations. This aspect should be explored in more detail.

2. Reference AEN/58/119(H) dated 18 August 1993 (Chinook HC Mk2 - Status of Engine FADEC Software) [B20]

This letter followed a request from the Rotary Wing Performance section leader (see above) for a statement from Engineering Systems Division (ESD) concerning the verification of the FADEC software in the Chinook HC Mk2, and any Limitations that should be included in subsequent recommendations to the Project Director. Engineering Systems replied:

'2. *With regard to the software, ESD's position is very clear; the standard of software is of such poor quality that in our opinion it cannot be independently verified. With the agreement of DHP therefore, the work being undertaken by EDS-SCICON has been terminated.*

3. The analyses completed by EDS-SCICON covered the less complex of the modules, but even so a significant number of anomalies involving both primary and reversionary lanes were identified. The software itself contains illegal code and the structure of some parts is so intricate it is impossible to determine the effect, even in those areas that we suspect are safety critical. On the basis of the above, it must be assumed that at some stage the FADEC will act in an unpredictable manner.

4. In view of our concerns with the software, we have been trying since May 1993 to obtain sufficient data to enable us to conduct a hazard analyses/risk assessment of the total engine control system. In addition, we have requested information concerning the amount of rig, bench and flight testing carried out on the actual standard of FADEC software embodied in the test aircraft (ZA718). To date, none of the data requested has been provided.

5. At present, our major concerns relate to;

  a. Engine overspeed/runaway

  b. Engine over temperature

  c. Undemanded rundown

7. Unfortunately, a lack of detailed understanding of the engine control system prevents us from assessing the likelihood of an over temperature or undemanded rundown, neither can we identify whether separate backup exists within the overall system that is independent of the FADEC software which would prevent or reduce the potential for such a failure. We are still looking at available data and have recently made a "last ditch" effort through AD/HP1 to try to obtain the information required before our first flight, although the chances of success are I believe remote'.

This is an excoriating condemnation of a corporate failure to support Boscombe, and a breakdown of contractual dependencies between DHP,

Boeing and Boscombe - something mandated by MoD's Safety Management System. Boscombe have, belatedly, been given the task of validating and verifying safety critical software. However, they have not been afforded the necessary resources, primarily access to crucial design information; rendering their task impossible.

Paragraph 4 is crucial to any subsequent declaration of airworthiness. Boscombe state, categorically, that the necessary Safety Case work has not been carried out. Lacking this, there can be no audit trail back to the build standard, or forward to the Release to Service. Given this black hole remained when the Assistant Chief of the Air Staff signed the Release to Service less than three months later, what evidence did he have to justify the statement (through signing the Release) that the work had been completed satisfactorily?

3. Reference AEN/58/119(H) dated 27 August 1993 (Task E1536 - Chinook HC Mk2 - CA Release Trials) [B21]

This letter is from Boscombe's Superintendent Engineering Systems Division to his Chief Superintendent, a degree of escalation indicating how serious the issue was becoming.[18] Its purpose is to bring to the latter's attention several points regarding FADEC, and expand upon them.

The letter of 18 August is referenced, serving to formally advise the Chief Superintendent of FADEC's status and Boscombe's concerns, and states:

'...we cannot show it meets the integrity levels normally expected of a safety critical system. We must therefore be prepared for FADEC to act in an <u>unpredictable manner</u>'.

It goes on to explain in detail the risks outlined above, and concludes:

'There is very <u>little meaningful evidence to support the clearance</u> of the standard software used in the UK FADEC... Within ESD (Engineering Systems Division), we can go no further with any integrity/safety studies'.

By now, we are within eleven weeks of the Release to Service being signed, with no indication a solution is in sight, or that the recommended modifications to FADEC have even been considered; never mind endorsed, designed, approved, manufactured, embodied and trialled. Furthermore, this period is notable for holiday absences and it would be a few weeks (September) before staffing levels would be normal again. Also, a busy period is looming, one of the two large peaks in a MoD(PE)

---

18 On airworthiness matters, Superintendent Boscombe Down reported direct to the Chief of Defence Procurement.

year - the consideration of Alternative Assumptions to the Long Term Costings. This is a 'drop everything' period so, in practice, little else could be achieved between this letter and the Release to Service being issued on 22 November.

4. Reference Letter Report TM 2174, incorporating Letter Report E989 and PE/Chinook/40 dated September 1993 (Chinook HC Mk1 Assessment of T55-L-712F FADEC) [B22]

This letter is from Superintendent Engineering Systems Division to MoD(PE)'s AD/HP1 (the Aircraft Project Director); copied to various RAF departments, including that responsible for the Chinook HC Mk1 Release to Service. It concludes:

'CA Release is NOT recommended for the T55-L-712F FADEC equipped engine to be fitted or used on the Chinook HC Mk1'.

It recommends, again, amendments to the Aircrew Manual, a modification to reposition the Overspeed Test switches, and that indications to the pilot be made more obvious. Critically, it states:

'A full electronic engineering assessment of the production standard hardware and software will be required before CAR can be recommended. In addition, as a number of detailed changes to the FADEC software are anticipated, it is recommended that A&AEE be tasked to carry out a brief appraisal of the operating characteristics and the EMC of an aircraft fitted with the production standard FADEC prior to the system's use in Service. It is anticipated that this work will be carried out on a Chinook HC Mk2 during the CA Release Trials for this aircraft'.

That is, as the work to date has been based on an unrepresentative build standard of aircraft, it is irrelevant to any decision regarding release of the Mk2. To complete the audit trail, Boscombe must be tasked to conduct the trials on a proper Mk2. And, as a prerequisite, the FADEC must be modified/redesigned. This work was still outstanding at the time of the accident. In fact, matters had got worse, as Boscombe ceased flying their aircraft in March and June 1994.

5. Reference AEN/58/119(H) dated 30 September 1993 (Chinook Mk2 - T55 Engine FADEC Software) [B23]

This letter, from Superintendent Engineering Systems Division to Boscombe's Trials Management and Planning Officer, confirms that Boeing's Hazard Analysis identified FADEC software as Safety Critical (something MoD and Ministers later denied), quoting Boeing:

'...any malfunction or design errors could have *catastrophic effects*.'[19]

He confirms Boscombe's concurrence, stating:

'Although only 17% of the code has been analysed, 21 category one and 153 category two anomalies have been revealed. One of these, the reliance on an undocumented and unproved feature of the processor, is considered to be positively dangerous'.

The procedures used for controlling and recording the software's development are described as good; but they were not implemented properly, resulting in *'35 category one and 39 category two anomalies'*. This has resonance with the Nimrod Review - the airworthiness regulations were robust, but they were not implemented.

He then places these numbers in context:

'This density of anomalies (code and documents) is large; one category one and three category two would be more reasonable. Worse, the nature of the software is such that corrective action is considered to be impractical, and independent verification is virtually impossible. The assessment has been abandoned, rather than completed, on the grounds that the software is of proven inadequacy. The results are in fact similar to those derived from a study of the development standard which was terminated in September 1990 for similar reasons'.

After confirming that *'some of the* (software) *versions tested are not even direct ancestors of the current versions'*, and disqualifying the testing conducted on these older systems, he concludes:

- The density of deficiencies is so high that the software is unintelligible.
- Because of the density of deficiencies, it would be impractical to maintain the software as re-verification of all the software would be required after every change.
- No assurance can be given concerning the fidelity of the software, hence the pilot's control of the engine(s) through FADEC cannot be assured.
- The standard of engineering is demonstrably not that expected of software intended for the purpose of controlling a safety critical function in the aircraft.
- Although it is never possible to quantify the risk associated with the use of software, in this case it is obvious that available measures to ensure the quality of engineering for safety critical software were not

---

19 Defence Standard 00-56/1 defines 'catastrophic' as causing multiple deaths, whereas 'critical' is a single death/multiple severe injuries.

employed.

- Controller Aircraft Release for Chinook Mk2 with this version of software in FADEC <u>cannot</u> be recommended.

And recommends:

'Since it appears impractical to retain the hydro-mechanical system used in Chinook Mk1, urgent consideration should be given to <u>re-writing</u> the FADEC software'.

This confirms Boscombe understands the significance of there being no manual reversionary mode. That, by definition the software is Safety Critical.

In summary, the Chinook HC Mk2 was not considered airworthy.

It is noted that, during later Inquiries, the Secretary of State for Defence (Dr John Reid MP) claimed this FADEC was used in Concorde; contrasting sharply with the facts.

6. Reference AAD/308/04 dated 12 October 1993 (Chinook Mk2 - CAR for T55 FADEC) [B24]

This short letter, from Boscombe's Chief Superintendent to MoD(PE)'s Director Helicopter Projects (DHP), encloses the above internal Boscombe correspondence of 30 September. As such, it is the formal notification to his Customer, at a more senior level than normally required of Boscombe Down, that the Chinook HC Mk2 is not airworthy. He states this information has already been relayed to DHP's staff, finishing:

'Should you accept our recommendations to re-write the software, we strongly recommend that it is done with some urgency, and introduced in to service at the earliest opportunity when the rate of flying should be least and the exposure of the aircraft to risk is least. This of course assumes a Release to Service for the existing software is provided in some form'.

This last sentence is very important. It contradicts MoD's claim (May & October 2010 - see Appendix 6) that there was no such thing as a Release to Service in 1993. That, these only came into being in '1995/96'. But it is the final words ('some form') that make clear to DHP that the regulations, requiring a Controller Aircraft Release before the Assistant Chief of the Air Staff (ACAS) can sign his Release, cannot be met.

This raises, again, the oft-mooted possibility of 'political' pressure on Controller Aircraft to sign his Release. And perhaps on ACAS (a 'mere' 2 Star) to get the Mk2 into service as soon as possible, by signing *his* Release. One thing is certain - they acted in concert. An extension of this political imperative can be seen in the inexplicable, and illegal, order to fly passengers on a transit flight when the aircraft was demonstrably not airworthy. Only by questioning Controller Aircraft and ACAS can the truth be revealed. The regulations require their decisions and reasoning to be on record in case they need to be defended. MoD will not supply this information.

At this point one can see the genesis of the INTERIM Controller Aircraft Release.

7. Reference - Boscombe Down AMS 8H/05, Letter Report AMS 107/93 dated 15 October 1993 (Chinook HC Mk2 - INTERIM CA Release Recommendations - Navigation Systems) [B25]

The available version is incomplete, containing the letter and Annexes C and D. This is the first known use of the term 'INTERIM CA Release' in Chinook HC Mk2 papers. Until this point, Boscombe's position was there could not, and would not, be CAR Recommendations. The implication is that, following the earlier statements that the aircraft was not airworthy and could not be released, discussions took place to determine a 'way ahead'. Significantly, the letter explains the definition of the term 'INTERIM' and its intended purpose:

'In order to carry out crew conversion and training an INTERIM (Switch-On) clearance was requested by the Sponsor. This report covers the results of the initial trials to provide INTERIM CA Release recommendations'.

The current issue of JSP553 defines 'Switch-On Only' as:

'Switch-On only means that it is understood that operation of the equipment does not interfere with the proper operation of any other equipment or system fitted to the aircraft. The equipment may be fitted and may be operated in flight within the Limitations defined (which may therefore restrict such operation to specific phases of flight and parts of the flight envelope) but cannot be relied upon to function correctly (which may include incorrect functioning of any failure indications). The aircraft must not be operated in any way that places any reliance whatsoever on the proper functioning of this equipment'.

That INTERIM and Switch-On Only are one and the same is fundamental. If Boscombe say 'INTERIM' for an equipment, and that is accepted by Controller Aircraft (as it was), then that equipment cannot be relied upon in any way. When fitting such equipment (e.g. for trials purposes) the important thing is to ensure that the aircraft reverts to being safe when it is switched off. The aircraft must have already been proven safe without the equipment, something that had not been achieved on Chinook Mk2 on 2 June 1994.

Boscombe's Switch-On Only recommendation applied to the entire Navigation and Communications systems. But taken together with there being no FADEC certification, then by definition it applied to the whole aircraft - and in fact 'INTERIM' was printed on every page of the INTERIM Controller Aircraft Release. Even if FADEC was satisfactory, this precluded meaningful operational use. In truly exceptional circumstances one might be permitted to start engines, but not to engage rotors (which requires the aircraft to be able to lift off, to alleviate ground resonance).

8. Reference - AAEE Letter Report NR 108/93, AMS 8H/05 dated 19 October 1993 (INTERIM CA Release Recommendations for Communication Systems of the Chinook HC Mk2) [B26]

This report fulfils a similar function to that above, only on the aircraft Communication Systems. Of the five Annexes, Annex C (ARC340 VHF(FM) radio) is missing. (ARC340 has a chequered history in MoD. At the time, the RN had removed the Homing function from Sea King HC Mk4 due to performance issues).

It states trials are due to continue until April 1994, saying the tests reported took place in October 1993. The different terminology is important. 'Test' pre-dates 'trial' in the system integration, evaluation and acceptance process. This indicates immaturity of process as far as establishing installed performance during flight is concerned. Switch-On Only clearance could only be replaced by Installation Only, Limited or Full (flight) clearance, following trials due to commence in April 1994. However, as can be seen by events of early June 1994, matters had not moved on. They had regressed, as Boscombe had ceased flying the PE Fleet aircraft on airworthiness grounds.

The following airworthiness issues are raised:

- Despite a signal dated 11 May 1992, the Air Publications for the HaveQuick (HQ) UHF radio remain out of date. It is recommended as **Essential** that this be corrected.
- The HQ radio is unreliable if the power supply falls below 24 volts, despite a specification of 18 volts. There is an associated problem of aircraft battery incompatibility. (See Appendix 8). This prevents correct operation in an emergency, if using battery power.

These issues are indicative of the funding cuts implemented in 1991, which prohibited such publication amendments. Also note, the GPS

Time of Day output to the HQ radio was faulty in ZD576.

However, and unlike the Navigation report, here the systems are listed.

- IFF/SSR Mk12
- PTR1751WWH HQII UHF
- ARC340 VHF(FM)
- AD380 ADF *
- AD120 VHF(AM)
- 718U/A4 HF *
- Keystone Role Radio VHF(FM)*
- APN198 Radar Altimeter
- AD2770 TACAN AD2770 (Tactical Air Navigation)
- Decca 671 VOR/ILS (VHF Omni-directional Radio / Instrument Landing System)
- Chelton 7 UHF Homing *
- Chelton 7 VHF Homing *

(In this sense 'communications' means they have emitters/receivers, and so must be tested together for Electro-Magnetic Compatibility, explaining why some are navigation equipments).

A few weeks later, and without explanation, those marked * were not listed in the Release to Service, and so prohibited in the aircraft.

Notably, there is no mention in either document (this Boscombe report or the Release to Service) of the aircraft intercom (Communications Control System), a prerequisite to using any radio or receiving any audio warning. By omitting it, the rest of the comms cannot be used. Again, even if there had been no FADEC problems, the aircraft could still not have flown because communication and navigation equipments are a prerequisite to safe flight.

But the most serious issue is that Boscombe are testing an aircraft in October 1993 containing equipment due to be removed during the Mk2 conversion. This is confirmation that they did not have a representative Mk2, or specific knowledge of the desired build standard. By definition any work they are doing is nugatory, especially regarding Electro-Magnetic Compatibility.

9. Reference Letter Report PE/Chinook/41, APF/247/Annex dated 22 October 1993 (Chinook HC Mk2 - INTERIM CA Release Recommendations) [B27]

This report is signed by the Superintendents of Flying and Aircraft Dynamics. It places severe Limitations on the flight envelope, among them a maximum altitude of 5,000 feet and All Up Mass of 18,000kg. The operational requirement was 15,000 feet and 22,700 kg respectively. It can be seen the altitude Limitation would be very severe in operational terms, and both represent a degradation over the Mk1. Key points:

- The RAF had requested an INTERIM CAR so that Training and Familiarisation could commence (implying a formal process for INTERIM, contradicting MoD - see Appendix 7). This status had not changed on 2 June 1994. Plainly, the RAF hoped for a clearance to actually fly, but the INTERIM status applied to the whole aircraft.

- The software standard of FADEC had *'changed from that initially tested in 1991'*, negating any previous Boscombe work. This probably explains the short period they had to conduct extensive validation and verification. Importantly, the Software Issue flown by Boscombe should be stated in the Release to Service - it is not.

- The positioning of Caution/Advisory captions was wrong: *'The most important ones did not occupy the most prominent positions'*.

- Engine Fail captions were amber (Caution), not red (Warning), and there was no associated audio warning (and no intercom permitted to route and present that warning).

- *'The DASH (Differential Airspeed Hold) Low Rate caption was not consistent with the DASH feedback signal, and was not an indication of any rate of actuator movement. The title of the caption was inaccurate'*. The report ties these issues to (e.g.) altitude clearance.

- The design of Caution/Advisory Panel lighting *'denied the aircrew important cues to a major malfunction'* and Advisory lights (amber) were difficult to see in bright sunlight.

- There was no Auxiliary Power Unit/Battery interlock, so groundcrew could inadvertently start the Auxiliary Power Unit. (Which in turn would cause power interrupts and equipment failures).

- The cockpit lighting convention, supposedly improved by the Mid-Life Upgrade, was *'unnecessarily complicated and confusing'*.

- Lighting balance was unsatisfactory, with red-lit panels difficult to see.

- *'It was not possible to read the code set on the Identification Friend or Foe with normal cockpit lighting, requiring floodlighting or a torch. This was unsatisfactory'*. (This assumes importance in the context of the IFF code found post-crash).

- A torch is required to see the pilot's emergency flare dispenser. This was unsatisfactory.

- All flying must be conducted in Torque Matching mode, as Power Turbine Inlet Temperature Matching induces torque and rotor speed oscillation during pull.

- *'The vibration characteristics were similar to the Mk1 and were unsatisfactory'.* At 150kts *'Vibration is immediately apparent to experienced aircrew even when fully occupied. Performance of primary task is affected or tasks can only be done with difficulty'.* At 140kts Instrument flying was *'uncomfortable and distracting for instrument flight'.* This contradicts MoD claims that vibration improved in the Mk2.

The report concludes by recommending various amendments to the Aircrew Manual and Flight Reference Cards. (Noting the Board of Inquiry heard these remained grossly immature in June 1994).

Such observations are routine during aircraft development, but one expects them to be identified and fixed long before the aircraft is presented to Boscombe. Again, this indicates Boscombe (and perhaps aircrew) were not present at Design Reviews or the Installation Design Conference.

10. Reference - AAEE AEN 58/012 dated 26 October 1993 (Engineering Systems Division letter Report E1109 Chinook HC Mk2 - INTERIM CA Release) [B28]

This report is signed by the Superintendent Engineering Systems Division (ESD). It concludes:

'ESD is unable to recommend CA Release for operation of the Chinook HC Mk2 due to the inadequate standard of the safety critical software in the FADEC system. A software rewrite to RTCA/DO-178 level 1 standard, which can be independently verified, is considered to be essential.

With the exception of FADEC, ESD can support operation... up to 5000 feet.

It is recommended that all flying control and hydraulic pipe clearances are checked during the acceptance procedure of each aircraft. Corrective action to alleviate fouls and chafing should be taken where necessary.

An incident on the second production aircraft, ZA681 that resulted in the main plug on the #1 engine DECU becoming loose in-flight has highlighted a possible lack of security of a critical item. It is recommended that all electrical plugs on each engines' DECU be checked for security prior to every flight'.

These are flight safety critical issues. The comment about clearances is utterly damning indictment of the aircraft design, and of those who approved and accepted this design after the Installation Design Conference. The DECU connector issue is discussed in detail separately at Appendix 10, due to the possibility of it being a contributory factor, or even cause, of the accident.

Summary

Aircraft Dynamics, and Engineering Systems Divisions, have different roles, and came to slightly different conclusions. The former recommends CAR subject to severe Limitations. The latter does not recommend CAR due to problems with the FADEC safety critical software.

It is not a case of choosing a recommendation that suits. As stated, the regulations governing system maturity dictate the level defaults to that achieved on the lowest sub-system. (See Appendix 2). The reports are assessed as a whole, and the inescapable conclusion is that, while there are satisfactory features of the Mk2 (as one would expect), the conversion programme has introduced a critical and, at the time insurmountable, safety issue - FADEC. The decision of Boscombe Down as a whole is that the Mk2 does not meet the airworthiness requirements and Controller Aircraft Release is <u>not</u> recommended. This conclusion is entirely consistent with airworthiness regulations.

The key issue, however, is the use of 'INTERIM CAR'. The entire concept is alien, as there is no point whatsoever. It is clear that unpublished discussions took place to devise some form of 'clearance' for the Air Staff to 'justify' flying the Mk2, but that Boscombe refused to compromise on their advice that the aircraft should not be flown. Hence, their use of INTERIM (not to be relied upon in any way) and making clear this was a <u>type</u> of clearance, not a temporal term. It is equally clear that the Air Staff, disingenuously, chose to interpret this as a temporal term, despite being told by Boscombe it was not. Plainly, this was a deliberate deceit.

Section 5 - The issuing of INTERIM Controller Aircraft Release Recommendations by A&AEE Boscombe Down

Executive Summary

Chinook HC Mk2 did not meet the necessary airworthiness criteria [B22]. On 26 October 1993 Boscombe Down submitted to Director Helicopter Projects a Letter Report TM2210. Its Annex A was a document *'in the form of an INTERIM CA Release'*. [B29]

Boscombe warned that this document <u>had</u> to be read in conjunction with the reports detailed in the previous Section, in which they had already made clear the definition of INTERIM. It meant Switch-On Only clearance - not to be relied upon in any way.

Introduction

To recap, Boscombe issued AEN 58/012 dated 26 October 1993 (Engineering Systems Division letter Report E1109 Chinook HC Mk2 - INTERIM CA Release), signed by the Superintendent Engineering Systems Division. The report concludes: *'ESD is unable to recommend CA Release for operation of the Chinook HC Mk2'.*

Discussion of Annex A to Letter Report TM2210 dated 26 October 1993 ('Chinook HC Mk2 - Document in the form of an INTERIM CA Release') [B29]

First, one must ask what the purpose of this Letter Report is. It is not a Controller Aircraft Release (CAR) recommendation, which is the required output of Boscombe's tasking from MoD(PE). The Annex is *in the form* of a CAR, but its content is almost entirely non-compliant with the requirements of Controller Aircraft Instructions. (See Section 2 - Compliance Matrix).

The evidence suggests MoD(PE) and the Air Staff discussed the consequences, the latter seeking an INTERIM Release to commence Training and Familiarisation (a formal programme phase). These discussions are fundamental to understanding why the Chinook HC Mk2 was prematurely released. None of the principals have been interviewed, and MoD claims the interdepartmental exchanges, which the Secretary of State requires to be retained, cannot be found.

Plainly, the RAF always expects the CAR to say an aircraft as airworthy, but perhaps with Limitations. But it had no such expectation in late 1993, as it knew Boscombe had stated the Chinook HC Mk2 was <u>not</u> airworthy. It would be entirely remiss of Boscombe to confuse matters by (a) refusing to recommend CAR, and (b) recommend it a matter of days later, when nothing had changed. And they did not.

But Controller Aircraft was stuck between a rock and a hard place - his independent technical and safety advisors were saying the aircraft was not airworthy, his Customer was demanding he say it was. Boscombe correctly stuck to their guns and the Secretary of State's regulations (for which they were later criticised by Secretary of State Dr John Reid MP), leaving Controller Aircraft to deal with the Air Staff.

While an INTERIM CAR was entirely routine for equipment, so long as it could be switched off and the aircraft remain safe, Boscombe would seldom, if ever, have been in this position (being completely ignored) with a whole aircraft. This would have generated much debate, both internally and with DHP, as to how this should be managed. The agreed 'solution' was obviously a progress report *'in the form of an INTERIM CAR'*, with a covering letter reiterating CAR should not be granted. And, importantly, saying the INTERIM report should be read in conjunction with recent detailed reports.

In addition to defining Switch-On Only, the use of the words *'INTERIM'* and *'in the form of'* would, in Boscombe's mind, do three things:

- Clearly indicate it was not a formal recommendation, so should not form part of a CAR or Release to Service, or be misrepresented as a Boscombe recommendation that the aircraft was airworthy.

- Demonstrate that trials were in their very early stages (due to not having a representative Mk2); with the major hurdle, FADEC, being a DHP dependency, as Boscombe had recommended a software re-write.

- Crucially, the almost total lack of clearances for avionic equipment, and the Navigation and Communications systems in their entirety, would indicate that, until the FADEC software standard was resolved, and agreement reached as to what standard was to be embodied, it would be a complete waste of resources to conduct Electro-Magnetic Compatibility (EMC) or new/disturbed systems testing, because any results would be invalidated when the software/hardware was changed.

This last can be seen in the Letter Report TM 2174 of September 1993 [B22], in which Boscombe make it clear EMC testing has yet to commence. This aspect is particularly relevant on Fuel Computers. An aircraft can withstand many Electro-Magnetic Interference problems - indeed they are normal in a platform where ideal antennae and Line Replaceable Unit physical separation is nigh on impossible - but the one area that cannot be compromised is Fuel Computers. Such testing is conducted largely in the Radio Frequency Environment Generator (REG) at Boscombe. So important is the REG, it is a Strategic UK Asset, and the primary reason why such airworthiness clearance work cannot be contracted elsewhere. So high was the demand placed upon it, at the time it had to be booked 18 months in advance. The only logical explanation for the lack of clearances or statements regarding installed performance is that Boscombe had not yet started the work in earnest because of FADEC problems, which were proving insoluble. In practice, Boscombe's Chinook project manager would be allowed to book the REG, but would have to give up his slot if another requirement arose.

Furthermore, under normal circumstances Boscombe would use the Mk1 CAR as a template, and one would expect the Mk2 document to be similar. It is not. The Mk2 INTERIM report is sparse compared to the Mk1 CAR, missing large tracts of basic, mandated data - illustrating gross immaturity of process. This would be immediately obvious to both MoD(PE) and the RAF. (See Section 2 and Addendum A).

In addition to reiterating their existing position (CAR not recommended) Boscombe also stated, at paragraph 3:

'Although not covered within these reports, there remains a requirement for a Differential Airspeed Hold (DASH) actuator runaway warning device. This requirement, often stated by (Boscombe Down) and most recently justified at Reference C (Letter APF/246/13 dated 11 April 1990) was considered Essential for CA Release for the Chinook HC Mk1, and remains so for the HC Mk2. This matter will be covered in detail in the definitive CA Release recommendations, but it is considered relevant to restate the Establishment's position once again at this stage'.

Again, this is a thoroughly damning statement. A modification, considered Essential to the safety of the Chinook HC Mk1 following a previous fatal Chinook accident, had not been developed, trialled or embodied. (ZA721, Falkland Islands, February 1987, seven killed).

In this one statement Boscombe are, in effect, stating that the Release to Service for the Mk1 is invalid (because the Safety Case is incomplete and there is no audit trail). This is of vital import, because that Mk1 build standard (including the Safety Case, which should express this concern) would have formed the contractual baseline for the Mk2 programme. As this baseline is contaminated, or non-existent, one must ask what chance the Mid-Life Upgrade programme had of ever succeeding in obtaining a timely CAR recommendation from Boscombe.

While, in theory, the regulations permit Controller Aircraft to ignore such a recommendation, they also require him to record his reasoning and obtain independent advice which is both valid and verifiable. Even then, and faced with this conflict, one should go one step further and seek conflict resolution through another independent and suitably qualified party (but who is more qualified than Boscombe?). The obvious question is: *What action was taken or being considered?* Boscombe's frustration is clear at having to quote a 4-year old letter which they have obviously not received a reply to, so the answer must be 'none'. And what were the Aircraft Design Authority's (Boeing) thoughts on this, as (presumably, because of their input to the Safety Case) they accepted a contract to modify an aircraft knowing that the contracted baseline contained this fundamental flaw?

Section 6 - Issue of INTERIM Controller Aircraft Release and Initial Release to Service, November 1993

Executive Summary

'INTERIM' and 'Switch-On Only' have the same meaning. Controller Aircraft reissued Boscombe's report to the Assistant Chief of the Air Staff (ACAS) with *'INTERIM RECOMMENDATIONS'* printed on every page. Therefore, by definition he (a) rejected any other advice he received, or (b) that advice was the same as Boscombe's. This disproves MoD's claim he accepted other advice over Boscombe's.

There is no evidence Controller Aircraft articulated what INTERIM meant (as MoD claims the correspondence cannot be found). But ACAS would be expected to know, and certainly Controller Aircraft's staff would. In any case, Boscombe had reiterated the meaning shortly before.

The Release to Service is the Master Airworthiness Reference in the Aircraft Document Set, as it represents the In-Use build standard(s). In issuing his Release to Service, ACAS misrepresenting the facts to RAF Users. That was maladministration and a failure of duty of care.

It was incumbent upon Controller Aircraft to then re-state to ACAS the obligation he was under. If he did not, that was negligence and maladministration.

Introduction

On 9 November 1993 Controller Aircraft issued a letter of promulgation:

'CA 23/3

9 November 1993

Chinook HC Mk2 - CA Release

The Chinook HC Mk2 post Mid-Life Update is issued for Service Use subject to the Limitations stated in this CA Release.

(actual signature) *Donald Spiers'*

This is attached to Boscombe's INTERIM CAR recommendations, but does not reference the various Boscombe letters explaining that (a) INTERIM means Switch-On Only, and (b) the aircraft is not considered airworthy - despite Boscombe specifically requesting this in the covering letter to their report.

RAF staff knew the detailed background, if only because Boscombe departments such as the Trials Management Planning Office and Rotary

Wing Test Squadron included many RAF personnel. Also, various Support Authorities, Role Offices, RAF officers in MoD(PE), and the RAF Handling Squadron at Boscombe, were demonstrably aware. Ironically, the Board of Inquiry's engineer was posted to Boscombe as a Trials Management and Planning Officer at his next posting. It is worth speculating what the Board would have said if he already had this experience.

It is also clear that the Air Staff knew something was seriously amiss. ACAS was in possession of the August 1992 Chinook Airworthiness Review Team report, the content of which would have placed systemic airworthiness failings uppermost in his mind. This is discussed in detail later.

Comparison of the Boscombe Down report *'in the form of INTERIM recommendations'* and the INTERIM CAR issued by MoD(PE)

Based on the documents provided by MoD when asked for the CAR, the two are substantially the same (although different recipients were given different versions). There is one major difference. Boscombe considered the embodiment of various modifications, including a DASH runaway modification, as *'Essential'*. That is, to be embodied before the aircraft could be considered safe. Yet, in Section Z, paragraph 2 'Essential Modifications', the INTERIM CAR states:

'NO ESSENTIAL MODIFICATIONS ARE REQUIRED'.

Section Z (2) is usually taken to refer to modifications that have already been designed. However, this convention rather assumes MoD would not ignore the need for an essential safety modification. This (blank) section also confirms that the recommended modifications to FADEC software and hardware, and to the Automatic Flight Control System to correct Undemanded Flight Control Movements, were not in the build standard.

In summary, the INTERIM CAR does not reflect the in-service build standard, and there is no evidence of any testing or trials having been carried out on that standard.

With hindsight, and under the circumstances (Boscombe having been ignored over a period of time), it may have been better to annotate the INTERIM report *'CA Release Not Recommended'* rather than state it in a covering letter. But Boscombe would never have imagined they would be ignored on such a crucial matter, so this is not a criticism.

ACAS's staff include individuals whose entire *raison d'être* is the control and upkeep of Releases to Service. Even without seeing the covering letter, they would immediately recognise the report described an unairworthy aircraft. Even a cursory comparison with the Mk1 Release would reveal gross differences, each constituting a risk to life. Ignoring these issues would be negligence and maladministration.

Initial Issue of the Release to Service

Air Vice Marshal Anthony Bagnall issued the Release. The document carries no precise date, the cover sheet saying *'Dated November 1993'.* However, recent Freedom of Information requests (May 2011) reveal it was signed on 22 November 1993. This is significant, because hitherto MoD denied the existence of the mandated Letter of Promulgation or other relevant correspondence, only stating that *'one must exist'.*[20] [B16] Yet it clearly possesses a document with this precise date.

This audit trail must be retained, permanently. The Letter of Promulgation should be inserted at the beginning of the Release document. Such a letter was not issued with subsequent Amendments 1-5, but *was* issued at AL6 on 10 January 1996 - by which time ACAS was Air Vice Marshal Timothy Jenner. That is, the Chinook HC Mk2 was only formally released to service in January 1996.[21]

The body of the Release is that of the INTERIM CAR, and (correctly) renamed 'Part 1'. Notably, there is no Part 2 (Service Deviations), which would imply all Chinook HC Mk1 Service Deviations are either (a) not applicable to Mk2, or (b) have been superseded during the conversion process. There is no evidence either way. Omitting mention of the Mk1 Deviations would be confusing to aircrew, especially as a dual fleet was operating. When flying the Mk1 they used kit covered by Service Deviations. Some of the same kit was fitted in the Mk2 and expected to be used, but was not covered in the Release to Service, so its use was prohibited. This is a serious airworthiness failing, and again illustrates the immaturity of process in November 1993, and at the time of the accident (when only two Service Deviations were extant).

On 2 June 1994, both Releases were still annotated *'INTERIM Recommendations'.*

---

20 Letter RTSA RW/11/5/3, 8 March 2010.
21 D/DD Mar & Hels 270/2/1, 10 January 1996. First Letter of Promulgation for Chinook HC Mk2.

MoD replies to Freedom of Information Requests

There seems to be confusion in MoD as to what constitutes a Controller Aircraft Release (CAR) and Release to Service (RTS). When asked for the CAR, it has variously provided the RTS, or an INTERIM CAR with pages from an RTS inserted. When asked for an RTS, it has supplied an INTERIM CAR or one with the cover sheet removed. (And variations thereof). Crucially, it has often removed specific pages before supplying copies, these pages providing clear evidence pointing to the possible, and perhaps even probable, cause of the accident.

However, in May and October 2010 MoD trumped this by stating, in letters to Dr Susan Phoenix, there was no such thing as a Release to Service in 1993; that they only came into being in 1995/96, replacing the CAR. This lie is discussed in Appendix 6.

Section 7 - Assessment of the INTERIM Controller Aircraft Release and Release to Service, at Amendment 1, March 1994

Executive Summary

As there existed only an INTERIM Controller Aircraft Release (CAR), it is important to assess the single amendment issued before the accident, as this sets the baseline for any discussion of the aircrew's knowledge of the aircraft. (Noting there was no copy of the Release to Service at RAF Aldergrove). Amendment 1 was the first time Service Deviations were promulgated. These were issued after the deceased aircrew had undertaken their Mk1/Mk2 'Differences Course'.

A key administrative error is discussed whereby the Icing Limitation of the aircraft was, probably inadvertently, removed. There was a related anomaly in the Board of Inquiry report.

Introduction

When the CAR (or any document under configuration control) is updated, an Amendment Pack is compiled by the Issuing Authority and sent to those on the Distribution List. In this case, the Issuing Authority was Controller Aircraft, who delegated the task (via Departmental Management Plans) through Director General Air 1 to Director Helicopter Projects. In turn, Assistant Director / Helicopter Projects 1 (AD/HP1, responsible for Chinook and Lynx at the time) was required to have a process whereby technical and administrative staff combined to compile and issue amendments. This is routine work in any MoD Aircraft Project Office. The Amendment Pack consists of:

- Covering Letter and Front Sheet.
- Amendment Instructions - a 'monkey sheet' detailing the actions to be undertaken by, usually, an Administrative Assistant or Administrative Officer (the two most junior administrative grades in the Civil Service). This officer is not required to understand the content of the Pack, merely to have the skill to follow the Instruction Sheet to the letter (e.g. *remove and destroy existing page 2, insert new page 2*).
- Instructions on updating the Amendment Record Sheet in the top-level document (e.g. *Insert AL1, date of amendment, and sign*).

Thus, this part of the audit trail is maintained.

INTERIM CAR - Amendment 1

The content of Amendment List 1, dated March 1994 (unspecific, but in the latter part of the month), would seem routine, but contained a crucial error regarding Section R 'Cold Weather, Snow & Icing Operations'.

To recap, the Icing Limitation for any aircraft plays a vital role in determining what altitude the aircraft can be safely flown at - a particular concern for the flight of ZD576. Clearance is usually a progressive process. That is, it is not unusual to have an altitude/icing Limitation, but it should not be so restrictive as to prevent 'normal' operation. In this context, 'normal' should include comparison with the HC Mk1, because a dual Mk1/Mk2 fleet was being flown during the Mk1 to Mk2 conversion programme. It would constitute a Human Factors hazard to have aircrews operating, alternately, Chinooks with vastly different clearances; and would be operationally ineffective if, for example, a Mk1 and Mk2 were required to fly in tandem, and take account of each other's Limitations. Here, there was a 10°C difference between the aircraft Icing clearances, with the Mk2 more restrictive.

It follows the Chinook HC Mk1 and Mk2 Interface Definition Documents (as distinct from Interface Control) would have been significantly different, and the operational impact assessed. This is a fundamental component of Safety Management and Systems Integration, and hence functional safety. While this may seem relatively minor and, indeed, manageable, it is the cumulative effect of the many Human Factors hazards mentioned in this submission that is important. Here:

- ZD576 was the first Mk2 to enter service in Northern Ireland, arriving on 30 May 1994. The other Chinook in theatre was a Mk1.

- The crew of ZD576 had completed a short 'differences' course in early 1994, but reverted to flying the Mk1 until 2 June 1994.

- The crew's relative unfamiliarity with the Mk2 was compounded by the immature/incomplete nature of the Flight Reference Cards and Aircrew Manual, which form part of the Aircraft Document Set. This failing alone should have been sufficient to preclude issuing the Release to Service. The underlying reason for this immaturity was the single biggest failure. That is, Boscombe were still seeking, from the Aircraft Project Office, basic data to support trials. They had nothing to provide to the RAF Handling Squadron or Air Technical Publications, whose job is was to prepare and issue the publications.

- The installed performance of, for example, avionics systems had not been established - to such a degree that the entire Navigation and

Communications systems were not to be relied upon in any way.

- The performance of the power plant and controls was not fully understood due, primarily, to the inability to validate and verify the FADEC safety critical software.

The cumulative effect persuaded Flight Lieutenant Tapper to make an extraordinary request to use a Chinook Mk1. This was refused.

INTERIM CAR/Release to Service, Section R

At INTERIM Issue in November 1993, Section R was headed 'Cold Weather, Snow & Icing Operations'. Amendment List 1 (AL1) changed this to 'Snow and Icing Operations'. It only has a page R1, and does not include an Icing paragraph, despite the title.

At this point, it is simpler to detail the sequence of actions the clerk would take when amending Section R.

- The instruction sheet says *'destroy R1 and replace with the new R1'*. No more, no less, leaving no Icing paragraph in a properly amended INTERIM CAR (i.e. amended in accordance with the Instruction Sheet). The clerk would simply move on to Section S.

- A page R2 is actually supplied, containing an Icing paragraph. However, in practice, the clerk destroys discarded pages as he/she progresses through what is a tedious task. If he/she realises there is a spare page left over (and there always is, because the Pack includes blank backing sheets), the tendency would be to sign the Amendment Record as job done, in accordance with the Instruction Sheet, and discard what is left.

That is, it is entirely possible that some of the recipients, and there were 39, did not insert R2, meaning the reader would not have access to Icing Limitations. Also, in 1994 it had been at least three years since project offices were afforded adequate manpower for such tasks, so it was common to save up amendments and blitz them periodically. It is possible many recipients still hadn't seen AL1 on 2 June 1994. (Subsequent to the accident, pages R1 and R2 were replaced at AL2, with a page R3 added).

This was a sloppy mistake, yet it may be that most or all clerks recognised the error and inserted page R2, even though the instructions said not to. But the Amendment Pack was not updated to correct the error, indicating no-one reported the problem. However, the basic error does little to engender confidence in that area of the Safety Management System.

Where were the checks and management oversight? These little errors accumulate. One begets another. In safety management terminology, a bigger hole was created in one slice of cheese, thus weakening the defences in depth. (A reference to the Reason Model of accident causation).

Of perhaps greater concern is this. When the pilots undertook the basic Mk1 > Mk2 Differences Course, were they 'converted' at the INTERIM Issue standard, or the AL1 standard? The content of the conversion course would have had to change to include AL1 changes. Did it? When?

Board of Inquiry Report - Annex AI 'Extracts from the Chinook HC2 CA Release'

To illustrate the Icing Limitations of the Chinook HC Mk2, the Board reproduced pages R1 and R2 in its Annex AI. The two pages are seemingly from a different source. R1 is exactly like that provided under Freedom of Information. However, R2 uses a different font size and is visually different in other subtle ways. The impression is of a page scanned with Optical Character Recognition software. MoD has provided copies of the INTERIM CAR and Release to Service many times under Freedom of Information, and none have contained a page R2 like this. Could it be that, in seeking a copy of the INTERIM CAR, the Board were supplied with one that omitted page R2? Were they forced to seek a copy of the missing page, only to be provided with someone else's scanned copy?

In isolation this may not seem significant, but when viewed with the administrative error it emphasises that investigations must view the entire chain of events, not cherry pick convenient facts. Especially when a contributory factor available to the Board is 'Organisational Fault'.

This page R2 issue is a vital link in the airworthiness chain. That the crew knew of the *intended* Icing Limitation is accepted, but it is unclear if this was from the written word, or word of mouth. It is not necessarily what is there that reveals systemic failings, but what is missing. The Board of Inquiry and MoD only looked at what was there.

The two Service Deviations introduced by AL1 are discussed in Section 10.

Section 8 - Events in MoD after Release to Service, and why Boscombe Down ceased flying

Executive Summary

Internal Directorate of Helicopter Projects correspondence reveals AD/HP1 (Captain Mike Brougham RN) was extremely concerned about immaturity of both equipment and process, writing to his superiors asking them to heed Boscombe Down.

Boscombe ceased flying the MoD(PE) Fleet twice in 1994, on airworthiness grounds.

Events in the Directorate of Helicopter Projects (DHP)

It is important to look at events immediately after INTERIM CAR, in particular the actions of Captain Brougham, who reported to Director Helicopter Projects (DHP, Dr David Hughes). He was in charge of all Chinook and Lynx programmes, with project management teams under him, including a resident team at Boeing Helicopters in Philadelphia. Dr Hughes' immediate superior was Director General Aircraft 1, Air Vice Marshal Peter Norriss, who reported to Controller Aircraft, Donald Spiers. (Later Sir Donald).

A Guardian article, calling on Computer Weekly's work, summarised matters:

'A previously unseen handwritten memo dated 29 April 1994 - a month before the crash - reveals that Captain Brougham, the MoD official appointed project manager for the Chinook, was urging his superiors to "understand and take full account of" Boscombe Down's views to ensure that in future negotiations with the manufacturers, the MoD would be able to secure the "satisfaction of all Safety Case issues".

The memo also raised concerns about misleading comparisons between different FADEC systems, calling in to question another key element of Dr Reid's defence of the Chinook programme: the positive experience of other countries which use it. For example, he told the select committee last year that the United States was "...perfectly happy. They have a huge fleet of Chinooks - and they are applying the standards of NASA". He failed to mention, however, that the RAF's version of FADEC was different from those used by other countries.

The magazine has obtained a second memo from Brougham, dated 11 January 1995. In a handwritten footnote to the report of a meeting with Textron Lycoming, he referred to a "series of problems" with the Chinooks, "many of which were traced eventually back to software design and systems integrations problems...". The period in which these incidents occurred, Brougham wrote, was between February and July 1994 - the same period as the crash.'

These memos [B30] from Captain Brougham to superiors (plural, implying Hughes and Norriss, at least) were seen by the House of Commons and House of Lords, but were assessed against a backdrop painted by MoD. That is, MoD was disparaging about Boscombe, implying the problems Captain Brougham cited were minor and not an obstacle to releasing the aircraft. However, one wonders what their (Commons, Lords) reaction would have been had they been advised the background was not a minor disagreement, but a statement that the software implementation was *'positively dangerous'*? Or that Boscombe's advice was the aircraft should not be flying at all? Or that Donald Spiers actually issued this mandate?

Even without such condemning evidence, each of these Inquiries found in the pilots' favour, but the basis for their conclusions would have been even more concrete had they been able to cite this background. Even though they quoted Captain Brougham, they apparently did not understand the full implications (that he was reporting a breakdown in the airworthiness process), yet this is where MoD is known to be guilty of systemic failures - now admitted post-Nimrod Review.

Captain Brougham (apparently) did not spell this out, but he would have no need to. He was writing to (at least) Dr Hughes, to whom the 12 October 1993 Boscombe letter was addressed (stating CAR could not be recommended, and covering the 30 September 1993 *'positively dangerous'* report). Dr Hughes would have known precisely what Captain Brougham meant. Both were senior staff responsible for delivering safe helicopters. There would be no need to preface internal correspondence with a simple statement of policy effectively teaching Dr Hughes to suck eggs. It would be condescending and rude.

Highly significant is the mention of *'system integration'* problems. No-one seems to have asked what these were, yet if systems are not integrated properly, one cannot verify functional safety and there can be no evidence to support a Limitations-based Release to Service. Nor can its behaviour and performance be measured against the aircraft/system specification - so it is impossible to state if a given performance represents a Limitation. This uncertainty can be seen in just how few systems were cleared to any level on 2 June 1994.

Visit to Textron Lycoming

On 21 January 1994 Captain Brougham undertook a visit to Textron Lycoming in Stratford, Connecticut, USA. The subject of the meeting was 'The way forward with Chinook HC Mk2 FADEC software'. The notes of the meeting [B31] state the primary aim was to:

'Discuss the overall position and to see Textron's full agreement, co-operation and urgent participation in our proposed short-term course of action. Specifically, on the HSDE proposal for additional work, the aim would be to seek technical and commercial agreement, so that this could be authorised to proceed, and contracted without delay.' (HSDE, Hawker Siddeley Dynamics Engineering, were Textron's sub-contractor on FADEC software).

The secondary aim was:

'To discuss the longer-term options for revisions to the software which would enable the UK to satisfactorily complete the CA Release process.'

It cannot be emphasised enough how extraordinary this is. The personal involvement of an RN Captain is indicative of the high profile FADEC was receiving, and the seriousness of the problems. Here we are, 2.5 months <u>after</u> the aircraft has been declared airworthy by the Assistant Chief of the Air Staff, discussing how to *'move forward'* on safety critical software - which Boscombe have cited as the main reason why the aircraft is <u>not</u> airworthy.

Moreover, this visit, and any discussion of FADEC, must always be viewed in the context of ongoing legal action MoD was taking against Textron following severe damage to a Chinook in 1989. MoD later won this case, the basis of which was the poor quality of FADEC software (i.e. it was not fit for purpose).

Why did Boscombe Down cease flying the Chinook HC Mk2 in 1994?

After the accident, MoD sought to refute an allegation that the test pilots had refused to fly the Chinook HC Mk2, stating: [B32]

'As to the allegation that some pilots refused to fly the Chinook HC Mk2 during CA Release trials at Boscombe Down, this is an over simplification of what actually happened and perhaps it would be helpful if some of the background was explained.

On 7 March 1994 during one of the specified FADEC checks on the ground, the engine of an HC Mk2 flamed out. Trials at Boscombe Down were halted while the failure was investigated. The failure was not due to a software fault and flying resumed on 20 April 1994.

However, in the period up to 2 June 1994 there were a number of incidents

*involving airborne HC Mk2 of which approximately five were due to FADEC
malfunction whilst operating in normal mode. There had also been incidents on the
ground. The MoD(PE) project office sought explanations of the various incidents
from the aircraft and engine manufacturers but in the absence of satisfactory
explanations Boscombe Down suspended trials flying.*

*The trials aircraft as transferred to RAF Odiham for servicing and subsequently
returned to Boscombe Down in mid-October 1994. It was subsequently fitted with
instrumentation for the remaining flight trials which commenced in November
1994.*

*The postponement of trials at this time was therefore an <u>expediency within the
proper exercise of airworthiness considerations by Boscombe Down</u> and was not
seen as a refusal by individual test pilots to fly the Chinook HC MK2'.*

First and foremost, MoD is admitting long-standing critical airworthiness
concerns existed on the day of the accident. The admission of five
FADEC related in-flight incidents in a 6-week period is alarming, more
so because they occurred on the single PE Fleet trials aircraft. Failure to
explain this arising <u>rate</u>, and the associated erosion of aircrew confidence
in the product, misled by omission.

The admission that the MoD(PE) project office (DHP) sought an
explanation from manufacturers, demonstrates they were fully involved
in this process and decision making. Key questions include (a) when were
the manufacturers tasked to investigate?, (b) were they given a deadline?,
and (c) did they offer any advice, such as cease flying? And, crucially, was
Boeing's Safety Case amended?

Because RAF Chinooks had a unique FADEC variant, Boeing and Textron
would have immature data on failure modes and effects. They would not
have been complacent about such a failure <u>rate</u> on a Safety Critical
system. Under these circumstances, why did Service flying continue after
the first of the failures in the period from 20 April 1994? What discussions
took place between DHP and the RAF? Was the RAF Director of Flight
Safety consulted?

Boscombe's decision to cease flying <u>must</u> be viewed in the context of
their consistent declaration that the Chinook HC Mk2 was not airworthy;
and that matters got progressively worse.

Section 9 - Status of the Release to Service at time of accident

Executive Summary

The Release to Service is the Master Airworthiness Reference in the Aircraft Document Set, and must be available to all aircrew where practicable. It is the first document one looks to if asked to demonstrate airworthiness, with the audit trail flowing backwards through Safety Case, Controller Aircraft Release (CAR), build standard, etc.

If one signs a Release to Service, that signature is relied upon by aircrew, groundcrew and passengers as evidence the regulations have been complied with, the aircraft and its systems have been tested and trialled, and installed performance established; so facilitating the promulgation of Limitations. That was not the case on 2 June 1994.

This section assesses the Release as that date, concluding it was so immature, so lacking in mandated information, as to be a fabrication. (Knowingly presenting false or incomplete information as true or complete with the intent to deceive). It concludes there were serious and systemic breaches of the airworthiness regulations.

Freedom of Information requests

When asked by the author to provide the CAR and Release to Service, as of November 1993, MoD provided:

- The Boscombe Down report *in the form of an INTERIM CAR*, dated 26 October 1993, (and subsequent ALs 1, 3, 4, 7 & 8 to the CAR; but not AL2, issued after the accident, or 5 and 6).

- The Release to Service at Initial Issue 1, Amendment 6, dated 10 January 1996.

When then asked to provide the Release to Service current at the time of the accident, MoD provided a copy of the INTERIM CAR, plus Service Deviations 1/94 and 2/94. When asked to provide the final Chinook HC Mk1 Release to Service, MoD provided Issue 2 at Amendment 20, dated 8 September 1988.

Several issues and questions arise, among them:

- The covering letter to Boscombe's report of 26 October 1993 states it must be read in conjunction with previous reports detailing why the aircraft is not to be relied upon in any way. This was not reflected in the Release to Service.

- It was known other Service Deviations were signed in April 1994, but had not been promulgated before the accident.

- Why provide a Release to Service dated 1996, when asked for one dated 1993? The answer is that it is the first legal Release.

- The Assistant Chief of the Air Staff (ACAS) had merely added a Cover Sheet to the INTERIM CAR, calling it the 'Air Force Department Release'. (An old RAF term for the Release to Service). Despite the requirement to issue a Letter of Promulgation, which is the authority to commence Service regulated flying, and insert it in the Release, there was none. That is, there was no legal Release to Service in November 1993, or on 2 June 1994. The fact it was almost entirely non-compliant was discussed in Section 2.

- It is highly unlikely the final Mk1 Release was in 1988, if only because of the plethora of Special Trials Fits embodied for Gulf War 1 in 1990/91. This would also imply it was not up-issued to reflect the Mk2 (for example, the immature status and erroneous *ERROR* warnings in the GPS). This introduced Human Factors hazards because aircrews were expected to migrate between the two Marks. If, indeed, it remained at this 1988 Issue, then the failure to update it was a serious breakdown of the airworthiness process. If there was a subsequent Issue, why did MoD withhold it?

Other parties also sought this information, and each received different versions, which had plainly been 'tailored' according to who asked. This is common. Nevertheless, these papers have been collated and, as far as possible, a full suite has been reconstructed facilitating the detailed analysis in this report.

To summarise the background:

- On 26 October 1993 Boscombe issued a document *'in the form of an INTERIM CAR'* outlining the current status of their work - the aircraft was not airworthy.

- MoD(PE) re-issued this progress report to ACAS as an INTERIM CAR, dated 9 November 1993, but made no reference to the status.

- ACAS prepared a new cover page and regurgitated the INTERIM CAR as an 'MoD(AFD) Release', dated 22 November 1993.

- In late March 1994 an amendment was issued adding two Service Deviations.

- On 10 January 1996, Issue 6 of the Release to Service was the first to include a Letter of Promulgation. This was the first authority to conduct Service regulated flying.

Configuration control of the INTERIM CAR and Release to Service

If asked for a copy of a document under configuration control, only the document owner/controller can provide a certified copy. If the recipient is not to be provided with updates, then it must be marked 'Not Maintained'.

Every such document, if under correct configuration control (a key component of airworthiness), must have an Amendment Record Sheet in which the insertion of successive amendments is <u>individually</u> recorded. This process demonstrates when and by whom each amendment was incorporated, in each copy of the document. *Inter alia*, it demonstrates to investigators <u>when</u> changes were promulgated to users of that copy.

So, at Amendment 6 (10 January 1996), there should be seven entries in the Amendment Record Sheet (Initial, plus ALs 1-6 inclusive). There was not. It merely contains a statement that ALs 1-5 have been *'incorporated'*, the implication being they had not been incorporated earlier. It does not say when or by whom. This suggests a clumsy attempt to 'correct' the audit trail after the event.

Amendments 2-8 are important, as they provide an indication of actions taken in the aftermath - particularly relevant given the Reviewing Officers' assertion that the aircraft was serviceable, and MoD's denial that there were any airworthiness issues.

MoD has refused to provide ALs 2, 5 and 6. For obvious reasons AL2, issued in July 1994, is crucial. However, most of their contents can be reconstructed by comparing other issues. They reveal six Service Deviations were issued immediately after AL1 (in April 1994), but not promulgated in the Release to Service as of 2 June 1994.

Amendment List 1 (AL1) to the Release to Service, dated March 1994

The two Service Deviations promulgated at AL1 are:
- 1/94 - 14 February 1994 - Secure HF Role Radio
- 2/94 - 14 February 1994 - Repositioned IR Jammer Transmitters

These remained the sole Service Deviations at the time of the accident. Was the use of these equipments included in the Mk1 > Mk2 conversion course undertaken by the ZD576 crew? When asked for a list of Mk2 Deviations current on 2 June 1994, MoD provided a retrospectively (and

81

using past tense) produced list containing a further seven Deviations. [B33] That is, it was not a working, maintained document. They are all dated April 1994 and, in the context of the Freedom of Information request, the clear intent was to give the impression they formed part of the Release to Service at the time of the crash. They did not. Also, if a proper Release existed, there would be no need to waste such effort - all MoD would have to do is copy the relevant index. Again, this is evidence of an invalid Release on 2 June 1994. Subsequent requests yielded actual copies of the Service Deviations.

Intentional or otherwise, this misrepresentation gives the false impression of <u>nine</u> Service Deviations being extant on 2 June 1994, when there were only <u>two</u>. Compounding matters, the delay in issuing the other seven is unexplained. The seven unissued Deviations were:

- 3/94 - 15 April 94 - Fast Roping Insertion and Extraction
- 4/94 - 22 April 94 - Use of Chaff/Flare Dispenser *
- 5/94 - 22 April 94 - LORAL AN/AAR 47 Missile Approach Warner *
- 6/94 - 22 April 94 - M60D Armament System *
- 7/94 - 22 April 94 - Cougar/Keystone Secure Radio Installation #
- 8/94 - 22 April 94 - Use of Night Vision Goggles
- 9/94 - 22 April 94 - Extended Range Fuel System

Ideally, Service Deviations should not be saved up for consolidated issue. They should certainly not be held back for three months when they include vital self-protection systems (*) and communications equipment for use in Northern Ireland (#). They should be issued at the time of signing, subject to MoD(PE) being advised and given the opportunity to assess any possible impact on the CAR. Notably, MoD(PE) *must* prepare engineering Service Deviations, but there is no indication this mandate was adhered to.

MoD correspondence on this subject (from Adam Ingram, Minister for the Armed Forces) is disingenuous, omitting to mention Service Deviations. It implies the Chinook HC Mk2 was a new build aircraft, stating the short period between Release to Service (November 1993) and the accident (June 1994) was insufficient for any configuration control problems to arise. This is manifestly untrue, and a crucial misrepresentation of facts relating to the Mk2's basic airworthiness.[22]

---

22 Letter D/Min(AF)/AI 4573/05/C/LN, 10 November 2005 (Adam Ingram MP to Steve Webb MP).

Furthermore, there is a discrepancy between the above list and the INTERIM CAR issue that first mentioned Service Deviations 3/94-on. The former states 3/94-9/94 were issued in April 94, the latter that 9/94 (and 10/94) were withdrawn. Given the list was drawn up retrospectively, this is a further indication of a serious disconnect in the MoD's Chinook configuration management system.

Additionally:

- It is incumbent upon MoD to test and trial the aircraft at this new, post-Service Deviation build standard, to establish any changes or degradation to the installed performance (which should have been established during Contractor/CAR trials). This is mandatory, because it is the basis of any Limitations expressed in the CAR. MoD implied this had been carried out. But it had not, witness so much information missing from the INTERIM CAR and Release to Service.

- Of the nine Service Deviations, six are avionic related and would be expected to generate comment, and probably Limitations, in the INTERIM CAR; especially as the entire Navigation and Communications systems have Switch-On Only clearance. For example, both 1/94 and 2/94 (secure HF radio and IR Jammer) routinely caused Electro-Magnetic Compatibility problems. Also, any radio is dependent on the intercom. The Release to Service does not permit the intercom to be fitted, rendering 1/94 erroneous.

- The list of Boscombe Chinook reports, as of May 1994, includes only one giving advice on a Service Deviation for Chinook Mk2. Where are the others?

The only reasonable conclusions are that these Service Deviations were:

- Not prepared by MoD(PE).

- Hastily embodied by Service Engineered Modifications or Special Trials Fit (none of which are mentioned in the Release to Service).

- 'Approved' in the Mk2 without proper or timely promulgation, and lacking what would be regarded as a normal Integrated Test, Evaluation and Acceptance process.

It seems likely Boeing either did not heed existing Mk1 Service Engineered Modifications, or were not contracted to subsume many of them into the Mk2 design. Either way, it is clear this came as a belated surprise to the Assistant Chief of the Air Staff. Nor, it seems, were Boeing tasked to appraise the installations. There is no evidence of Boeing being tasked to up-issue the Safety Case for each change to the build standard (and each Service Deviation constitutes such a change). These are common breaches of regulations.

Crucially, for avionic systems, and especially those with high power emitters and sensitive receivers, it would seem the brief Electro-Magnetic Compatibility assessment of Mk2 *preceded* these Deviations. This reinforces the comments made in the '3 Fellows' (of the Royal Aeronautical Society) report of 2000. [B5]

The obvious risk is that of the Deviations, individually or collectively, not being compatible with the baseline build standard, causing adverse effects on existing systems. The full extent of this cannot be known, except that MoD admitted serious problems with the IR Jammer and HF installations; but for the purposes of this submission it does not have to be. The issue is that regulations, designed to establish airworthiness and ensure it is maintained, and installed performance and subsequent degradations or changes measured and notified, were not implemented. It is entirely possible these Service Deviations caused degradation but the pilots were not advised. This would cause uncertainty and distrust.

Section 10 - The audit trail

Executive Summary

The maintenance and permanent retention of an audit trail is a fundamental component of airworthiness. This regulatory requirement was not implemented on Chinook HC Mk2 or in the wider MoD.

Relationship between Release to Service, Controller Aircraft Release, the Safety Case, and the build standard.

To briefly recap:

The Release to Service (RTS) is the Master Airworthiness Reference in the Aircraft Document Set. Its content and structure are laid down in Controller Aircraft Instructions. Additionally, JSP553 (Military Airworthiness Regulations) states:

'The RTS is the release document giving authority for Service regulated flying. The RTS is derived from the initial CA Release but includes a safety justification of subsequent changes. It is thus based on a Safety Case covering the as-flown configuration of the aircraft to which the RTS applies'.

(It is the covering letter of promulgation that provides authority).

In 1993 Controller Aircraft Instructions defined the Controller Aircraft Release (CAR) as:

'The statement of the operating envelope, conditions, Limitations and build standard for a particular aircraft type, within which the airworthiness has been established as meeting the required level of safety'.

MoD(PE)'s Airworthiness, Design Requirements and Procedures (ADRP) department amplified this by saying:

'CA Release is a notification by Controller Aircraft to the Service department concerned (Royal Air Force, Royal Navy or Army) that a new type of aircraft has been developed to the stage where it is suitable for use by Service aircrew. By the same token the Service requires CA Release before they can operate a new type of aircraft'. [B6]

At all times it should be noted that if reference is made to the CAR, then by definition this also refers to Part 1 of the Release to Service.

Defence Standard 00-56 defines a Safety Case as:

'A structured argument, supported by a body of evidence that provides a compelling, comprehensive and valid case that a system is safe for a given application in a given operating environment'.

The Safety Case (and hence CAR and Release to Service) is constructed against a defined build standard; in turn traceable to a Statement of Operating Intent and Usage (SOIU). Any change to the build standard or SOIU must be reflected in a new issue of the Safety Case. To be valid, the build standard must be maintained. Defence Standard 05-125/2, called up in JSP553 and mandated in all aviation contracts by Controller Aircraft, lays down the procedures for doing this.

Configuration Management, safety and the build standard

Design configuration must be controlled and maintained.[23] When a design has been brought 'Under Ministry Control', the responsibility for maintaining the build standard rests with MoD. The contractual vehicle is the Post Design Services (PDS) contract, and PDS is defined as 'maintaining the build standard'. There are 17 core components, and Configuration Management (and the Safety Case) is a common thread running through each. (See Appendix 1 for a fuller explanation).

If the build standard has not been maintained, the Safety Case, Controller Aircraft Release and Release to Service cannot be properly validated or verified, and become progressively invalid. In saying this, MoD takes a degree of acceptable risk because, in practice, this work must often lag behind the engineering or trials work, if only to prevent nugatory work in the event of minor or late changes as a result of test and evaluation. However, this delay should at most be weeks, not years; and there is a process to swiftly promulgate urgent information. For example, it is not acceptable for a new Mark of aircraft to be released to service lacking up-to-date Flight Reference Cards or an Aircrew Manual, or for modifications to be missing from publications or the Release to Service. Yet this is precisely what happened on Chinook HC Mk2.

Therefore, the single most important process in maintaining airworthiness is PDS. If the through-life cover has not been continuous, then the audit trail is broken. That does not mean the aircraft is unairworthy - 'merely' that MoD cannot demonstrate, as it is required to, that it *is* airworthy. In time, this risk will accrue to a point where it is too great to say, with any confidence, that the aircraft remains airworthy. This transition point is a matter of engineering judgment.

Of relevance, in his evidence to the Public Accounts Committee on 3

---

23 Defence Standard 00-57 'Configuration Management of Defence Materiel'.

March 1999 the Chief of Defence Procurement (CDP), Sir Robert Walmsley, acknowledged that the Chinook was not under proper configuration control.

(Q) *'It seems your management information systems have not been able to establish their design status or keep up with the modifications to Chinook helicopters. Is that right?'*

(A) *'I think you have understood it absolutely correctly. That is true.'*

As the Committee was investigating, *inter alia*, the Chinook HC Mk1 to Mk2 modification programme, it is fair to say they were referring to this period. Thus, Adam Ingram's claim of 2005 wholly contradicts CDP on a critical component of airworthiness. It is inconsistencies like this that demonstrate the weaknesses in MoD's case against the pilots. The misbriefing of Mr Ingram was a serious offence. Worse, it ignored the August 1992 CHART report in which the RAF Director of Flight Safety reiterated that failure to maintain configuration control had led to previous Chinook accidents, concluding:

'The current organisational structure for tasking and fleet management, and the lack of resources, is not a healthy recipe for the future sound airworthiness of the Chinook.'

As the Safety Case, Controller Aircraft Release and Release to Service must all reflect a build standard that is under full configuration control, it follows that none of these documents could be fully validated or verified. It is recommended the motives of an organisation and its staff who are prepared to deceive a Minister to such an extent are investigated. What desperation drives them when they must know their words are so easily refuted?

Evidence of negligence relating to the rundown of Post Design Services

Having established the need to maintain the build standard, one must assess MoD's actions in the period before 2 June 1994. Defence Standard 05-125/2 was mandated by Controller Aircraft in every aircraft related contract, and calls up PDS Specifications 1-20. [B11] As the use of these publications has been discontinued (in fact, prohibited), and they have not been replaced, it unclear where MoD's corporate knowledge now lies. Notwithstanding, any reputable company would insist on them being invoked in contracts; and if they weren't, would use them anyway.

In 1991 PDS funding for avionics was cut by 28% by MoD(PE)'s Director of Air Radio (Mr Barry Cox). Responsibility then transferred to Air Member Supply and Organisation (AMSO - Air Marshal Sir Brendan

Jackson), who applied similar cuts over the next three years. Despite the 1992 cut being noted in the CHART report, MoD has denied all knowledge. For example, in letter dated 17 May 2007 from Adam Ingram, also claiming the airworthiness regulations were implemented properly. Mr Haddon-Cave QC disagreed.

Increasingly, non-technical AMSO staff refused to release funding to maintain build standards. Technical Publications were not to be kept up-to-date. Fault Investigations were curtailed. In mid-1992 an edict was issued that only safety related tasks should be let, ignoring that all PDS is safety related. Finally, in January 1993 funding for flight safety critical tasks was denied. Addendum C maps these failures to the recommendations of the CHART report, illustrating the immediate effect they had on Chinook airworthiness.

Example

A prime example of the effect was the case of RN Lynx aircraft making heavy landings due to toxic fumes in the cockpit, injuring aircrew (thankfully, not seriously). Junior RAF Supply Managers denied more senior engineering staff funding to conduct an investigation and make the aircraft safe. (A disregard for real fire hazards that has resonance with the Nimrod XV230 case). The problem was resolved in the first instance by disobeying a direct order, and diverting money from a lower priority RAF task to fund redesign of terminal blocks associated with the radar.

This was notified to senior staff. No action was taken, yet it is now known that the same failings, leading to the CHART report of 1992, were occurring concurrently on other fleets. This was a failure of management oversight and leadership by the RAF Chief Engineer, and his senior staff.

Director Internal Audit conducted an audit, in June 1996 making 19 recommendations to the Permanent Under-Secretary of State for Defence. [B34] MoD no longer has this report and cannot say if these have been implemented but, for example, if #15 had been implemented it would be immediately apparent build standards were not being maintained, rendering Safety Cases, Controller Aircraft Releases and Releases to Service progressively invalid. (*'The system provisioning parameters are reviewed periodically and evidence retained of the review'*. This was mandated policy anyway).

This 1996 report can be viewed as a forerunner of the Nimrod Review. They have the same originator (myself), cover the same issues, and reveal the same culprits.

Annex - Organisation of MoD in 1993/94

This Annex seeks to complement Chapter 12 of the Nimrod Review 'History of RAF In-Service Support (1990-2009)' by discussing practical implementation of regulations and instructions and the effect on all In-Service. The Review claimed *'systemic failings'* commenced in 1998, coinciding with the disestablishment of the RAF Chief Engineer post; naming and blaming two very senior officers for *'cuts, change, dilution and distraction'*. This date, and hence the criticism of these officers, is wrong, and Mr Haddon-Cave knew it was. In his CHART report the RAF Director of Flight Safety confirmed they existed in the late-80s - see Addendum C. One must ask why Mr Haddon-Cave ignored this evidence, and who his claim served to protect.

Airworthiness family tree

The best contemporaneous example of the tree was promulgated in Defence Council Instruction (General) 89/93 [B6]; current when the INTERIM Controller Aircraft Release and Release to Service were issued. Below is an extract (the original is of similar poor quality).

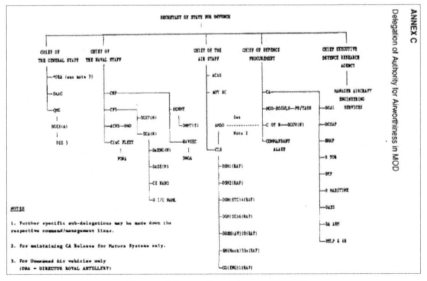

Airworthiness family tree (1993)

The Secretary of State meets his airworthiness responsibility by delegating matters to the Chief of Defence Procurement (CDP), the Chiefs of Staff, and the Chief Executive of the Defence Research Agency (for the PE Fleet). Briefly:

1. CDP <u>attains</u> airworthiness.

2. Air Member Logistics (AML, formed 1 April 1994, and formerly Air Member Supply and Organisation) <u>maintains</u> the airworthiness of aircraft types.

3. The Services ensure the <u>continuing</u> airworthiness of individual aircraft.

Responsibility for new aircraft transfers from CDP to AML at or around the point the design is brought Under Ministry Control. That is, when the PDS contract is let. However, if CDP is charged, for example, with conducting a major upgrade, the responsibility may temporarily transfer back. This is not so much a formal process, but usually arises through necessity caused by AMSO's 1991 policy of not maintaining airworthiness. Put another way, a standing risk (or certainty) in every upgrade programme is that airworthiness will have to be resurrected and stabilised. This applied to the Chinook Mk1 to Mk2 upgrade, and this submission sets out the reasons why stabilisation was never achieved.

The key column in Figure 1, as far as the Chinook INTERIM CAR is concerned, is CDP down to Controller Aircraft, then to his 2 and 1 Stars (the column starting with DGA1 (Director General Aircraft 1), then to DHP (Director Helicopter Projects). For the Release to Service, it is the column headed Chief of the Air Staff.

In the context of a Mid-Life Upgrade programme such as Chinook HC Mk1 to Mk2, Note 2 is crucial, illustrating the functional link between AMSO/AML and the MoD(PE) Directorates. That is, AMSO was responsible for maintaining the airworthiness and Safety Cases of many components and systems of the Mk1; and DHP was wholly dependent on this work.

In turn, DHP (in practice, AD/HP1) had a duty to satisfy himself that the Mk1 was indeed airworthy, the build standard maintained, the Safety Case valid and verifiable, and the Mk1 Release to Service up-to-date and valid. In project management terms, for the purposes of the Mid-Life Upgrade contract this comes under the heading 'Induction Build Standard', which must be agreed between DHP, the Service User and AMSO; and then between DHP and Boeing.

All the above requirements were wholly compromised by the ongoing policy not to routinely maintain build standards. That meant any Safety Case was unverifiable, compromising the INTERIM CAR and Release to Service. The airworthiness delegation system had broken down.

Practical Implementation

MoD(PE) staff expected such changes in structure to commence around 1992/3, following repeal in 1987 of Section 10 of the Crown Proceedings Act 1947, which had hitherto effectively prevented the possibility of a legal action against Crown Servants. While those with airworthiness delegation had been notified long before (letters of delegation were first issued in October 1991, and all were briefed as to how to inform and direct Design Authorities and Custodians), the new Defence Airworthiness Group (established February 1992) issued its first amendment to JSP318B and Controller Aircraft Instructions in January that year, with further details promulgated to staff by DCI GEN 89/93.

Those affected by changes in legislation are given a reasonable period in which to comply. After that period of grace, the clock runs on litigation. All staff with airworthiness delegation understood this principle, especially the Technical Agencies whose job it was to prioritise airworthiness work at contractors.

Briefly, the resultant changes in how airworthiness was managed would cost more. The senior management (2 Star and above) response was to cut funding, so what changes took place were negative. That is, instead of being given a higher profile and bolstered, airworthiness was severely degraded. It was treated as an even greater waste of money (especially by AMSO(RAF), who now controlled funding). But not by those with airworthiness delegation who were now under threat of legal action. Engineering staff responsibilities were no longer complemented with the necessary authority and resources to meet their legal obligations; compounded by non-engineering staff in AMSO being permitted to make engineering decisions directly affecting airworthiness - a malaise that spread to MoD(PE) and was approved by CDP. This is discussed in greater detail in Appendices 4 and 5.

The issue of how delegation is managed remains important, given its contribution to recent fatal accidents. The regulations are robust, but poorly implemented. For example, while a non-engineer cannot be given airworthiness or technical and financial approval delegation, he/she is permitted to overrule/make engineering design decisions - which in an aircraft always affects safety. This, of course, is ludicrous (and demonstrably fatal), but is universally condoned. It became common in the early 1990s; and in MoD(PE) Sir Robert Walmsley (Chief of Defence Procurement - CDP) specifically ruled so in 2001. Full Ministerial support has been expressed consistently since 2003. For example, on 30 April 2003 Dr Lewis Moonie MP cited CDP's rulings that (a) it was an offence to refuse an order to make a false written declaration regarding Requirement Scrutiny (encompassing airworthiness), and (b) it was not an offence to issue such an order.[24]

A Release to Service Authority (RTSA), knowing the above, would be wise to permanently engage legal counsel. The problem they face is they may be the *authority*, but have no *control*, which rests with, primarily, the Technical Agency. Similarly, the project offices do not have control over everything in their aircraft, and such is the dearth of experience most no longer know how to implement the regulations, even if they have the resources. (A rather blunt way of expressing the views shared by Mr Haddon-Cave QC). The system relies on adequate funding, experience, competence and trust. When senior staff and Ministers do not insist on any of these, and are quite happy to state this, the RTSA becomes a lonely man.

Key staff posts (At time of INTERIM CAR/Release to Service/accident, unless otherwise stated)

Royal Air Force
ZD576 Crew

Flight Lieutenant Richard Cook - Handling Pilot

Flight Lieutenant Jonathan Tapper - Aircraft Captain and Non-Handling Pilot

Master Air Loadmaster Graham Forbes - #2 Crewman (forward)

Sergeant Kevin Hardie - #1 Crewman (aft)

Board of Inquiry (Members)

Wing Commander Andrew Pulford (President, Pilot)

---

24 Chief of Defence Procurement letters CDP 117/6/7, 19 November 2001, and CDP 117/6/7, 13 December 2001.

Squadron Leader Peter Cole (Engineer)

Squadron Leader Edward Gilday (Pilot)

Board of Inquiry (Reviewing Officers)

Group Captain Peter Crawford - Station Commander, RAF Odiham

Group Captain Roger Wedge - Station Commander, RAF Aldergrove

Air Vice Marshal John Day - Air Officer Commanding 1 Group, Convening Officer

Air Chief Marshal William Wratten - Air Officer Commanding-in-Chief Strike Command, Senior Reviewing Officer

Directorate of the Air Staff

Chief of the Air Staff, professional head of the RAF - Air Chief Marshal Michael Graydon

Assistant Chief of the Air Staff - Air Vice Marshal Anthony Bagnall

RAF Director of Flight Safety

Air Commodore Martin Abbott, succeeded by Air Commodore Rick Peacock-Edwards on 1 July 1994.

RAF Chief Engineer

Air Chief Marshal Michael Alcock was appointed on 8 August 1991. He became double-hatted as Air Member Logistics (replacing Air Member Supply and Organisation) on 1 April 1994, and retired on 25 June 1996.

Notes:

Appointment dates and taking up post are often months apart.

I have endeavoured to refer to Air Chief Marshal Day by his rank at the time being discussed, as it is important to appreciate he was subordinate to Air Chief Marshal Wratten at the time of the Board of Inquiry, but later attained the same rank.

MoD (Procurement Executive)

Chief of Defence Procurement, responsible for all Defence procurement expenditure:

1991-1996 - Sir Malcolm McIntosh

1996-2003 - Vice Admiral (retired) Sir Robert Walmsley

Controller Aircraft, head of Air Systems Controllerate in MoD(PE):

1989-31 March 1994 - Sir Donald Spiers

1 April 1994-29 October 1996 - Air Marshal Roger Austin

Director General Aircraft 2, responsible for delivery of helicopters and maritime aircraft - Air Vice Marshal Peter Norriss, who later became Director General Air Systems 1, Controller Aircraft, and Deputy Chief of Defence Procurement.

Director Helicopter Projects, responsible for delivery of all helicopters except Merlin. Also, peculiar-to-type avionics and aircraft equipment:

1993-June 1996 - Dr David Hughes

July 1996-March 1999 - Dr David Colbourne, whereupon the post was disbanded due to the reformation of Integrated Project Teams.

Assistant Director Helicopter Projects 1, responsible for delivery of all Chinook and Lynx programmes and, from August 1997, Sea King, Health and Usage Monitoring System, and VVIP (Queen's Flight replacement). The post holder is the Aircraft Project Director:

1993-1996 - Captain Mike Brougham RN

1996-February 1999 - Colonel Barry Hodgkiss

APPENDICES

Appendix 1 - Airworthiness submission to the Nimrod Review (2007-09)

Executive Summary

The following was submitted to the Nimrod Review by the author. It is essentially a summary of issues that had already been submitted as evidence to the Oxford Coroner, and so available to the Review. It does not pretend to cover all aspects of airworthiness, but is an authoritative source from the viewpoint of practical implementation of the airworthiness regulations. The intention was to signpost the way for the Review, whose final report incorporated all the main points. However, as stated, it wrongly dated the start date of the RAF's *savings at the expense of safety* policy. [B1]

Note: Minor amendments have been made to remove references and names. In convening the Nimrod Review, The Right Honourable Des Browne MP confirmed past and present Crown Servants would be immune from prosecution if they gave evidence. The Mull of Kintyre Review could not confirm the same applied.

Submission to the Nimrod Review

Introduction

The purpose of this submission is to expand upon the points made by Commander in Chief Air Command, Air Chief Marshal Sir Clive Loader, in the Nimrod XV230 Board of Inquiry report; in particular:

> 'I conclude that the loss of XV230 and, far more importantly, of the 14 Service personnel who were aboard, resulted in shortcomings in the application of the processes for assuring airworthiness and safe operation of the Nimrod. I am clear that further activity must be undertaken for our other aircraft types to check whether there is any read-across of lessons we have learned from this accident at such enormous (and immensely sad) cost.'

His conclusion influenced the statement to the House by the Secretary of State for Defence (and Scotland) that MoD accepted liability. However, given the narrow remit of the Nimrod Review, it is unclear if his recommendation to check other aircraft has been accepted.

In discussing the issues I will endeavour to illustrate, through practical examples and benchmark rulings, that Sir Clive's conclusions were far from revelatory. They have been made before by MoD staff, and rejected. If heeded, other fatal accidents would have been prevented.

With a few exceptions (examples noted below) I believe the processes and procedures for attaining airworthiness are implemented well. Much of what follows discusses maintaining airworthiness.

Definition of Airworthiness

Airworthiness is defined as:

'The ability of an aircraft or other airborne equipment or system to operate without significant hazard to aircrew, ground crew, passengers (where relevant) or to the general public over which the airborne systems are flown'. [1]

It is important to differentiate between attaining and maintaining airworthiness, and indeed JSP553 [2] deals with the subjects in two different chapters (4 and 5 respectively). One must also understand the different dynamics at play in the MoD departments responsible for each.

Airworthiness is not a one-off process, it is a through-life obligation. Components of an airworthiness system include, but are not confined to:

- Qualification testing of components and systems including software validation and verification to the appropriate standards.
- Safety and Risk Management
- Quality Systems and Standards, Control and Assurance [3]
- Flight Trials - both Manufacturer's and MoD's
- Certification
- Release to Service Recommendations from Boscombe Down and the way they are dealt with by MoD
- Release to Service including flight Limitations
- Configuration Management, including Configuration Milestones such as Critical Design Review, Functional Configuration Audits, etc.
- Ageing Aircraft Audits/management
- Training of air and ground crews, and by definition provision of all necessary facilities, including their validation and verification
- Documentation, Publications and Orders including vital publications such as the Operating Data Manual, the Aircrew Manual and Flight Reference Cards
- Maintenance Standards and Responsibilities [4]

- Recording Systems, Fault Investigation, Feedback and Corrective Action

Airworthiness and Fitness for Purpose

Airworthiness should not be confused with fitness for purpose, which is an operational term. To make an airworthy aircraft fit for purpose often requires it to be significantly enhanced, at great cost. A typical example would be a Defensive Aids Suite in response to a perceived threat in a new operational theatre. But the concept also recognises the imperative to operate an aircraft at a sub-optimal build standard. This is usually referred to as operating at 'military risk'.

It is my opinion that the way fitness for purpose is managed and approved has veered too much toward the latter, the emphasis being on reducing cost at the expense of safety.

The relationship between the Safety Case, Build Standard and Release to Service

For an aircraft to be airworthy or fit for purpose, a valid Safety Case must exist. As the Safety Case <u>must</u> reflect the current in-use build standard(s), it follows that the build standard <u>must</u> be maintained for the Safety Case to be valid.

Therefore, by definition, if the build standard is not maintained, or there is no continuous unbroken audit trail of its maintenance, then the Release to Service is tainted and cannot be validated.

Materiel and Financial Provision, and Requirement Scrutiny

Materiel and Financial Provision is the process whereby the Customer (i.e. a representative of one of the Services) is seen to quantify his requirement and ensure adequate financial provision is made to sustain the requirement, through-life.

Requirement Scrutiny is the separate but related process whereby any stated requirement is scrutinised against a checklist [5], ultimately resulting in a written statement by the project manager that the requirement is *'fair and reasonable'*. Lacking this written declaration, the finance and commercial officers cannot append their signatures and convert the requirement into a contract. To make a false statement is maladministration by making false record.

In the same way fitness for purpose has deviated away from

enhancements (see above), Requirement Scrutiny now concentrates on paring down the requirement ('salami slicing'). The emphasis is not on ensuring provision for what is needed, but on using the process to apply cuts, regardless of impact. This leads to important requirements being omitted.

A practical example is that of an uninformed scrutineer not appreciating the importance of certain airworthiness components, like maintaining the build standard. There is no tangible delivery, so it is seen as a waste of money. For this reason the regulations require Requirement Scrutiny to be conducted from the Customer's point of view. This rarely happens. Thus, vital requirements are often omitted, and safety compromised. It follows that, if Requirement Scrutiny is not conducted properly, the airworthiness audit trail is compromised.

The link to Airworthiness and Through Life Management

Before programme expenditure can be approved, a Through Life Management Plan must be prepared, and maintained. It must articulate how JSP553 Chapters 4 and 5 are to be satisfied, and must be re-validated and verified each time an underlying assumption changes during the project cycle. In short, one states what processes and procedures shall be used, and demonstrates that sufficient materiel and financial provision has been made to implement them. If sufficient provision has not been made, then the regulations cannot be a satisfied and the 'requirement' must fail scrutiny. Every other component of airworthiness flows from this initial act of making sufficient materiel and financial provision for the stated requirement, and applying robust Requirement Scrutiny. A failure to make sufficient provision is, at this point, relatively easy to correct. But if not corrected it quickly becomes difficult to increase funding and/or resources as one falls foul of what the Treasury calls 'entryism' - the perceived act of bidding low to establish a requirement, then asking for the true resources.

For aircraft and their associated equipment, scrutiny must ensure that adequate provision has been made not only to deliver a safe and airworthy aircraft at the 'as built' build standard, but to keep it as safe as reasonably practicable, and airworthy, as the build standard evolves during service. That is, the build standard must be maintained. The process for carrying out this work is called 'Post Design Services'.

The Sponsor [6] must ensure, in consultation with stakeholders [7], that the requirement is properly formulated; especially for what, in broad terms, is called Logistic Support [8]. This includes, for example, spares, repairs, test equipment, training [9] and Post Design Services [10]. If adequate provision is not made, is denied, or subsequently cut, then airworthiness is compromised.

It follows that any subsequent 'requirement', for example a modification, or change to the aircraft or associated equipment, must be scrutinised to ensure adequate provision is made for maintaining safety and airworthiness at the new standard (and maintain the old one until the fleet is at the new standard).

It is not enough to just buy the kit - it must be possible to safely put it to its intended use, and maintain its build standard through-life. If no such provision is made, the 'requirement' must fail scrutiny and should be returned to the sponsor for action, as it is not viable or sustainable. This is an obligation, carried out on behalf of the Chief Accounting Officer (PUS) by staff having delegated technical and financial authority. (A single delegation, to engineers; and letters of delegation are issued, in the same way airworthiness is delegated). That is, when one conducts scrutiny, one is seen to work directly to PUS, not a line manager.

Critically, however, there exist formal rulings that:

- An officer holding technical and financial delegation may be instructed to make a false declaration to the effect that a 'requirement' passes scrutiny, when it is known it does not.

- The instruction to make the false declaration is not a disciplinary offence.

- Refusal to make a false declaration (and thereby commit a serious offence and avoid one's obligation to PUS) is an offence.

It can be seen that these rulings [11] compromise safety and airworthiness.

Processes and procedures

The processes, procedures and regulations for delivering airworthiness are relatively robust [12] but, as Sir Clive Loader reiterated, their implementation is often poor. The source documentation comprises a series of Defence Standards, Joint Service Publications and the like. They are based on long established best practice, but do make a number of assumptions, including:

- There is adequate resource to implement them properly. [13]
- The staff charged with implementation are suitably qualified and experienced. In the past (pre-1990) competence, integrity and

suitable training was included, but these attributes are no longer required. Nor is 'experience' defined. Source documents are written in a manner which assumes all these attributes, but many are little more than aide memoires - inadequate if the user lacks a specific background, or resource to employ extramural assistance.

- A management structure and ethos exist that supports these staff.
- The processes, procedures and regulations will be adhered to and implemented properly.

Maintaining airworthiness

The main enabler and contractual vehicle for maintaining safety and airworthiness is Post Design Services (PDS), defined as 'Maintaining the Build Standard'. For aircraft and their equipment, the procedures are outlined in two key Defence Standards - 05-123 and 05-125/2. [14] (The latter is the more detailed, the former a summary). It is worth setting out the 17 core components of PDS (which can be tailored to requirements) to illustrate how wide-ranging and important the subject is, and how closely it is aligned to, and complements, airworthiness regulations.

1. Appointment of an Aircraft, Equipment or System Design Authority - and Co-ordinating Design Authorities where necessary. The PDS contract is his contractual vehicle.

2. Investigation of faults.

3. Design of modifications.

4. Submission of modification proposals.

5. Design incorporation of approved modifications and changes.

6. Holding and maintaining master drawings (or secondary masters).

7. Management of component replacement/unavailability. (Often, wrongly, called obsolescence, which is merely one reason why a component can be unavailable. Failure to understand this explains many supply problems).

8. Responsibility for complete systems (as opposed to a single 'black box'). That is, a contractor may be the designer of a single box, say a radio, while the Communications system (multiple radios, intercom, etc.) may have numerous contributors; so an overall System Coordinating Design Authority is required. This structure is the basis of system integration, and hence functional safety, but largely ignored in MoD.

9. Provision of technical advice to MoD and their agencies.

10. Visits to User units (primarily to discuss system performance with users in the light of Service experience, and brief Capability Working Groups, while fulfilling part of the continuous reporting and feedback obligation).

11. Packaging and handling.

12. Maintenance and Supply of documents (to Integrated Project Teams and agencies).

13. Management of sub-contractors, and monitoring their capability. (If they suddenly go bust, they cannot supply components to build/repair systems and the expertise must be replaced - a key PDS activity).

14. Preparation of amendments to Technical Publications.

15. Conduct of Trials Installations (a TI is when a modification is first installed and proven at a pre-production build standard).

16. Holding and maintaining the Sample and Reference systems. The Sample, sometimes called the 'hack', is a system or unit (depending on the Design Authority's responsibility) on which he can develop modifications and conduct initial fault and general investigations. It is not at the in-service build standard as it has been 'hacked' by such development activity. The Reference, however, is a fully functional system or unit, maintained to the Design Authority build standard (not the in-service build standard, which usually lags). The Reference is used to embody and install the first-off production mod set or change (the Proof Installation). Few companies are now funded to hold and maintain either, but if there is no traceability back through the Reference the airworthiness audit trail is broken.

17. Dealing with day to day correspondence from MoD, their agencies and suppliers.

At all times configuration control must be maintained, and Safety Cases must have an identifiable Issue for each change.

Most of these core components are not volume related. That is, they cost the same regardless of how many aircraft or equipments are in service. Therefore PDS, historically, was a separately funded and managed discipline.

When PDS was subsumed into the wider support structure (spares, repairs, test equipment, etc. which *are*, broadly, volume related) in 1991, it was subject to financial cutbacks each time there was a fleet reduction or Treasury 'savings measure'. Inevitably, this compromised airworthiness. For example, sufficient funding no longer existed to conduct Fault Investigations or maintain Safety Arguments. In time, instructions were issued in 1993 that even safety related issues were not to be investigated and corrected (missing the point that all PDS is safety related). [15] Component unavailability was no longer addressed. Aircraft Technical Publications were not maintained, and many became useless. [16] The application of PDS, and hence maintaining safety and airworthiness, became fragmented. Some aircraft or equipment would be adequately funded, others less so. [17] The effect was cumulative, over some years. While the outcome was clear to experienced staff, there were few immediate problems so protests were ignored in favour of short-term gains (i.e. savings).

Importantly, these decisions, affecting engineering and safety, were often being made by non-engineering staff (primarily suppliers and financiers), whose only objective was to reduce expenditure. There was little regard for the advice of those who had to exercise airworthiness delegation, or had to continue using equipment and aircraft whose safety could no longer be demonstrated.

In short, those now making safety and airworthiness decisions:

- Had a casual approach to Risk Management, Configuration Management, Systems Integration and other core disciplines.
- When advised of problems they were causing did not seek (or understand) detailed information. An ethos persisted whereby the person who understands detail (and that the Devil is in the detail) was ignored and belittled.

Aircraft Document Set (ADS)

The ADS is produced and maintained for each aircraft type. It comprises:

- The Controller Aircraft Release, the Project Director's statement to the Release to Service Authority (RTSA) that the aircraft is airworthy at a stated build standard, which then forms Part 1 of...
- The Release to Service (the Master Airworthiness Reference) which includes Service Deviations and reflects the in-use build standard.
- Aircrew Manual (explains and describes aircraft systems, operating drills and Limitations). [18]
- Operating Data Manual (definitive performance definitions and data on the aircraft).
- Flight Reference Cards (*aide memoire* for checks and drills). [18]
- Engineering Air Publications for the aircraft and all associated air and

ground equipment.

- Aircraft Maintenance Record (MF700).
- Statement of Operating Intent and Usage.

—   The ADS forms an integral part of the Safety Case and should be validated and verified prior to release to service. Any subsequent changes should also be validated and verified and the subject of (a) an Integrated Test, Evaluation and Acceptance Plan, and (b) a separate issue of the Safety Case. It follows that, if any part of the ADS or its supporting documentation is not maintained, the airworthiness audit trail is broken. [19] Any individual observing a deficiency, omission or inaccuracy in any part of it should raise the issue in, for example, an Unsatisfactory Feature Report. [20] However, these must be progressed under Post Design Services which, as discussed, has been decimated.

Risk Management

Failure to implement any airworthiness component (above) constitutes, to a greater or lesser extent, a risk. Risk Management is a complex business governed by simple rules. The main components are:

1. Identify
2. Notify
3. Assess and quantify
4. Agree ownership
5. Nominate Risk Manager
6. Formulate and agree a mitigation plan
7. Implement the mitigation plan

Again, it is the implementation where the MoD system is lacking. MoD does not resource Risk Management very well. To many, it is sufficient to compile a Risk Register and satisfy Items 1-2. Some will satisfy 3-7, but this requires a deeper knowledge and experience, which is no longer required by management. This is compounded by poor management oversight to ensure compliance. [21]

Risk Managers are seen as a nuisance. By definition, their role is to manage problem solving, which costs time and money. A typical reaction is to accuse him of *thinking up problems which may not be there*. [22] Also, from 1996-on the Chief of Defence Procurement encouraged staff to 'trade out' more performance (which includes safety) to enable time and cost targets to be met.

The Risk Manager is better seen as a collator. Risks can and should be notified by everyone. They seldom are - to do so is to be seen as a troublemaker. [23] The difference between MoD and Industry is that Industry will frequently appoint a senior and suitably experienced manager as Risk Manager. (Experience and seniority are often mutually exclusive concepts in MoD, but far less so in industry). The MoD Risk Manager will not necessarily be senior, and rarely given authority commensurate with his responsibilities, the role regarded as a minor task to be set aside if anything else crops up. [24]

Nor should the Risk Manager necessarily develop and implement mitigation plans - he allocates tasks and timescales, and people report back to him on progress. But he is seldom given sufficient resource, so the default position is that he must carry out all seven components himself. This has been upheld by Director General Air Systems 2 (the Chinook and Nimrod 2-Star) and CDP. Yet, it is common for a single risk mitigation plan to require significant resource. Whole projects can emerge from a single risk. (And the main programme may have hundreds of risks). This expectation and ruling are therefore unreasonable, and is itself a significant resource risk. To seek to manage risk correctly is to be chastised and marked down in annual reports. Consequently, many experienced staff avoid Risk Management.

DGAS2 and CDP have also ruled that it is acceptable to create a second and even third Risk Register omitting (hiding?) MoD-owned risks. [25]

Notably, managing risk and the Safety Case requires the same attributes. The same person often does both - not least because it has not been funded policy since 1991 to have valid Safety Cases - which is always a standing risk on programmes. Both are viewed as sources of potential trouble, cost and delay. Therefore, the creation or upkeep of the Safety Case is invariably the aim of a risk mitigation plan, not a core activity. I believe this to lie at the root of the Nimrod case.

Safety Management

Again, MoD's processes and procedures are relatively robust, except there are none designed to ensure compliance - which is rather assumed. I do not intend describing the safety management process, only outline key elements which are often overlooked.

Safety Management is concerned with having a consistent approach to potential causes of harm and targeting effort where it will have most benefit. Like the above PDS example, which requires the same consistency or else gaps appear in audit trails, achieving this is compromised by, for example, inexperience, lack of corporate knowledge, funding restrictions, stove-piped project teams, and lack of management oversight.

The pace of technological change means it is no longer possible to just rely on designs and practices which have been 'safe' in the past. This tendency manifests itself most frequently in the concept of 'read across', whereby equipment, their installation designs, and concepts of use are simply copied from other aircraft without adequate design, review, testing or trialling. That is, they are neither validated nor verified. (Read across is a valid concept, indeed impossible to do without, but it must still be validated and verified on each occasion). [26]

Safety Management requires a proactive approach rather than reacting to harm once it has occurred. This is impossible without resources, or in the face of the prevailing management ethos. Only senior managers have the authority to correct the attitude, resource and organisational deficiencies which commonly cause accidents.

Professional judgment continues to the most important part of Safety Management. On aircraft and equipment this primarily means engineers. But this concept was compromised by CDP's 1996 announcement that he was to vastly reduce MoD's pool of engineering project managers, and hence corporate knowledge, without compensatory provision. (That is, at the same time resources for extramural support were being cut, so inexperienced MoD staff had less access to advice and assistance, and the remaining experienced staff were grossly overburdened).

A decision may have to be defended on the basis of judgment, so the process must be fully documented [27] (the audit trail), and assumptions validated. *It has never happened before or since* is not valid evidence on its own that a particular event will not happen, yet this is a common position adopted by MoD. For example, on Chinook ZD576.

A system cannot be considered in isolation from its environment. Safety assessment must cover how it interacts with its environment, including the physical environment (location, weather, vibration). Also, with other systems and utilities with which it interfaces and is integrated.

Both physical and functional safety must be addressed. It is not sufficient, despite DGAS2/XD1 and CDP rulings [28], for a system to work and be physically safe in isolation (e.g. on the factory bench). It must be properly integrated and the system of systems assessed for functional safety. An item which is safe in one application may be unsafe in another where it is intended to achieve a different function. See 'read across' above.

Because its assessment requires exploratory analysis, functional safety cannot be assured just by complying with prescriptive legislation and regulations. This is where professional engineering judgment comes in, combined with the expertise provided by, for example, PDS engineers and Design Authorities - none of which are adequately funded by MoD.

It is important to identify and record (in the Hazard Log) all the hazards which might possibly arise during the life of a system. By the very nature of the task, those who practice this are often seen as pessimistic. Often they are denigrated, especially by non-engineers in the MoD who view the process as a vast potential variable in their time, cost and performance targets. These opposing attitudes highlight two issues:

- The aforementioned need for scrutiny to be from the Customer's viewpoint (mandated by PUS, but routinely ignored).
- Risk and Safety Management starts at the Concept stage (i.e. the Service sponsor should initiate the Risk Register). In practice, the subject is often an afterthought, commenced some way through the acquisition cycle - when costs, timescales and performance have been firmed up, if not set in concrete. The practical effect is that time, cost and performance must be traded out to mitigate risks and achieve adequate safety. This explains many well publicised 'procurement' disasters.

The diagram below is fundamental to understanding risk and safety assessment, classification and decision making. In the case in point (Nimrod XV230) and the wider fleet, and with reference to the QinetiQ and BAeS reports on fuel leaks, one should review what class each risk falls into and compare this with the MoD's own assessment.[25] [26]

25 QinetiQ D&TS/AIR/RF051726/14, 17 March 2006. 'Nimrod Fuel Leak Study'.
26 BAeS MBU-DEF-C-NIM-SC0710, August 2004. 'Nimrod MR Mk2 and R Mk1 Safety Case Baseline Report Phase 2 - Fire/Explosion Hazard Assessment'

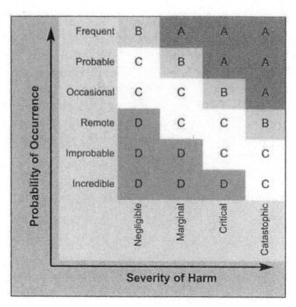

Risk Matrix

Risks must be justified on a case by case basis as being 'Tolerable and As Low As Reasonably Practicable' (ALARP). ALARP criteria should be defined to allow a judgment of how much risk reduction is practicable in the B and C regions (i.e. where risk exists but may be tolerable if ALARP). This can include balancing the costs of reduction measures against the expected financial benefit, to correctly target resources. This involves placing a financial value on human lives, injuries or environmental damage, and so can be an emotive matter. Nevertheless, guidelines are provided.

Importantly, if the Severity of Harm includes loss of multiple lives (i.e. Catastrophic), then any risk, regardless of probability of occurrence, must be reduced to ALARP. (Note, the Probability of Occurrence column stops short of 'Always'. This is called a 'certainty' and must be reduced to a mere probability before being allowed to proceed. A good example of a certainty is that the build standard, and hence Safety Case, will not be maintained).

Safety Management is not a one-way street. The process relies on constant feedback from users, and robust reporting and corrective action systems. The contractual vehicle for this is PDS - yet it is grossly underfunded. The March 2006 QinetiQ report on Nimrod fuel leaks makes it clear that the build standard has not been maintained. For example, Flight Reference Cards, Aircrew Manuals and other Air Publications are outdated, maintenance procedures are inadequate, lack of test equipment and proper tools means repairs cannot be verified, and so on. It should be ascertained whether the User (RAF Kinloss) fulfilled their obligation in this 'two-way street' by assiduously reporting all such incidents. Put another way, has the QinetiQ report come as a surprise to anyone in Kinloss or the Integrated Project Team? It should not, as most of the problems it highlights are well known and have been reported on other aircraft and equipment over a period of many years. Direct parallels can be drawn with other fatal accidents.

To continue this theme, the delegation of safety tasks (in fact any delegation) within MoD requires the person delegating to:

- Ensure the person tasked is competent to undertake the task.
- Provide the necessary resources.
- Continue to monitor the progress of the task.

In turn, the delegated person must:

- Report back on progress.
- Identify shortfalls in achievement or necessary resource.
- Implement the technical reporting procedures laid down in, for example, Defence Standards 05-123, 05-125/2, etc.

Importantly, the delegation transfers authority, not responsibility.

Reports of equipment failures, design faults or procedures which might cause a hazard must be encouraged, without fear of censure. This is difficult to achieve when DGAS2/XD1, CDP and Mins(AF) have consistently ruled that refusing to make a false declaration on airworthiness and safety is a disciplinary offence. By way of contradiction, MoD professes to have a 'blame free' culture. A better way may perhaps be a 'just' culture, where individuals are not free of blame if they are culpably negligent, and where the organisation gives due regard to honesty, rather than disciplining those who strive to meet legal obligations.

Common breaches of the airworthiness regulations

- Failure to maintain the build standard (thus invalidating the Safety Case).

- Out-of-date Engineering Publications, Aircrew Publications (Operating Data Manual, Aircrew Manual and Flight Reference Cards) and drawings.

- Failure to maintain corporate knowledge by diluting the experience and knowledge required before being granted airworthiness delegation.

- Failure to ensure those making airworthiness and safety decisions are properly approved.

- Non-technical staff permitted to make engineering decisions.

- Non-technical staff permitted to over-rule engineering decisions made by the Technical Agency (the named individual responsible for maintaining the build standard).

- Absolving contractors of responsibilities designed to ensure safety and airworthiness is achieved e.g. design reviews, configuration milestones.

- Failure to heed Boscombe Down advice (and that of MoD's own experienced staff) that design features are unsafe / create hazards and, related to this, no process to ensure reasoned explanations for rejecting such advice are promulgated.

- Failure to resource Risk Management, Safety Management, Quality Assurance.

These systemic failings have led to an ambivalence when applying the processes, procedures and regulations. There exists an attitude that, lacking resources or knowledge, one must merely 'do the best you can' and if a problem occurs the blame lies elsewhere. The danger here is that the people making the decision to withhold resources or not apply the regulations do not, ultimately, sign to say the aircraft or equipment is safe or the design is sound. If they have the authority to withhold these resources, and do so having been advised of the consequences, they should be held accountable for their decisions.

Is the Nimrod case unique?

The dismantling of specialist teams carrying out centralised functions (such as maintaining the build standard of avionic equipment) in 1991, and the stove-piping created in MoD by the (re)formation of Integrated Project Teams (IPTs) in 1999, was at odds with the airworthiness regulations. Serious cases of poor application of process, procedures and disregard for regulations were dismissed as isolated, in that the aircraft

IPT under scrutiny may have been able to demonstrate no other failures, but similar failures throughout the MoD were not visible to that IPT. But, often, the stove-piping is within the IPT, whereby one project team will recognise and mitigate a risk, while the team at an adjacent desk misses it altogether (or ignores the advice from colleagues). Knowledgeable management oversight is poor. Air Chief Marshal Loader's comments in the Nimrod XV230 Board of Inquiry report make this clear; but, again, were not a revelation.

The following examples from other cases demonstrate a trend:

- The House of Commons Committee of Public Accounts comment about lack of management oversight on Chinook HC Mk3, when the same problems were recognised and mitigated in Sea King projects under the same Director. [29]

- The Board of Inquiry report into the Tornado/PATRIOT shootdown on 23 March 2003 highlighted a serious safety issue whereby the IFF failure warnings were not properly integrated. [30] This is a well-known 'friendly fire' risk yet, at the time and in the preceding years, it was common for the warnings not to be integrated properly. [31] Twice, in 1999 and 2002, MoD 2-Stars (XD1 and XD5) were advised to have all aircraft checked, especially Tornado. They took no action.

- The Mull of Kintyre papers reveal that aircraft documentation was not at the standard required by the regulations when the aircraft was released to service. As much of this is a centralised function in MoD, by definition all aircraft are affected.

- In an unusually detailed question, the Committee of Public Accounts previously expressed concern over lack of configuration control. [32] Despite CDP's assurances to the Committee that configuration control was being addressed on the project in question (Sea King ASaC Mk7), on the direction of non-technical staff a Configuration Control Board had not been convened; and technical project staff were still voicing concern some time afterwards. [33] This extended to the conduct of Configuration Milestones, such as Critical Design Reviews; a contracted requirement and prerequisite of the airworthiness audit trail, which the same non-technical official waived.

- The Board of Inquiry report into the collision between two Sea Kings ASaC Mk7 on 22 March 2003 [34] reported that the forward/lower High Intensity Strobe Light (HISL) so distracted the pilot that it had to be switched off. The Board described the HISL installation as *'not fit for purpose and non-compliant with the requirement in Defence Standard 00-970 [35] Vol. 2, paragraph 2.1 in that.... emitted light shall not be detrimental to the crew's vision'.* [36] A serious, in fact fatal (seven dead), mistake was made concerning the installation, design and use of the HISL. The crews were forced to fly the aircraft in darkness and poor weather without anti-collision lights, yet the only other comment was that HISL should be replaced. This ignored that the programme manager's directive <u>not to fit</u> HISL, on airworthiness grounds, had been overruled by the same official.

Summary

The loss of Nimrod XV230 is rooted in MoD's systematic and conscious failure to adequately fund implementation of the regulations designed to ensure safety and airworthiness, in particular those laid down in Military Airworthiness Regulations (JSP553) - despite many warnings of the consequences over a long period.

To return to Sir Clive Loader's statement:

'I conclude that the loss of XV230 and, far more importantly, of the 14 Service personnel who were aboard, resulted in shortcomings in the application of the processes for assuring airworthiness and safe operation of the Nimrod'.

On <u>15 September 2005</u> I wrote to my MP - who passed the letter to Adam Ingram, Minister for the Armed Forces - that:

'In my experience, this ambivalent attitude toward configuration control, and indeed safety on occasions, is compelling evidence of a lack of robustness in the application of procedures within the MoD, which I have personally known to result in critical safety problems. Only slightly less serious, this ambivalence has been the direct cause of in-service aircraft documentation being many years out-of-date'.

On <u>17 May 2007</u> Adam Ingram replied at D/Min(AF)/AI MC06559/2006 stating:

'Mr Hill has stated that although the MoD has a robust airworthiness regulatory framework it is not applied robustly. I contend that the framework <u>is</u> applied robustly'. (His emphasis).

Please note the period taken by Min(AF) to respond in the context of XV230 (which crashed on 2 September 2006).

And on <u>22 August 2007</u> Bob Ainsworth MP reiterated at D/Min(AF)/BA MC03982/2007 that:

'Adam Ingram has previously provided responses (and) I have nothing further to add'. (A position repeated by Min(AF) on 2 August 2008 to my MP).

Cultural traits and organisational practices which are contrary to sound engineering practice, and detrimental to safety, have been allowed to develop as a result of many years of resource constraints, fluctuating priorities and operational pressure; often rendering time, cost and performance targets impossible to achieve. Effective communication of critical safety information, and intelligent debate, is stifled. There is a lack of integrated management and oversight across programs, and very often an informal and uninformed chain of command and decision-making process exists outside the formal airworthiness and safety delegations.

Notes

[1] JSP550 Military Aviation Policy, Regulations and Directives (formerly JSP318) AP 3456 Ch.4-3.

[2] JSP553 Military Airworthiness Regulations (formerly JSP318B).

[3] The everyday definition of Quality is 'fitness for purpose'. However, in this aircraft context the phrase is rarely used in Defence Standards - while they state it is an operational term, it is undefined.

[4] The term 'maintenance' in this context refers to all technical, administrative, managerial and supervisory actions supporting the objective to retain or restore an item so that it is fit for purpose (in the Quality Assurance sense).

[5] The checklist is not exhaustive, and it is an underpinning principle that the scrutineer's engineering judgment can prevail - in the same way it is the most important part of Safety Management. It follows that if the scrutineer is not an engineer, then the scrutiny is not robust.

[6] Sponsor - the appropriate Director of Equipment Capability (DEC).

[7] Stakeholders - interested parties such as the Integrated Project Team, Design Authorities, Users, Civil Aviation Authority.

[8] See Defence Standard 00-60 Integrated Logistic Support. Note: until April 1992 'ILS' had a different meaning. The ILS Manager was an identifiable individual responsible for managing all aspects of a project, as opposed to there being separate departments managing development, production and in-service support.

[9] While training is an ILS subject, a contradiction exists whereby a Training Needs Analysis must be prepared in order to identify and cost the training requirement for purposes of scrutiny. But the resources to do so are seldom available so early in the project. Thus,

very often training is an afterthought, and there are many examples of projects having funding shortfalls or late In Service Dates because insufficient heed has been taken of the subject. Apache is the prime example.

[10] PDS does not procure spares, effect repairs or enhance equipment. It maintains the build standard. This fundamental misunderstanding, first promulgated in the ill-fated Chief of Defence Procurement Instructions in 1994, and in direct contradiction of the mandated PDS Defence Standard (05-125/2), was the first true indication in an official document that the art of maintaining the build standard (and hence Safety and Airworthiness) was being lost.

[11] Defence Procurement Agency Executive Director 1 XD1 (304), 15 December 2000, and XD1 (325), 10 January 2001.

Chief of Defence Procurement CDP 117/6/7, 19 November 2001, and CDP 117/6/7, 13 December 2001.

Dr Lewis Moonie MP D/US of S/LM 2214 & 1401/03/Y, 30 April 2003.

Adam Ingram MP D/Min(AF)/AI MC06559/2006, 17 May 2006.

Bob Ainsworth MP D/Min(AF)/BA MC03982/2007, 22 August 2007, and D/Min (AF)/BA MC03883/2008, 2 August 2008.

[12] While robust, many standards and source documentation need updating as they assume a degree of detailed knowledge of the processes, procedures and of the equipment itself that is no longer taught in MoD. This is a fatal flaw, and in 1996 CDP declared his intention to reduce the number of technical project managers in MoD(PE), to be replaced by staff who were not required to retrospectively attain the competences others routinely gained in up to five previous grades. Thus, the key airworthiness requirements of experience, competence and maintenance of corporate knowledge were compromised, and no compensatory provision was made to, for example, fund the necessary updates to Standards or training; or the inevitable cost of seeking extramural assistance.

[13] But note that applying the mandated rules to ensure adequate resource is a disciplinary offence.

[14] While it is often said that Defence Standard 05-125/2 is a 'Chinese copy' of 123, the reverse is true. The former subsumes a series of specifications (PDS Specs 1-20) which explain in greater detail *how* to implement the procedures, whereas other standards merely say

what the procedures are. Notably, these specifications are not available from Defence Standardisation, yet 05-125/2 remains available on their website. One should ask how a procedural Defence Standard can possibly be implemented in the intended way when 20 key specifications are not available. (If 05-125/2 were to be updated from the current 1991 issue, six of these specifications would need to be replaced, and the other 14 updated to reflect organisational changes. Nevertheless, they remain valid and perfectly useable. In 2001-2 an Army programme - Future Integrated Soldier Technology - used 05-125/2 as the basis for its main contract, updating it where necessary; so much of the work has been done).

[15] For example, smoke in Lynx cockpits, caused by an overheating radar terminal block. RAF supply managers refused to sanction funding to correct the problem, despite it being a critical flight safety issue and a current life-threatening hazard to aircrew.

[16] Technical Publications not being maintained is specifically noted in Mull of Kintyre papers and the Nimrod XV230 Board of Inquiry report.

[17] All the listed rulings encompassed this issue, supporting the concept that physical safety was sufficient - that a contract could be deemed complete and paid off in the knowledge that the aircraft was functionally unsafe.

[18] Items referenced published by RAF Handling Squadron, Boscombe Down.

[19] The QinetiQ report on Nimrod Fuel Leaks, dated March 2006, reports Technical Publications are not up-to-date, test equipment not available, test procedures not verifiable, etc. Similarly, the Chinook Operating Data Manual, Aircrew Manual and Flight Reference Cards were not current at the time of the Mull of Kintyre accident. That is, the Safety Cases were not valid.

[20] AP 3456 - A key question in any accident investigation is *What MF765s were raised, and what action was taken?* If this process has not been implemented, or compromised, then those responsible must share liability.

[21] Noted, for example, in the Public Accounts Committee report into Chinook Mk3 procurement. 9 February 2009.

[22] Stated to me on 9 May 2000 when I voiced concern over the High Intensity Strobe Light (HISL, mentioned elsewhere), an unproven system colleagues want to fit without any trials or testing. My

assessment of the risk was rejected, and my directive that it not be fitted until proven safe, was illegally overruled. Seven aircrew subsequently died (Sea Kings ASaC Mk7 XV650 & XV704, 22 March 2003). The Board of Inquiry unwittingly repeated my concerns.

[23] For example, on the above Sea King AEW Mk2 to ASaC Mk7 Upgrade, only a solitary risk was notified by someone in MoD other than the Risk Manager, in the period 1994-2000.

[24] See Sea King AEW Mk2 to ASaC Mk7 Upgrade Risk Register, and DHP's directives not to progress risk mitigation during office hours, or procure extramural support to mitigate, *inter alia*, airworthiness risks. That is, risks must be mitigated in one's own time, at home, other 'home' tasks permitting. Subsequently upheld by DGAS2/XD1 and CDP.

[25] See above. Secondary and tertiary Risk Registers notified to DGAS2/XD1 and CDP. No action taken.

[26] See above. The Support Authority sought read across on HISL, whose functional safety had not been validated or verified. Read across was refused, but (my) decision was later overruled in my absence by an unauthorised non-technical official. The Board of Inquiry cited the design as a Contributory Factor, but without knowing of this background.

[27] See above. In 2004 the Sea King IPT claimed to investigators they had no record of the process leading to the fitting of HISL, yet in 2007/8 Min(AF) quoted that very record. Similarly, key maintenance documentation is missing from the Nimrod and Chinook audit trails.

[28] The Sea King AEW Mk2 Identification Friend or Foe system was deemed safe and operational because it *'worked on the bench'*, despite Boscombe Down declaring it unsafe because it was not properly integrated - rendering the aircraft vulnerable to friendly fire and collision. Nor was a specific issue of the Safety Case raised or the simulator modified. See also the Tornado ZG710/PATRIOT accident (2 killed) Board of Inquiry which subsequently noted the same problem. The issues were raised with DGAS2, XD1, XD5, Director Personnel, Resources and Development and CDP; and ignored.

[29] House of Commons Committee of Public Accounts - 'Battlefield Helicopters' dated 23 February 2005.

[30] 'Aircraft Accident to RAF Tornado GR Mk4A ZG710', paragraph 19b.

[31] See above - Sea King AEW Mk2 IFF under MER(S) 28/89. IFF Mode

4 failure warning was not integrated and verified as functionally safe, the project office and Support Authority refusing to do so. DGAS2/XD1 and CDP confirmed that the project manager did not have to ensure aircraft safety, despite it being a contractual obligation, and he could make a false declaration that it was.

[32] House of Commons Committee of Public Accounts - 'Modifying Defence Equipment', 26 July 1999 proceedings of the Committee dated 3 March 1999, paragraphs 34-36.

[33] D/DHP/24/4/93 dated 31 January 2000, arising from design changes to Sea King HC Mk4 on safety grounds, which were then overruled. The Design Authority was directed to disregard this illegal overrule and comply with the Secretary of State's regulations.

[34] Unreferenced report dated 29 April 2003.

[35] Defence Standard 00-970 - Design and Airworthiness Requirement for Service Aircraft.

[36] Sea King ASaC Mk7 XV650/XV704 Board of Inquiry report, paragraph 101.

Appendix 2 - The measurement of technical maturity

Executive Summary

Maturity, or rather immaturity, is key to this case. This Appendix discusses how MoD manages and assesses maturity of an aircraft and its systems, concluding that the Chinook HC Mk2 and much of its equipment did not meet the minimum criteria for entering production, never mind entering service. This was reflected in Boscombe Down's advice to MoD(PE).

The Acquisition Cycle

In MoD this has taken various forms. For example, the Downey Cycle was used at the time of the Chinook Mid-Life Upgrade. The cycle breaks down project lifespan into sequential, but overlapping, steps:

- Concept Formulation
- Feasibility
- Project Definition
- Full Development
- Production
- In-Service
- Disposal

The cycle applies equally to new products and modification programmes. In this case, an airworthy Chinook HC Mk1 is seen to be a technical and contractual prerequisite as it formed the design baseline for Mk2 and the cost of the contract. If it was not airworthy that would be a major risk, and a Risk Reduction exercise would be required to bring it up to standard before proceeding to Full Development. If MoD does not comply, it is in contractual default, costs escalate and delays occur. If one does not want delay or increased cost, then often the only way out is to proceed with Development while concurrently mitigating the risk. This is permitted, but entering Production before mitigation is complete is prohibited. On Chinook HC Mk2 the airworthiness risks were knowingly carried throughout Development, Production and into the In-Service phase.

It follows that maintaining the airworthiness of the legacy aircraft, in accordance with JSP553 Chapter 5, is a prerequisite to the success of modification programmes. Failure to do so, and it was policy in the preceding years <u>not</u> to, explains many MoD programme delays - the ongoing Nimrod MRA4 upgrade is simply one example.

Technical and System Maturity

The basic methodology is to apply tests of maturity. Today, these are termed:

- Technology Readiness Levels (TRLs)
- System (Integration) Readiness Levels (SIRLs)

During Chinook HC Mk2 development the terminology was different, but the approach essentially the same. The project manager is responsible for assessing and managing <u>all</u> aspects of risk during every stage of the project, whereas the staff of the Chief Scientific Advisor (CSA) have a remit to provide advice to the Chief of Defence Procurement on technical risks only. CSA Guidelines for Technical Scrutiny, Appendix 7K, Amendment 22 set out the same basic requirements - the need to demonstrate a given level of maturity before proceeding to the next stage.

This is explained because the decision to ignore this aspect on Chinook, and the associated risk, was not recorded and remains unexplained. MoD's Independent Safety Auditors, at Boscombe Down, notified Director Helicopter Projects (DHP) that the immaturity of various systems, notably the Full Authority Digital Engine Control (FADEC) software, Navigation and Communications systems, was such that the aircraft could not be considered airworthy and should not be released to service. The Project Director, Captain Michael Brougham RN, took heed of this advice and advised his superiors that they should too. His Loose Minute dated 11 January 1995, cited in evidence by the House of Lords Committee, refers to known *'software design and systems integration problems'* between February and July 1994.

Notably, on 24 October 1995, Captain Brougham's successor, Colonel Barry Hodgkiss, wrote saying the official DHP position was that Boscombe's advice (not to release the aircraft) still stood.[27]

Technology Readiness Levels

1. Basic principles observed and reported. Lowest level of technology readiness. Scientific research begins to be evaluated for military

---

27 Letter D/DHP/HP1/4/1/4/1, 24 October 1995.

applications. Examples might include paper studies of a technology's basic properties.

2. Technology concept and/or application formulated. Invention begins. Once basic principles are observed, practical applications can be postulated. The application is speculative and there is no proof or detailed analysis to support the assumptions. Examples are still limited to paper studies.

3. Analytical and experimental critical function and/or characteristic proof of concept. Analytical studies and laboratory studies to physically validate analytical predictions of separate elements of the technology are undertaken. Examples include components that are not yet integrated or representative.

4. Technology component and/or basic technology sub-system validation in laboratory environment. Basic technology components are integrated. This is relatively 'low fidelity' compared to the eventual system. Examples include integration of 'ad hoc' hardware in a laboratory.

5. Technology component and/or basic sub-system validation in relevant environment. Fidelity of sub-system representation increases significantly. The basic technological components are integrated with realistic supporting elements so that the technology can be tested in a simulated environment. Examples include 'high fidelity' laboratory integration of components.

6. Technology system/subsystem model or prototype demonstration in a relevant environment. Representative model or prototype system, which is well beyond the representation tested for TRL 5, is tested in a relevant environment. Represents a major step up in a technology's demonstrated readiness. Examples include testing a prototype in a high fidelity laboratory environment or in simulated operational environment.

7. Technology system prototype demonstration in an operational environment. Prototype near or at planned operational system. Represents a major step up from TRL 6, requiring the demonstration of an actual system prototype in an operational environment, such as in an aircraft or vehicle. Information to allow supportability assessments is obtained. Examples include testing the prototype in a test bed aircraft.

8. Actual technology system completed and qualified through test and demonstration. Technology has been proven to work in its final form

and under expected conditions. In almost all cases, this TRL represents the end of Demonstration. Examples include test and evaluation of the system in its intended weapon system to determine if it meets design specifications, including those relating to supportability.

9. Technology System 'qualified' through successful mission operations. Application of the technology in its final form and under mission conditions, such as those encountered in operational test and evaluation and reliability trials. Examples include using the system under operational mission conditions.

System Integration Readiness Levels

1. Key requirements identified. The requirements, which are assessed as key to the achievement of the systems aims are identified and collated.

2. System Requirements Identified. System 'blocked-out' at high level with major sub-systems identified. System Requirements Document complete or nearing completion. Paper studies only still.

3. Analytical and experimental validation of major functions of system. Modelling and experimental studies carried out to validate analytical predictions of system performance.

4. Sub-systems validation in laboratory environment. Each sub-system is demonstrated to perform as required when subjected to simulated system conditions.

5. Sub-system validation in relevant environment. Fidelity of sub-systems representation increases significantly. Some sub-systems realistically joined with realistic supporting elements so that sub-systems can be tested in a simulated environment.

6. System prototype demonstration in a relevant environment. Representative model or prototype system with all major sub-systems integrated and operating, which is well beyond the representation tested for SRL 5, is tested in a relevant environment. Represents a major step up in a system's demonstrated readiness. Examples include testing a prototype in a high fidelity laboratory environment or in simulated operational environment.

7. System prototype demonstration in an operational environment. Prototype near or at planned operational status. Represents a major step up from SRL 6, requiring the demonstration of an actual system prototype in an operational environment, such as in an aircraft or vehicle. Information to allow supportability assessments is obtained. Examples include testing the prototype in a test bed platform.

8. Pre-production system completed and proven though test and demonstration. The system has been proven to work in its final form and under expected conditions. Examples include test and evaluation of the system in its intended weapon system to determine if it meets design specifications, including those relating to supportability.

9. System proven through successful mission operations. Application of the system in its final form and under mission conditions, such as those encountered in operational test and evaluation and reliability trials. Examples include using the system under operational mission conditions.

SIRLs 1-2 focus on the need to properly define the requirements for the system under consideration. Lacking this, it is impossible to measure the success when producing the system.

SIRLs 3-5 relate to the integration and verification stage. SIRL 3 is intended to ensure that the proposed system can meet the requirements placed on it by carrying out modelling and experimental studies. These studies may be operational analysis or computer-based simulations. SIRLs 4 and 5 represent the first real testing of physical sub systems, firstly in the laboratory environment and then in a more relevant environment with more realistic supporting elements.

SIRLs 6-9 highlight the installation and validation phase. All major sub-systems are assumed integrated and operating for SIRL 6, and the system prototype is tested in a relevant environment. SIRL 7 is a major step up from SIRL 6, with the system prototype tested in an operational environment i.e. fitted to a platform. SIRL 8 is where the system has been proven to work in its final form (though this may be a pre-production version still) in the required conditions. SIRL 9 is achieved when the system is proven operationally through successful mission operations.

Governing principles

1. It is not possible to say that a particular TRL/SIRL has been completed until the criteria for that level has been achieved.

2. The SIRL should not be higher than the lowest contributing TRL.

3. The SIRL of a system should be assessed as equivalent to the lowest SIRL of the contributing individual sub-systems.

4. In general terms, MoD Project Managers need to demonstrate Level 6 or 7 to obtain approval to proceed to manufacturing/conversion. Self-evidently, as the Chinook avionics system integration (including trials to establish performance) was dependent on FADEC maturity (due to

Electro-Magnetic Compatibility considerations), it could not be deemed better than Level 4. This immaturity is evidenced by Switch-On Only clearance on the date of the accident. In other words, the level of maturity required to enter production, never mind issue a Release to Service, had not been achieved.

Key Integration Parameters

In addition to considering the status of the technologies (through TRLs), when assessing the SIRLs Key Integration Parameters (KIPs) should be considered. Again, terminology has changed over the years, but the basics remain the same. Examples of KIPs are:

- Physical Size and Weight
- Testing and Evaluation
- Training requirements
- Availability, Reliability, Maintainability
- Production
- Human Factors Integration
- Software
- Power Management
- Thermal Management
- Performance
- Interfaces
- Integrated Logistic Support
- Command, Control, Communications, Computers and Intelligence (C4I) connectivity
- Operating Environment e.g. vibration, noise, temperature, humidity, corrosion, shock

The definitions of each KIP set out the expected level of achievement required to judge that the system is at a particular SIRL. By considering the KIPs together with the SIRL definitions, it is possible to identify the necessary level of achievement of each KIP, at each SIRL.

Case Study - The technical immaturity of FADEC

In September 1993 Boscombe Down had stated this safety critical software should be re-written, due to the sheer number of anomalies and the inability to verify it in accordance with MoD regulations.

As discussed, the immaturity of FADEC is evidenced by a meeting held at Textron Lycoming in Stratford, USA on 21 January 1994, chaired by Captain Brougham. The purpose was to discuss the way forward on FADEC software. Assistant Directors simply do not get involved in such matters unless all else has failed and/or there is a serious flight safety risk. (In over 30 years' service, the only other occasion I can recall this occurring was when DHP's AD/HP2, Mr Kevin Thomas, chaired a meeting on 30 May 1996 following AML (RAF) refusal to implement airworthiness regulations - an act which placed all his programmes, and those of AD/HP1, at risk.[28] The issues were precisely those noted in the 1992 CHART report - further proof that no action had been taken. That is, refusal to maintain the build standard and, hence, Safety Case).

But it is the conclusions in the minutes, written by Captain Brougham and intended for his Director (Dr Hughes), that reveal the immaturity of process. To summarise:

- HSDE (Hawker Siddeley Dynamics Engineering, manufacturers of FADEC) had submitted a proposal for further work, which Captain Brougham agreed with.

- His staff were actioned to raise a requisition (which, when technically and financially approved, would initiate contract negotiations).

- UK Defence Project Office in Washington DC were to agree costs.

- The Test Specification was to be reviewed by MoD by end-February 1994 (the minutes do not specify by whom).

- Captain Brougham was to write to Textron Lycoming with a proposed Statement of Work, copying the EDS-SCICON report on FADEC software, requesting a detailed account of the methodology used to comply with RTCA/DO-178A (software standard). Also, their proposals for the longer-term solution to outstanding software quality issues.

- H/CPG (a DHP officer immediately under Captain Brougham) was to take the lead with Boscombe Down, EDS-SCICON and HSDE in taking forward the EDS-SCICON proposal for a Feasibility Study to contract.

At this point it should be noted that, on 1 May 2011, MoD confirmed a 'Block 0' upgrade to FADEC software had been contracted in November 1993, and 'Block 1' was contracted in April 1995. Block 0 is not mentioned in the minutes of this meeting. The Board of Inquiry confirmed the

---

28 Minutes of meeting, D/DHP/24/4/93/25, 30 May 1996.

original software standard was in ZD576, not Block 0. That is, the standard whose implementation was *'positively dangerous'*. Also, the wording of the minutes in no way reflects an upgrade having been recently contracted. They are discussing the 'way ahead' for the existing (original) build standard. It is recommended the Review investigate this aspect and determine the precise timeframe and nature of FADEC software upgrades.

So, some months after the safety critical software implementation was branded *'positively dangerous'* by Boscombe, yet declared safe by ACAS:

- Proposals are being sought from the FADEC supplier for further work.
- Contract action has yet to be initiated (never mind let).
- A new Test Specification for safety critical software has yet to be reviewed (never mind validated and verified).
- MoD has agreed the need for further studies, requiring a Statement of Work to be negotiated, agreed and contracted.
- There are outstanding Quality issues on safety critical software.
- A proposal for a Feasibility Study is to be agreed.

By no stretch of the imagination does this describe mature software. The language and description of the proposed action are more akin to a risk reduction exercise before initial approval to proceed with development. It is almost as if Captain Brougham wants to start again - which in fact was Boscombe's recommendation. But this is January 1994, two months <u>after</u> ACAS has rejected Boscombe's recommendation, and ignored Controller Aircraft's mandate.

With his predecessors having taken almost a decade to get to this *'positively dangerous'* stage, what chance had Captain Brougham of succeeding a mere five months before the accident? But at least he tried, and certainly put his career on the line by so openly disagreeing with ACAS's false declaration. There can be no better illustration of just how immature he regarded this safety critical software.

The above sets out a series of high priority risks emerging from extant risks, which have themselves not been mitigated. The Review is invited to consider if this constitutes Technology and System Readiness compliance.

Appendix 3 - A discussion of the National Audit Office report 'Accepting Equipment Off-Contract'

Executive Summary

This Appendix is an analysis of the National Audit Office (NAO) report which included the Chinook Mid-Life Upgrade as a case study, and concludes there were disturbing errors which hid systemic failings.

The most serious is that the safety critical software in the FADEC was not subjected to the laid down Certification and Acceptance regulations; meaning there was no authority or justification for using FADEC in Chinook HC Mk2. Evidence is presented that FADEC software was Safety Critical, despite Ministers insisting that it was not.

National Audit Office report

The NAO issued its report on 11 February 2000. [B35] Seemingly, the committee was briefed almost exclusively by the RAF: both MoD(PE) and Boscombe Down would have immediately pointed out the many errors. The effect was to cast Boscombe Down in a poor light (consistent with the RAF's general approach).

The underlined parts of the following extract give cause for concern. They contain errors which deflect attention from systemic failings within MoD. The issues they raise are discussed. It is appreciated individual members of the NAO or Public Accounts Committee could not be expected to know or understand the detail, but it was incumbent upon MoD to give truthful and unambiguous briefings and evidence. Failure to do so served to hide the ongoing systemic failings - a serious breach of the Civil Service Code.

'Box 5: Chinook MK 2 Mid-Life Update

1. In 1990, the Department placed a £143 million contract with Boeing Helicopters to upgrade 32 Chinook Mk1 helicopters to the Mk2 standard. The conversion involved the replacement of the transmission, hydraulic and electrical systems, various structural modifications and fitting converted modified Textron-Lycoming T-55 engines and a Full Authority Digital Electronic Control system (FADEC). The FADEC maintains the correct balance between the fuel flow, and therefore power output, of the Chinook's two engines which reduces pilot workload and makes the aircraft 'easier' to fly. It is made up of a computer system which utilises inputs from various sensors to measure the amount of fuel that the helicopter's engines need, and a mechanical system which delivers the correct amount of fuel.

2. Because of the extent of the upgrade, the Mk2 was designated a new type within the United Kingdom fleet and the aircraft therefore had to receive United Kingdom military airworthiness certification - then called Controller Aircraft Release - before being returned to operational service. This involved the aircraft being put through a series of ground and flying trials costing some £1 million by the Defence Evaluation and Research Agency based at Boscombe Down.

3. As part of these trials, Boscombe Down wished to verify the software in the FADEC system using their preferred method known as Static Code Analysis. This element of the trials programme accounted for roughly 10% of the overall costs and a contract was placed on EDS-SCICON, an expert software engineering and testing company, for this purpose. In verifying the software, EDS-SCICON divided the anomalies which they found in to four categories, with category 1 being the most significant. In their view, well developed software should contain none or very few category 1 and only a small number of category 2 anomalies. However, by the time EDS-SCICON had tested 18 per cent of the lines of code in the FADEC software they had already identified 21 category 1 and 154 category 2 anomalies in the software structure and documentation. Having discovered such a high incidence of anomalies at such an early stage, EDS-SCICON stopped testing because the way the software had been written made it unsuitable to full verification using the Static Code Analysis technique. The Department chose to terminate the EDS-SCICON contract at this point because the requirement for Static Code Analysis was an internal Boscombe Down policy, not supported by Defence Standards. The anomalies identified by EDS-SCICON were all reviewed by the equipment's Design Authority, who confirmed that whilst undesirable, none of them represented an airworthiness concern.

4. On the basis of EDS-SCICON's work, in October 1993 Boscombe Down advised the Department that they could not recommend Controller Aircraft Release for the Chinook Mk2 because of the "unquantifiable risk associated with the unverifiable nature of the FADEC software", and concluded that rewriting the software was essential.

5. In making their recommendation, Boscombe Down recognised that operational use of the Mk2 might be necessary before re-written software became available and provided a set of recommendations which were intended to allow flying if necessary but which would mitigate any consequent risk associated with their concern over potentially unpredictable FADEC software behaviour. In recognition of Boscombe Down's continued, but unsubstantiated concerns, the Department accepted their advice and restricted the loads carried by the Mk2 to ensure that the helicopter's all-up mass did not exceed 18,000 kg - the level at which the helicopter can fly normally with only one engine functioning - and a reduction of 26.5 per cent in load carrying capacity compared with the Staff Requirement. This precautionary Limitation had a minimal impact as 90% of all operations are carried out within the 18,000 kilograms limit. In March 1994 the restriction was relaxed to apply only to internal loads since underslung loads to an all-up mass of 22,700 kilograms (as specified in the Staff Requirement) could be jettisoned in an emergency.

6. As a result of the concerns raised about the software, the FADEC manufacturer has addressed some of the anomalies within the software, and produced an improved version which was then subjected to a Sneak and Traceability analysis to gain further confidence in its integrity. In September 1998 the Department, with the Royal Air Force's consent, issued full Controller Aircraft Release for the Chinook Mk2, removed the internal carriage all-up mass restriction for internal loads and allowed the Mk2 fleet to operate to the maximum payloads specified by Boeing which are 21% higher than those specified in the Staff Requirement. In making the decision to issue full Controller Aircraft Release, the Department, as is their right as executive airworthiness authority for the aircraft, weighed the advice of Boscombe Down against other factors, including the equipment's Design Authorities and the consequences of failure, and concluded that the aircraft could be cleared for safe flight within the parameters identified. Notwithstanding the internal differences of opinion over FADEC, there were no significant impacts on acceptance in to service and the Chinook Mid-Life Update was delivered on time, below budget and provided a significant increase in payload capability compared to the Staff Requirement.'

Analysis

Paragraph 1

FADEC was only later subsumed into the Mid-Life Upgrade due to significant programme delays. It was not *'on time'* (paragraph 6).

Paragraph 2

'The aircraft therefore had to receive United Kingdom military airworthiness certification - then called Controller Aircraft Release - before being returned to operational service'.

As explained, the Release to Service (RTS) is the Master Airworthiness Reference, issued by the RAF's Assistant Chief of the Air Staff (ACAS). It reflects the In-Use build standard. Omitting the RTS diverts attention from the RAF's role, and that it was responsible for the Safety Case at that build standard.

The RTS was a misrepresentation of the facts in that it concealed Boscombe's advice, and Controller Aircraft's statement, that the aircraft was not yet airworthy. The NAO gives the impression Controller Aircraft issued this false declaration. He did not, it was ACAS.

Paragraph 3

'As part of these trials, Boscombe Down wished to verify the software in the FADEC system using their preferred method known as Static Code Analysis'.

This is wrong. The argument centres on the definition of safety critical software and whether FADEC software met that criteria. In turn, that determined how Boscombe would approach their task of validation and verification. This aspect is utterly crucial, because it was the inability to validate and verify that led Boscombe to state implementation was *'positively dangerous'* and that the aircraft was not yet airworthy.

Boscombe's role was that of MoD Independent Safety Auditor, an activity carried out under Quality Assurance and configuration management procedures. Given the basic premise of the 1992 Chinook Airworthiness Review Team report is that configuration control had not been maintained for 12 years, and the Chief of Defence Procurement admitted this failure remained in March 1999, it can be seen that no valid Independent Safety Audit was possible.

Definition of safety critical software

On 14 December 1989 the Deputy Under-Secretary of State (Defence Procurement) issued a 'Joint MoD(PE) / Industry Computing Policy for Military Operational Systems' policy [B14] stating that the definition of Safety Criticality used in JSP188, Chapter 1 shall be used:

'Components whose failure <u>could</u> result in loss of life or serious damage to the environment in circumstances where there is <u>no possibility of reversion to manual control</u>'.

This joint Policy statement agreed by MoD, the Electronic Engineering Association, the Computing Services Association, and the Society of British Aerospace Companies further stated:

'This policy <u>shall</u> be adopted by all MoD(PE) branches procuring operational software-based systems'.

In evidence to the Public Accounts Committee (PAC 1999-2000/85 March 2000), MoD stated:

'...a letter dated 21 April 1999 from Mr John Spellar, MP, then Parliamentary Under Secretary of State for Defence, to the Chairman of House of Commons Defence Committee, who went on to advise that "Our judgment remains that

FADEC is not flight safety critical by the standards to which MoD authorities work, namely that failure would lead to catastrophe, as opposed to the US definition could'".

According to Mr Spellar, if the policy said 'could', then it was Safety Critical. It did. Not only that, it met the second criteria - there was no manual reversionary control possible. This single act of deception prevented crucial evidence and failings being explored, and taints much of MoD's evidence in this case.

Furthermore, Defence Standard 00-56/1 (Hazard Analysis and Safety Classification of the Computer and Programmable Electronic System Elements of Defence Equipment, later re-named Safety Management of Defence Systems) requires a Statement of Component Safety Criticality to be agreed at three distinct stages of the project:

- After Preliminary Hazard Analysis (provisional statement)
- After Project Definition (interim statement)
- Acceptance into Service of the system (final statement)

If this requirement was met, it could only have said that the software was Safety Critical.

The Requirement for Static Code Analysis

DUS(DP)'s policy [B14] invokes Static Code Analysis. Subsequently, Defence Standard 00-55 confirmed and detailed two basic approaches to safety critical software:

- The use of formal methods (correct by design), and;
- The static analysis of the code (conformance with the design)

The nature of FADEC software required (in the words of DUS(DP)'s policy) *'sophisticated mathematical proving'*. Static Code Analysis is such a methodology.

With reference to [B14], Static Code Analysis is defined as:

'Analysis of computer code when it is not running on the machine. Static analysis may range from simple visual examination to sophisticated mathematical proving'. (Annex B-6).

'Safety critical software must be coded according to the guidelines laid down by RSRE Malvern and subjected to such additional validation and verification as those authorities or the project office may determine, to establish the safety accreditations of the system'. (Annex A, A8.1 Policy).

Annex A-7, paragraph A8.3.1 ('Safety Critical Software Analysis') notes the following tools are available for Static Code Analysis - MALPAS, SPADE and SPARK. Policy devolved the selection and use of these tools to RSRE Malvern. MALPAS and SPADE were provided to Boscombe.

It goes on, at paragraph 3.8:

'(Software) dealing with safety-critical aspects requires further attention and is to be subjected to formal mathematical analysis'.

And continues:

(If independent validation procedures are carried out e.g. by Boscombe Down or a contractor) *'It is more than ever important that MoD should secure adequate rights of access and use to design information and code for itself and its agents'.*

Paragraph 2.6 states that if the project manager wishes to depart from this policy, he should consult his technical advisors before deciding. In this case, Boscombe <u>were</u> the technical advisors and, as they conducted Static Code Analysis, it is highly unlikely they criticised themselves by agreeing with any proposal not to conduct it.

It is noted, however, that the formal methods approach had not been widely adopted in preceding years. Some 'legacy' aircraft, such as Chinook, started development when formal methodology was immature, and tools and support were severely limited. FADEC development commenced at such a time, making it even more important that Boscombe Down conducted robust 'sophisticated' validation and verification. As MoD has a Tolerable and ALARP (As Low As Reasonably Practicable) approach to risk, the retrospective evaluation of safety critical code was the only reasonable method available (at the time) to mitigate safety critical anomalies.

It is clear there was a breakdown in this validation and verification process. It would appear the software was not amenable to Static Code Analysis. Nevertheless, to quote from the Public Accounts Committee proceedings:

'At the House of Commons Defence Committee hearing, MoD argued this merely meant Boscombe Down could not read the software. This is not, in fact, a trivial issue. A hardware component for an aircraft can be checked for quality by inspecting it against its drawing. If the part and its drawing do not match, either the part or the drawing is wrong. Either way, the component cannot be used. For software the process of checking is called "verification", not inspection. High quality software cannot be seen and measured but it can be verified against its design documents. If you cannot verify it, software is not suitable for a Flight Safety Critical system. The

NAO report refers to attempts made by Boscombe Down to apply Static Code Analysis to verify the software, and to the use of EDS-SCICON as additional independent verifiers. Leaving aside the detail, most of the FADEC software should have been amenable to such analyses, even if not designed for it from the start. Certainly the documentation should have matched the programme, and there would have been few errors if the necessary rigour had been applied to the design process'.

This does not justify MoD's criticism of Boscombe to various Inquiries, including the Public Accounts Committee. Instead of acknowledging that Boscombe were <u>required</u> to use Static Code Analysis, it is implied that they ploughed ahead regardless. The report omits that DUS(DP)'s policy places the onus on the project office to prepare and agree a valid Trials, Evaluation and Acceptance Plan at the outset, stating at A15.1:

'The procedures for the acceptance of a system, or components of a system (e.g. software) must be determined during the early stages of procurement, not later than Project Definition and certainly before the award of the contract'.

Instead of saying the software was *'not amenable'*, one should ask why this state of affairs existed in late 1993, on a contract let in 1985. If MoD did not intend Boscombe to use Static Code Analysis, what did it require of them? Did it apply a different interpretation of policy? And, despite the above policy requirement, why was the acceptance criteria still not agreed after the accident?

Ultimately, MoD's claim that Static Code Analysis was unnecessary is proven false by its own actions. In 1995 it contracted a Static Analysis using the SATA (Sneak Analysis and Traceability Analysis) technique, not previously available to Boscombe. This analysis confirmed 125 anomalies. This work was part of the Block 1 upgrade (see below) to FADEC software, and was accompanied by a re-documentation exercise - precisely the recommendations Boscombe made many years earlier.

Paragraph 5

'In recognition of Boscombe Down's continued, but unsubstantiated concerns, the Department accepted their advice and restricted the loads carried by the Mk2 to ensure that the helicopter's all-up mass did not exceed 18,000 kilograms'.

It is misleading to say Boscombe's concerns were unsubstantiated. Barring a catastrophic accident involving their single trials aircraft, of course they were unsubstantiated - at first. The very nature of Risk Management is such that there is an initial, and then continuous, assessment of perceived risks. It was Boscombe's job to notify and assess any such risks. They did so. They identified serious concerns during software validation and verification. As an airworthiness centre of excellence, it was their job to move to practical assessment - flight trials. After numerous FADEC related problems during these trials, they concluded their concerns <u>had</u> been substantiated, as the risks had materialised. As validation and verification of FADEC proved impossible, Boscombe took further action, ceasing flying twice in 1994 and advising MoD(PE) that Controller Aircraft Release (CAR) could not be recommended. In fact, matters deteriorated between their refusal to recommend CAR on 30 September 1993, and the date of the accident.

It is disingenuous to claim MoD accepted Boscombe's advice regarding All Up Mass. This implies it was Boscombe's only concern and they agreed with MoD's actions. They did not; witness the statements that the aircraft should not be released, the FADEC software re-written, and the DASH (Differential Airspeed Hold) system modified - quite apart from the gross immaturity and Switch-On Only status of the Navigation and Communications systems.

Paragraph 6

'In September 1998 the Department, with the Royal Air Force's consent, issued full Controller Aircraft Release for the Chinook Mk2'.

The report cites a 1998 decision within a paragraph discussing the events of late 1993. Also, and again, the report gives the impression all that was necessary to declare the aircraft airworthy at the In-Use build standard was the CAR. This is the function of the Release to Service, issued by the RAF, not MoD(PE).

Interestingly, *'consent'* implies an exchange of correspondence between Controller Aircraft and ACAS, but MoD has stated this cannot be found. Was it made available to the NAO? Controller Aircraft required ACAS's formal statement that he was content with the proposed CAR, and would subsume it as Part 1 to his Release to Service. At no time does the PAC report (or any other Inquiry) discuss this obligation or whether it was complied with. The statement also ignores the 'INTERIM' issue, discussed above.

'In making the decision to issue full Controller Aircraft Release, the Department, as is their right as executive airworthiness authority for the aircraft, weighed the advice of Boscombe Down against other factors, including the equipment's Design Authorities and the consequences of failure, and concluded that the aircraft could be cleared for safe flight within the parameters identified'.

Again, the presentation conflates 1993 and 1998. In 1993 the *'Department'*, represented by Controller Aircraft, stated the aircraft was not to be relied upon in any way. While (his staff) may have considered 'other factors', the mandated placed upon ACAS was precisely what Boscombe had written. There could be no *'safe flight'* within such a parameter. ACAS then defied this mandate, telling aircrew that the aircraft was airworthy.

Finally, the claim that *'the Chinook Mid-Life Update was delivered on time'* is highly misleading - in fact, patently wrong. One cannot separate delivery, acceptance and quality of product. The aircraft was deemed unairworthy at point of delivery, and remained so for some years.

MoD(PE)'s obligations to Boscombe Down

DUS(DP)'s policy [B14], paragraph 3.2, requires MoD to obtain:

'All rights it needs for in-service support of the software and for critical analysis if this should be needed'.

On 18 August 1993 Boscombe Down's Superintendent of Engineering Systems wrote (to the RAF):

'We are still looking at available data and have recently made a "last ditch" effort through AD/HP1 to try to obtain the information required before our first flight, although the chances of success are I believe remote'.

Paragraph 3.4 requires MoD to ensure any tools (e.g. those used during validation and verification) conform to the software interface standard. That is, the onus rested with MoD(PE) to ensure Boscombe had the correct tools.

These policy requirements were not complied with. It is therefore wrong to say:

'Boscombe Down wished to verify the software in the FADEC system using their preferred method known as Static Code Analysis'.

It is irrelevant what Boscombe *'wished'* to do. The responsibility to reconcile the FADEC specification, contract terms and conditions, Trials, Evaluation and Acceptance Plan, Boscombe tasking, and their ability to carry out that tasking, lay entirely with MoD(PE).

For reasons already explained, this is also wrong:

'The Department chose to terminate the EDS-SCICON contract at this point because the requirement for Static Code Analysis was an internal Boscombe Down policy, not supported by Defence Standards'.

The requirement to conduct Static Code Analysis was enshrined in MoD policy, which (obviously) sits above Defence Standards in the standards hierarchy. In fact, the policy specifically warns, at Annex A, A8.2

(Standards), that RTCA/DO-178A and Defence Standard 00-31 are less than rigorous as they do not include Static Code Analysis. RTCA/DO-178A was the standard against which FADEC was developed. It is a commercial standard, not military. Such a specific warning in the policy should have sounded alarms. The issue comes down to the mandated questionnaire before the contract was awarded, in which the criticality status of the software should have been established, agreed and acted upon. What does that questionnaire say? Does it even exist?

The mandated requirement for independent scrutiny renders it irrelevant (even if true, which it is not) that equipment Design Authorities:

'Confirmed that whilst undesirable, none of them (software anomalies) represented an airworthiness concern'.

The major contribution required from industry in this respect is from the Aircraft Design Authority (ADA) and System Co-ordinating Design Authority (SCDA). The essential difference is that Equipment Design Authorities assess Physical Safety of their system in isolation; and, perhaps, Functional Safety within the confines of a System Integration Rig (noting successive cuts in PDS funding had resulted in many Integration Rigs being dismantled or scrapped). Whereas, ADAs and SCDAs assess and certify both Physical and Functional Safety in 'System of System' Integration Rigs, and when installed in the aircraft. (In this case, safety critical software, embedded in the Digital Electronic Control Units, integrated within the entire FADEC system, then integrated with the engine and, finally, integrated with the airframe and flown).

In short, FADEC and its software (in fact any system) may be functionally safe in one application, but not in another. Therefore, it is wrong to quote the *equipment* Design Authority without establishing what role the ADA and SCDA had.

Certification and Acceptance into Service of safety critical software

Here, it is worth repeating the basic, mandated requirements of Defence Standard 00-55 (Part 1):

- *Certification shall be a pre-condition for delivery of safety critical software.*

- *The (software) Design Authority shall submit a Safety Critical Software Certificate to the MoD(PE) project manager prior to delivery. The certificate shall be an unambiguous, clear and binding statement by accountable signatories from the Design Authority, countersigned by the Independent Safety Auditor (Boscombe Down), that the software is suitable for service in its intended system and conforms to the requirements of Defence Standard 00-55). Certification shall be supported by the evidence in the Safety Records Log and supporting documentation.*

- *The Design Authority shall prepare an Acceptance Test Schedule for approval by the MoD(PE) project manager (noting the Aircraft Design Authority must clear safety critical software).*

- *Acceptance into service shall be based on acceptance tests and trials plus the Safety Critical Software Certificate.*

- *Shortfalls against the agreed requirement that are not apparent at acceptance shall be rectified promptly, without additional cost to MoD.*

The Safety Critical Software Certificate

In addition to normal statements of conformity, the Certificate shall contain:

- *Certification of conformance to the standards stated in the contract.*

- *Reference to any Limitations recommended by the MoD Safety Assurance Authority (that is, Boscombe Down).*

On 11 May 2011 MoD admitted uncertainty over what standards were applied to the FADEC contract.[29] Given Boscombe Down could not validate or verify the software, the Certificate and/or supporting papers should detail their concerns. MoD should be invited to produce both.

Subsequent upgrades to FADEC software

In its letter of 11 May 2011, MoD stated:

1. Block 0 upgrade to the original software was <u>contracted</u> in November 1993. The Board of Inquiry confirmed the *'original standard software'* remained in ZD576 on 2 June 1993.[30]

2. Block 1 upgrade was <u>contracted</u> in April 1995 and introduced in 1996, along with a new variant DECU Part Number 2-170-560-05.

The Block 1 change comprised:

- Enable Ground Crew Interface (Enable serial input/output in flight)
- 2.5Hz Notch Filter (N2 and Collective Pitch)
- Reversionary Power Interrupt Nuisance Faults

---

29 Letter DE&S Letter 16-03-2011-103347-004, 11 May 2011.
30 The Issue number of any software must be included in the Release to Service. It was not.

- Residual Torque Voltage
- Eliminate False Engine Out Indication
- Engine Rundown (Reversionary)
- Engine Run-up (Reversionary)
- Software Aliasing (Reversionary)
- Provisions for Reversionary Chip (BH Processor)

In 2006 a new engine, T55-L-714A, was introduced into the Chinook HC Mk2A for trials purposes. It used a new variant DECU Part Number 2-170-560-09, with FADEC 714A Block 1 software. In 2010, this was approved for Fleet Fit, the modification programme was ongoing, and completion due May 2012.

Please note the typical time elapsed between contracting and In-Service.

Conclusion

In the context of an investigation into 29 deaths, and in the interests of natural justice, the NAO report contains many disturbing errors in such a short section. As with other aspects of this case, there is irrefutable evidence of systemic failings in the application of MoD's airworthiness policy. The report misleads by omission. But it is also clear the Committee itself was seriously misled.

MoD spent the following years denigrating Boscombe's work on the software (in the same way it concealed the legal action being taken against Textron for defective software), yet behind the scenes belatedly contracted upgrades. In particular, the 1996 Block 1 upgrade is infinitely more comprehensive than hitherto admitted, with many of the elements seeking to correct or improve issues notified by test pilot Squadron Leader Robert Burke, whose evidence was dismissed with malice by MoD.

Self-evidently, the mandated Certification and Acceptance into Service procedures had not been implemented or completed at the time of the crash. On 2 June 1994 there was no authority or justification for using FADEC in Chinook HC Mk2.

Appendix 4 - Why did MoD cut airworthiness funding in the early 1990s?

Executive Summary

The Nimrod Review claimed systemic airworthiness failings commenced in 1998, linking this to the disestablishment of the RAF Chief Engineer post. This Appendix refutes that notion, providing evidence the systemic failings date to, at least, 1988. Examples are offered of profligate waste, resulting in airworthiness funding being cut to compensate. It concludes that the RAF Chief Engineer at the time either failed in his duty, or did not have the influence or skills attributed him by Mr Haddon-Cave QC.

MoD/RAF slashed airworthiness funding in the years 1990-94. Primarily, this relates to Post Design Services, whose role is to maintain the build standard. The Chinook Airworthiness Review Team (CHART) report of August 1992 refers to similar cuts affecting logistics support and other engineering activities. As explained earlier, this rendered the Safety Case and Release to Service progressively invalid and unverifiable.

Background

First, one must understand the concept of Maintenance Policy Statements. They are expressed thus (example): 1A, 2B, 3BC, 4BCD.

The number is the Line of Servicing. First Line is on-aircraft. Second Line is the workshop at the Air Station. Third Line is MoD workshops, manned by both civilians and Servicemen - such as RNAY Fleetlands, 30MU Sealand and 14MU Carlisle. Fourth Line is Industry.

The letter is the Depth of Servicing. For example, Depth A is commonly simple repairs such as switches and bulbs, and replacement of complete Line Replaceable Units (LRUs - 'black boxes'). Depth B will open the faulty LRU and replace modules or major components, such as Printed Circuit Boards (PCB). Depth C will repair that faulty PCB to component level. Depth D will repair the PCB when specialised, expensive tools, test equipment and expertise is required; for example, substrate repairs.

The Maintenance Policy is finalised during development, when MoD specialists determine the most cost-effective policy. An early decision is necessary because it determines equipment numbers to be procured, and the need to concurrently develop Special to Type Test Equipment (STTE) for Second and Third Line. The decision drives manning levels within the Service. Conversely, a cut in manning levels can force changes in policy, and a 'hidden' increase in support costs.

Thus, a 1A, 2B, 3BC, 4BCD policy means Third Line is capable of in-depth repairs, but there is an expectation that some complex repairs will be necessary at Fourth Line. Other equipments may be just 1A, 4BCD. Also, there is an acknowledgement that each Line can, statistically and reasonably, only expect to recover a certain percentage of arisings. In 1994 this policy, promulgated in Long Term Costings (LTC) Permanent Instructions, was:

- First Line - 8%

- Second Line - 68%

- Third Line - No target was set. Third and Fourth Line capability and capacity was shared because of the need to sustain a Depth D capability. If this was not achieved, the effect would be to increase either or both the Pipe Line Time and Beyond Economic Repair rate (the point at which an item is scrapped).

This policy has never been rescinded, but it ceased to be implemented in the early 90s, with the last attempt (by the RN) in 1994.

In-Service Support is governed by a simple formula called STOCKCAL (Stock Calculation). 'Stock' is the level of Depot Stock required to maintain the fit and maintenance policies.

$$S = \frac{NHP \, (1-R1) \, (1-R2)}{MTBR} \times \frac{100}{1}$$

Where:

S = Number of items required for Depot Stock, the theory being that a demand from a Service Unit can be met immediately by an item just returned from repair, without using contingency stocks or War Reserves.

N = Number of aircraft fitted.

H = Annual flying rate in Hours. This varies within aircraft fleets, as front line aircraft will fly more hours in a given year than those undergoing deep maintenance or held in reserve. The rates to be used were issued each January/February with the LTC Main Assumptions.

P = Repair Pipeline Time in Months. The time taken from the moment an item is deemed unserviceable, to that same item being returned to stores, serviceable. The average was established periodically by means of an asset tracking exercise. Until 1987 it was deemed 13 months for Third Line and 18 months for Fourth Line. In 1987 the RN reduced this to 9 and 13 respectively as a result of the Hallifax Report; which placed more emphasis on Third and Fourth Line efficiency, as manpower reductions at Second Line took effect. However, it can be seen this meant there was less room for error by, for example, Air Member Supply and Organisation (AMSO), who were charged with ensuring Third and Fourth Line spares availability was maintained. It also meant that, logically, there should be an increase in funding for Fourth Line, but this was withheld as part of the assumed 'savings'. So, not only were Fourth Line expected to reduce their Turn Round Time and do more work, they were to do so within smaller budgets. This was compounded, for the RN, when he RAF applied their own equivalent savings measures a few years later. By this time, RN assets and funding were under AMSO control, so the RN had to share the RAF's 'hit'.

R1 = First Line Recovery Rate. As above, 10% to 1987, 8% thereafter.

R2 = Second Line Recovery Rate. As above, 80% to 1987, 68% thereafter.

MTBR = Mean Time Between Removals (not Faults). It is the act of removal that generates the demand for logistic support, not the actual reliability. If an item is found not to be faulty, the arising cannot be counted in the Fault (reliability indicator) figure. MTBR must be constantly compared to MTBF (Faults), the aim being near parity, or nil 'No Fault Founds', which are a major drain on the repair system resources and responsible for large fluctuations in P.

For a given financial year there are fixed elements in STOCKCAL over which the Service HQ has no influence. Number of Aircraft and Flying Rate are relatively fixed. Pipeline Time and Second Line Recovery Rates are significant variables. For example, the simple act of moving an experienced technician to another repair bench, in the same Second or Third Line workshop, can result in major Fourth Line repair contract cost escalation. The consequent reduction in R2 results in increasing demands on LRUs, and is misconstrued by the automated system as a requirement to buy more LRUs; when the solution may be the provision of better training or allocating a properly trained person to the bench. And so on... To avoid such waste, it is vital to have knowledgeable human input - as a matter of policy this ceased in 1988.

As R2 is expected to be 68%, this is a key area to maintain; while it matters less if R1 falls below 8%. The rule of thumb is that if R2 falls to 50%, aircraft robbery will be necessary. That is, there was a conscious decision to make robbery more likely, something noted by witnesses at the Fatal Accident Inquiry. Complementary action was required to ensure properly trained HQ staff managed this. In fact, staff and their training were also cut.

The primary role of any Support Authority is to maintain the integrity of STOCKCAL for any given equipment or system. Every aspect of In-Service Support is contained in this single formula, and almost any In-Service Support problem can be identified and resolved by applying it. As the STOCKCAL of many equipments was maintained by one postholder, this is the classic 'spinning plate' scenario. However, to use the same analogy, spinning above the many small plates is one very large plate, called *implementation of airworthiness regulations*. If that stops, it comes crashing down on everything else.

What links STOCKCAL and airworthiness?

Let us assume R2 has fallen to 40% and aircraft are being robbed. The immediate impact is reduced Operational Effectiveness. Demands are at inability, pressure is on Second Line maintainers to recover more, and there will be a tendency toward shortcuts.

A knock-on effect is the expected arisings at Third Line. Broadly, they are resourced to deal with an R2 of 68%, meaning a maximum of 32% of arisings at Second Line will reach Third Line (but their resourcing remained at or below the pre-1988 20% arising rate). Without warning, there will be a sudden influx of arisings at Third Line. In the short term, they may be able to deal with this via overtime or transferring staff from another repair line. But if there is a pan-equipment problem, for example caused by a policy change (another large spinning plate), then Third Line will be quickly swamped.

When this occurs, they can let the unserviceable item sit on a shelf, but will not meet the Turn Round Time requirement. But the LRU value is seen as a debit in their accounts, so doubling the pressure to offload it. Therefore, the common response is to return the item to Fourth Line marked 'Beyond Unit Capability'. This is when significant problems arise.

Until now, the problem has been in-house, with the PE project manager largely unaware, unless he has constant feedback from Third Line, which few do. But, suddenly, Fourth Line has an increase in arisings and for the first time real money is needed (as Third Line was 'free', being centrally funded). Fourth Line needs an immediate uplift in funding and spares support. As we have seen, they were already under extreme pressure to reduce their Turn Round Time, while coping with an increased workload, within the same budget. A sudden change in either arisings or spares availability would be the straw that breaks their back.

What other factors affect R2? Training. Experience. Corporate knowledge. Up-to-date and accurate Technical Publications and drawings. Component unavailability, including obsolescence. The user having direct and immediate access to expert technical advice at the Design Authority. Fault Investigations being conducted efficiently... What is the process that provides or facilitates these Services? Post Design Services. These are all core components of 'maintaining the build standard' and, hence, airworthiness. As this is vital to the validity of the Safety Case and Airworthiness, the links are clear.

Maintaining the integrity of STOCKCAL for every item is fundamental to airworthiness. Some components are more important than others, but if STOCKCAL is not maintained then there is certainly a systemic failing.

Supporting Fourth Line repair contracts

To maintain Third and Fourth Line Turn Round Times (TRT), the MoD bought, stored, issued and replenished spares. A five-month TRT is impossible if a given spare takes 15 months to manufacture and there is nil stock. In other words, MoD either accepted a long TRT, in which case it had to buy more LRUs, or it bought fewer LRUs and supplied spares to ensure a quicker TRT.

For the purposes of spares management, Fourth Line were afforded the status of an MoD unit, and either demanded as-required or held 'buffer stock'. The latter was more cost effective, as the RAF would not be constantly delivering spares. They operated a max/min stock level system, similar to RAF stores, based on past and predicted arisings/usage.

This access to MoD stores was vital to maintaining the integrity of STOCKCAL. If Fourth Line could not turn round equipment, either on time or not at all, then by definition there was no-one else to do it. To compromise the Fourth Line TRT was to swiftly render aircraft fleets role-limited and, depending on the role of that equipment, ground them or force the use of an aircraft that was not fit for purpose.

In practice, if grounding was imminent resources would be redirected to prevent this, but to the detriment of other areas. But by 1990 even this had been abandoned, with AMSO content to permit whole fleets to be grounded instead of funding resolution of safety problems. And pleading lack of funds cuts no ice when elsewhere money is being consciously wasted...

Air Publication 830, Leaflet DM87

In 1987 the RAF introduced a policy termed 'DM87' - promulgated as Leaflet DM87 of AP830. Without any warning this denied Fourth Line contractors access to, for example, Section 10 (Electronic) stores. In most cases, these stores had already been bought for the sole use of Fourth Line (i.e. when the Maintenance Policy was 1A, 4BCD, and so were the only authorised user). Overnight, they were rendered surplus as they could not be put to their intended use. Simultaneously, AMSO issued instructions that not only was future access denied, but current holdings at contractors were to be destroyed. The immediate effects were:

- Extended Turn Round Times, which now included the Production Lead Time of the spares, negating the assumed P in STOCKCAL.
- MoD was placed in contractual default (for not supplying spares).
- Inability (in fact refusal) to meet demands from Air Stations and for Ship Storing.
- Second (especially) and Third Line swiftly adopted the practice of attempting repairs which they were not capable of, often damaging the item even more.
- Repair contracts had to be amended to increase financial sanction to allow the contractor to buy spares, on an *as required* basis. This had two major effects. First, the unit price increased, as they were not permitted to make economical buys. Second, and crucially in the context under discussion, MoD had to find this extra money - complicated by the funding for these spares having already been spent, spares delivered and then scrapped.

Immediately, the situation existed whereby front line Air Stations were desperate for kit, contractors had the necessary spares in their stores to effect repairs, but were not allowed access and were under orders to scrap them. All compounded by AMSO raising requisitions to duplicate the spares buys which could take 18 months or more to complete. MoD(PE) recommended that contractors be permitted to use up these spares, or buy them. AMSO refused.

As with all such policies, the true and lasting effect was immediately apparent to engineers, but Supply staff equated the reduced holdings at companies and MoD stores with efficiency. The *'savings at the expense of safety'* Mr Haddon-Cave claimed only commenced in 1998 had already gained momentum by 1988. Most Supply staff would finish their 2-year postings and not have to deal with the fallout. Nor would they brief their successors.

Something had to give. What other source of funding did AMSO have to make these duplicate buys? The answer, in 1988-1991, was that needed to buy LRUs, Modules and Test Equipment to (e.g.) replace attrition losses. Because the Long Term Costings Instructions required the holding of a Contingency (16% of Depot Stock) and War Reserves, the effect at first was gradual. These resources were committed to a purpose they were not intended for, hiding the problem for a while; but the longer-term effect was predictable, predicted (by PE), and ignored (by AMSO).

At this time Post Design Services (PDS) funding to maintain the build standard, the major component of maintaining airworthiness, was controlled by MoD(PE). As one would expect it was 'ring-fenced' because it is not volume related. While MoD(PE) recognised the problems AMSO were creating, this specific airworthiness funding was, initially, protected.

However, senior staff regarded the maintaining of airworthiness as *'the rump end of MoD(PE)'*.[31] A 28% reduction in funding was imposed, while concurrently action was put in hand to transfer these key skills to AMSO (effected 1 April 1992). At a stroke, MoD(PE) lost most of its experience.

No sooner was this transfer complete, than AMSO combined the financial pots, meaning (a) PDS monies could be used to compensate for the effects of DM87, but by doing so, (b) airworthiness was further compromised. As PDS maintained Safety Cases, by definition this work was curtailed.

While AMSO gained experience, its senior staff shared the disdain with which their PE equivalents viewed airworthiness. They ordered further cuts of at least 25% for the next two years (to end FY 1993/94). Their view was PDS did not generate a 'due-in' on the Stock Computer (as 'Maintaining the Build Standard' is an intangible in this sense) so it was regarded as a waste of money - fatally flawed reasoning along the same lines as DM87.

AMSO used much of this PDS funding to replace spares that had been scrapped but were still needed - urgently. This served to hide the problem for a year or two but, inevitably, the successive cuts bit and the critical effect - compromised airworthiness - came to the fore; ZD576

---

31 Director of Air Radio, Mr Barry Cox, when briefing airworthiness staff on their transfer to AMSO.

being the first major manifestation. Crucially, these replacement spares were then also scrapped under DM87. And then replaced... And then...

Requirement Scrutiny

No financial provision had been made, or would ever be approved, to make these duplicate buys. Requests would not (and did not) pass Requirement Scrutiny. The decision to commit PDS funding to compensate constituted a serious breach of PUS's Requirement Scrutiny regulations, as a series of false declarations were necessary.

As discussed earlier, in June 1996 MoD's Director Internal Audit issued a report entitled 'Requirement Scrutiny' [B34], notifying PUS (as Chief Accounting Officer) that Requirement Scrutiny was not being conducted properly. The accompanying evidence submitted to investigators revealed waste in excess of £100M in one small two-man avionics section alone, in one financial year. One affected equipment, Cloud & Collision Warning Radar, was, independently, characterised by the RAF Director of Flight Safety as the single greatest airworthiness risk to the Hercules fleet. PUS took no action.

Aftermath

The record shows that, eventually, and initially at a low level (Wing Commander), the penny dropped and a form of slow resurrection took place over the next few years (mid to late 90s).

However, this realisation did not extend to understanding of the links between DM87 and airworthiness. So, while the former was partially addressed, there was no retrospective action permitted to stabilise the latter. A significant effect was that the former PE staff who had been transferred to AMSO (and constituted MoD's corporate knowledge base) had been neutered. Many sought transfers back to PE as there was little to do, and no obvious career path as engineers of any grade had been decreed by AMSO to be junior to all administrative grades. (My new line manager, Ms Sylvia Clinton, was three grades below me - much to her alarm). Now back in PE, these experienced ex-PDS staff effortlessly delivered programmes to time, cost and performance, through applying the old policies and regulations.

A few examples

The above should be placed in some context. PDS, the primary vehicle for maintaining airworthiness, has very little materiel cost - it is mainly man hours. In the scheme of things, it is relatively cheap. However, the cost of general support activities (spares, repairs, modification sets, technical publications, attrition, etc.) is, broadly, proportional to aircraft or equipment numbers. Thus, PDS funding must be kept separate. This ceased when AMSO assumed responsibility for PDS.

During the above period, the Equipment Accounting Centre, Director Internal Audit, and Director Procurement Policy (Project Management) were given numerous examples of waste, including:

- 2 March 1989 - £3,626,000 on Lynx Surveillance Radar. Erroneous STOCKCAL caused by change in Pipeline Time and Recovery Rates, due to spares shortages. The actual requirement was a small number of key spares costing around £20k.

- 9 February 1991 - £1,924,731 on Sea Harrier Digital Guidance Equipment. Caused by DM87 requiring spares to be scrapped, and immediately replaced.

- 12 September 1991 - £3,840,000 on Sea King Surveillance Radar. Erroneous STOCKCAL caused by change in Pipeline Time and Recovery Rates, due to spares shortages.

At this time the PDS contracts for these three equipments were valued at approximately £250k each - and were taking year on year 25-28% cuts to help fund this waste. AMSO's direct response was to demand disciplinary action. When civilian heads of section refused, Air Vice Marshal Christopher Baker, Director General Support Management, and immediate subordinate of Air Member Supply and Organisation, visited London in December 1992 and threatened staff with dismissal. This prompted the aforementioned Director Internal Audit report 'Requirement Scrutiny', which was initially intended to protect these civilian staff.

These are not extreme examples, but indicative. These equipments were merely three of over 100 I managed at this time. A more complete list was submitted to DPP(PM) in January 1992 (see below). Again, historical context is important. In addition to this being during Chinook HC Mk2 development, Kuwait was invaded in August 1990. Every spare penny was needed for Transition to War. The sheer scale of this waste was out of all proportion to the funding required for PDS. The RAF was content to commit funding to unnecessary procurement (when even the Service Users stated they did not need the equipment), while knowingly compromising aviation safety.

In parallel, and unknown to MoD's airworthiness specialists, a Chinook Airworthiness Review Team was formed in May 1992, under the RAF Director of Flight Safety. It reported to the RAF Chief Engineer and Assistant Chief of the Air Staff in August that year, confirming the effects of the above. The cuts, and threats against civilian staff, continued. This ethos lies at the root of MoD's airworthiness failings.

Summary

If anyone with airworthiness delegation in MoD's Acquisition organisation or the new Military Aviation Authority does not understand all the above, implicitly, then the likelihood of deeper systemic failings increases. To make such an error, on something so basic, indicates deep rooted problems. More so, because the mistakes were immediately identified and notified; and, seemingly to save face, ignored, at the expense of safety. One mistake begets another - to allow this to happen so early in the process increased the likelihood of systemic failings, affecting whole fleets of aircraft and their equipment.

Similarly, if one has not worked within this system before being given airworthiness delegation, then the ability to do the job is compromised. There is a fundamental need to understand this level of detail. In the period under discussion, the procedural Defence Standard for maintaining build standards was declared obsolescent and the PDS system dismantled. (The last HQ Radio Modifications Committee sat in June 1991). Overnight, the risk of systemic failure occurring moved from *possible, but there are risk mitigation procedures*, to *has now occurred and there are no mitigation procedures*.

This was the situation in MoD at the time Chinook HC Mk2 was being developed and trialled at Boscombe Down.

Essentially, this is the background to the Nimrod Review. Mr Haddon-Cave did not address the depth and longevity of the failings, in particular failing to heed the evidence revealing why savings were deemed necessary *'at the expense of safety'*. However, he did summarise the problem correctly.

If money had not been wasted in the first place, these *'financial targets'* would have been more easily achieved without compromising airworthiness. The waste far exceeded the cost of doing the job properly. The root problem was a failure of leadership and management oversight.

Mr Haddon-Cave linked the demise of the RAF Chief Engineer post

(1998) to these failings. In fact, it can be seen they had their origins in 1987 (at latest). They came to full fruition in January 1993 when the last vestiges of a process designed to routinely maintain airworthiness were, as a matter of deliberate policy, abandoned.

At this time the RAF *did* have a Chief Engineer. Air Chief Marshal Michael Alcock held the post from 1991-96. This raises key questions:

1. Given the same airworthiness failings were outlined in CHART and the ZD576 Board of Inquiry Report, what action did he take to correct them?

2. Given these were systemic failings, not just Chinook failings, would timely corrective action have helped avoid the Nimrod Review?

If, as Mr Haddon-Cave implied, the Chief Engineer was able to influence such policies and prevent systemic airworthiness failings, then he failed. His subordinates (e.g. Air Vice Marshal Baker) were fully aware of the deliberate waste of money and its effect - I have cited evidence from mid-1992. They were duty bound to report this to the Chief Engineer. Similarly, did the Chief Engineer or Assistant Chief of the Air Staff report these failings to the Chief of the Air Staff (CAS)? It can be seen these four postholders are key players - have they ever been interviewed during Mull of Kintyre Inquiries?

On 21 February 1992 (four years after first notification), junior SS51(RAF) staff accepted (e.g. Section 10) spares should be removed from DM87. Reversing previous objections, their Section Head (a Wing Commander) agreed.[32]

On 15 July 1992 London staff briefed a Supply Group Captain at RAF Harrogate. He concurred. However, another meeting at the same level was held in London on 10 August 1992, at which the RAF hid behind the *'it is policy, we merely implement'* argument - indicating the Group Captain had sought advice from his seniors and been given a different party line.

By December 1992, when Air Vice Marshal Baker threatened his civilian specialists with dismissal should they persist in their refusal to commit fraud, it was clear what AMSO's formal position was - hide the waste and hope nothing happens.

As late as 11 August 1993 the problem had been bounced back down to the working level, civilian staff ordered to desist from challenging waste as it was not in their terms of reference. (But it was, through formal letters

---

32 Loose Minute D/ADSS 51(RAF)/421/3/38, 21 February 1992.

of delegation requiring they conduct Requirement Scrutiny).

This, then, is the detailed background to the criticism by Mr Haddon-Cave QC in his Executive Summary that:

There was a shift in culture and priorities in the MoD toward 'business' and financial targets, at the expense of functional values such as safety and airworthiness.

And wholly refutes his claim that:

Airworthiness was a victim of the process started by the 1998 Strategic Defence Review.

(Which he contradicted by citing the 1996 Nimrod ART, which in turn repeated the failings noted in the 1992 Chinook Airworthiness Review Team report, in turn repeating notifications by MoD's civilian airworthiness specialists in January 1988).

Senior staff were notified and refused to act. Despite industrial scale waste being notified to PUS in 1996 [B34], this ethos continued and has been condoned by successive Ministers for the Armed Forces (see Appendix 1).

By 2001, personnel being interviewed for transfer or advancement were being asked questions to ensure they understood that safety concerns should be ignored if it meant avoiding personal conflict and/or upsetting other staff.

Appendix 5 - A chronology of AP830, Leaflet DM87

Introduction

The purpose of this Appendix is to present detailed evidence of the effect of DM87. What follows has been gleaned from personal diaries and contemporaneous notes; kept because staff holding airworthiness delegation are required to retain records of decisions and actions in case of a need to justify decisions (in accordance with the Safety Management System) - a requirement that extends into retirement (as there is no time or geographical limit on Duty of Care). To ease understanding, two typical examples have been used. A Cloud and Collision Warning Radar fitted to, for example, C-130, VC10, Nimrod and Jetstream, and a Fire Control Radar fitted to Sea Harrier. These have been chosen to illustrate the pan-MoD nature of the problem.

By necessity, this Appendix contains detailed discussion of key events, so that the scale of the maladministration and financial waste may be fully appreciated.

Formulation of DM87

DM87 was being formulated as a policy throughout 1987. It is a significant Leaflet, some 30 pages long, with Annexes. Such a document would go through many drafts and changes. None of this preparatory work was discussed with the MoD(PE) project offices that would have to implement the policy. The first they were advised of changes at a working level (Assistant Director and below), was the circulation of a new Buffer Stock contract clause in January 1988, to be inserted in repair contracts with immediate effect. This denied contractors access to a number of 'excluded ranges' including Section 10 (Electronic) spares.

MoD(PE) (in this context the specialist Assistant Directorate within Directorate General Airborne Weapons and Electronic Systems responsible for 'cradle to grave' management of avionic systems) immediately realised such a policy could not be suddenly dropped on Industry. Extant contracts gave them access to MoD stores, so they had no need to enter into comprehensive supply arrangements with sub-contractors. Nor was there sufficient financial sanction on any contract to cover this new cost. There should have been (a) discussion with Industry, and (b) a period of grace to allow them to procure their own stocks (using MoD funding which would have to be bid for and approved). This period would have to be at least the longest lead time. Three years

150

would have been reasonable, accompanied by a direction to use up existing MoD stocks.

Upon querying this with Air Member Supply and Organisation (AMSO), PE were told there *had* been consultation with 'Industry' - the 13 January 1988 issue of THESBAC [B36], a circular 'for private circulation to members of the Society of British Aerospace Companies' had carried notification. It transpired the 30 pages of DM87 had been 'notified' in a short announcement next to an obituary. This was ineffectual and, more importantly, had no contractual or legal status.

MoD(AFD) EMBODIMENT LOAN
Revised procedures

The Ministry of Defence has advised that from April 1, 1988, Automatic Data Processing (ADP) demand vetting checks will be introduced into the Embodiment Loan (EL) demand process for all EL demands placed on SM4(RAF) MoD Harrogate. Member companies should note that all demands in the following categories will be referred to the appropriate Supply Management Branch for verification before issue action is approved:

a. Demands for P and L stores.
b. Demands for those items shown in contract documents as being excluded from issue on EL, and which should be obtained by the contractor from commercial sources.
c. Demands for like consumable items in excess of £1,000 per demand.

For P and L stores, the check will be to confirm that the item demanded is in accordance with the EL supply arrangements already approved for the contract quoted on the demand. Any demand in any of the above categories which is not approved for issue will be returned to the originating contractor for reconsideration. Member companies are reminded that if they wish to query the rejection of a demand for any particular item of equipment, or propose any amendments to spares schedules or contract conditions they should, in the first instance, refer to the MoD(PE) Project Office stated in the contract document.

OBITUARY
Mr Peter Harris

The Society has learned with deep regret of the death on January 3, 1988 of Peter Harris.
Mr Harris joined the Society as Assistant Secretary in 1947. He subsequently became an Assistant Director and, in 1970, the Deputy Director (Policy). He retired in mid-1977, remaining as a consultant for a further two years.

'Notification' of DM87, November 1987 *(SBAC)*

It took some time to uncover who was involved, but in August 1988 the author of DM87, SS9B(RAF), was tracked down and engaged. This RAF officer, a Wing Commander, confirmed AMSO's interpretation and implementation of DM87 was incorrect. AMSO disagreed.

Simultaneously, AMSO demanded that all repair contracts be firm price; which can only be prohibitively expensive on avionics as failures are random in nature so cannot be predicted.

Chronology from January 1988

14 January 1988 - Recognising the immediate effect this would have on Operational Effectiveness, especially on problematic/short supply equipments, MoD(PE) issued the required contract amendment as a test case on a Sea King Surveillance Radar, but tried to dilute the impact by adding a clause requiring the contractor (MEL, Crawley) to telex SM4(RAF) at Harrogate notifying them of spares shortages and inabilities. An extraordinary Local Equipment Repair Committee (LERC) was convened to try to work out a plan of action.[33] The amendment was issued, but AMSO did not give their support and refused to discuss, so it was ineffective. This confirmed PE's concerns and, within days, Service demands for a front line radar were at inability, compromising Anti-Submarine Warfare (ASW) and Search and Rescue (SAR) tasking.

12 April 1988 - Meeting at RAF Harrogate. Over the previous two months attempts to amend current contracts had been unsuccessful, and accepting DM87 in new contracts was proving impossible. The pricing conditions, Turn Round Time and cost would change dramatically, and what should have been routine renewals were taking months to negotiate, with little progress. Not only was DM87 wasteful, it was leaving Users with no repair cover at all. MoD(PE) extended the old contracts to provide emergency cover, using previous terms and conditions, which prompted formal AMSO complaints against civilian project managers. A higher-level meeting was convened.

Despite rapidly escalating costs, MoD(PE)'s points were rejected by AMSO. PE was forced to let high risk contracts which allowed the contractor to assume the worst case for every repair. For example, every

---

33 A LERC is unique in that decisions are contractually binding, and the minutes immediately become a contract amendment. It is not a routine repair meeting; it can be called at short notice by either MoD or the contractor. See DGDQA Standing Instruction 0136 and Def Con 112 (Repair).

Sea King radar transmitter was assumed to need a magnetron, the highest cost individual component. Given the restrictions in DM87, this was reasonable as, if the firm price did not include the device, and it was needed, the company would make a huge loss on that repair, through no fault of their own - in turn jeopardising the very existence of Fourth Line.

Previously, MoD had bought these devices in bulk for, typically, £8-10k each, and had constant production contracts as they could only be delivered at about three per month. Now, they had to be ordered on a much smaller scale, and the unit cost almost doubled. This was compounded when, in October 1990, AMSO cancelled the maintenance contracts for the MoD-owned Environmental Test Chambers used to test the tubes before certification. Thus, even if a production or repair contract was let, the items could not be delivered because they could not be tested. Again, this date was significant in the context of the Kuwait invasion and Transition to War.

AMSO's reasoning was: *If you put your car into the garage for an oil change, you don't provide the oil and filter.*

MoD(PE) replied: *Yes you do, if the garage takes 18 months to procure and you already have an in-house requirement for the same oil and filter, buy them in bulk at low cost, have them in stock, and there is an urgent operational need.*

MoD(PE) pointed out that Defence equipment is highly specialised, highly specified (e.g. environmental extremes), and often we are the only user. If it were a simple 'filter' costing a few pounds, MoD may have chosen to accept a slightly higher cost for convenience; but when the subject was an £10k magnetron whose price had doubled, and we were paying for 50 per year instead of 20, then that was unnecessary waste on a significant scale - and repeated across all Air Systems.

Finally, MoD(PE) asked where the funding was coming from. AMSO replied *'existing resources'*. One, the funding for Capital procurement, such as replacing attrition losses, coupled with reducing the cost of repairs by not repairing, and often scrapping, unserviceable kit (creating even more shortages). Two, the MoD(PE)-controlled funding for Post Design Services. That is, direct airworthiness funding. At the time this was 'ring fenced' in MoD(PE), but when the work was later transferred to AMSO the pot was immediately robbed to fund DM87.

June 1988 - Meeting at Ferranti Radar Systems, Edinburgh to discuss contract renewals for Lynx and Sea Harrier radars, at which the company rejected the proposed DM87 clauses. While their production staff knew of the issues through individual dealings with MoD(PE) project manager, the company position was they had not been advised by RAF or MoD Contracts Policy section, so had had no time to formulate a corporate response. Pricing and Turn Round Times were the major stumbling blocks, as previous contracts had a 10-week Turn Round, which had been achieved. But the sudden need to buy spares would push this out to 18 months or more. *Inter alia*, this would cause a cash flow problem and advance payments would be sought; further complicating negotiations and requiring MoD resources it did not have.

5 June 1989 - Radar Project Office memo to Contracts Branch. A contractor, Air Transport Charter Ltd, had notified MoD that the financial limit for Cloud and Collision Warning Radar (CCWR) repairs had been reached, and it was now bearing the burden of buying spares. Additional Financial Sanction was required, but the project manager notes no such financial provision was requested or made by the RAF, despite DM87 requiring such complementary provision. He states that the constant influx of such demands means that, just two months into the Financial Year, a whole-year overspend was looming. That is, additional money must be found, or repairs halted.

He also notes that some of these spares, such as Electronic Valves (e.g. klystrons, magnetrons) are procured by a specialist section. As they no longer have to buy them (as the contractor must, under DM87), the entire financial burden is placed on his own coffers. This is a double whammy, because what little funding exists is held by another MoD(PE) Directorate, who will have an underspend and lose the funding in the next costings round. He concludes by recommending higher level policy resolution. It can be seen this had been recommended and attempted before, but once at a certain level had just been thrown back at individual project managers - when what was needed was leadership.

October 1989 - Project Office letter to SS51(RAF) (responsible for consumable Section 10 Detail Part Spares, as distinct from repairable modules and LRUs). In response to previous correspondence of 14 September 1989, challenging the waste of money, an administrator in SS51 had replied on 9 October 1989 challenging the project manager's *'assumption'* of knowledge of the equipment. (The project manager is employed for his detailed technical knowledge and experience of repairing such equipment). SS51(RAF) had requested 'surplus' spares above a certain value (£20) be returned to 14MU for disposal. The company was to dispose of lower value items locally.

The project manager makes the point that, as they are Class C/3 spares (consumable and used at Third or Fourth Line), and there is no Third Line capability on that equipment (CCWR), the spares can only be used by the contractor. He also highlights that SS51's system is reactive, meaning they have not altered their computer programming to allow for DM87, and continue to raise requisitions when DM87 means there can be no further usage. In short, the initial buy of spares is to be scrapped, the contractor is to replace them at MoD's cost, and AMSO are also replacing them under separate contracts. A triple whammy!

The requisitions for both the repair contract and spares replacement could not possibly pass Requirement Scrutiny, as there is no 'legal' usage - yet MoD(PE) staff are being instructed to approve the former, and AMSO staff were approving the latter (which constitutes incitement to commit fraud, and fraud, respectively). This argument precipitated a parallel debate on Requirement Scrutiny, as AMSO were obviously not carrying out this obligation to PUS properly (if at all), while MoD(PE) were. Numerous requisitions signed by, say, a Wing Commander Supplier, would be rejected by a junior financier in MoD(PE), or the project manager himself, as a waste of money.

This is the vital link between Requirement Scrutiny, DM87 and Airworthiness. The ongoing waste and the 'need' to rob airworthiness funding to pay for it. Also, this activity was diverting these specialist MoD(PE) staff from their primary role, managing airworthiness. To them, the links were clear. If repairs, and hence availability of equipment to front line, were being compromised, then the obvious knock-on effect would be Second Line attempting repairs which could not be verified.

In time, this occurred, the prime example being RAF Lyneham attempting to repair CCWR scanner gearboxes. But lacking the crack detection capability of Fourth Line they failed to notice cracked casings. Had a gearbox shattered in the nose of a C-130, the engines might ingest the debris, damage props and mainplanes, etc.

This is why experienced project managers were responsible for all phases of the project, from Concept to Disposal. The primary aim was always to ensure airworthiness. Routine repairs and spares activity was, effectively, delegated to AMSO, with the project manager negotiating contracts, providing technical advice, chairing technical committees, and prioritising tasking/expenditure across a range of equipment (e.g.

Radars). This integrated approach ceased when MoD(PE) staff were absorbed into AMSO in 1992; at which point the project managers were seen to be complaining about their own Department's policy.

28 March 1990 - Letter from SM47b2(RAF) to the Radar project manager, complaining that he had not done the RAF's job for them. That is, the RAF had long since stopped making Materiel and Financial Provision for avionic support, so had not anticipated the problems DM87 would cause. SM47 were complaining about, and blaming the project manager for, the increased cost of repair contracts, ignoring the fact that the increase was due to DM87 and the sudden need to include cost of spares in the price. Additional funding had been sought. The project manager had applied the Requirement Scrutiny rules and the 'requirement' had failed, because the required spares had already been bought and the 'system' did not allow for the concept of perfectly serviceable spares then being scrapped and immediately replaced.

SM47 also stated *'reliability increases with age'*, citing this as the reason for not supporting or funding Fault Investigation requests raised by RAF Lyneham on the above cracked gearboxes (a critical flight safety hazard). That a junior supplier felt empowered to complain to, and about, a senior engineering project manager in such a manner, and make decisions on purely engineering matters affecting flight safety, is indicative of the emerging ethos.

Nothing encapsulates this entire period or attitude better than Loose Minute D/DDSM8(RAF)/PRU/4/41/11 dated 6 July 1993, which crows:

'The introduction of New Management Strategy and the creation of Multi-Disciplinary Groups has put Support Staff in control of the procurement process'.

These Support Staff (supply managers, financiers, filing clerks, etc.) now had primacy over senior specialist engineers, with authority to overturn their engineering decisions.

The project manager replied on 10 April, copying Finance and Contracts Branches, outlining the DM87 background, explaining why no funding was available and (again) recommending a review of the policy; stating it was now over two years since first highlighted.

13 June 1990 - Project Office letter to SM47(RAF), a Wing Commander. The predicted extended Turn Round Times and cost escalation had occurred, with SM47 and his superiors blaming MoD(PE) and Industry; Wing Commander being the level appointed to lodge complaints against

individual project managers.[34] That this was still occurring more than a decade later is recorded in the minutes of a hearing chaired by the Defence Procurement Agency's Director of Personnel, Resources and Development (DPRD, Mr David Baker), on 9 September 2002. His formal ruling was that the Chief of Defence Procurement (CDP) and Director General Air Systems 2 (DGAS2, responsible for, *inter alia*, Nimrod and Chinook) had been correct to rule the refusal to make a false declaration was an offence, but that the order to make the false declaration was not an offence. DPRD's ruling was conveyed to Prospect (Trades Union), who informed affected staff on 18 September 2002.[35] During this process, and in accordance with MoD Manual 2, this was brought to PUS's attention (Sir Kevin Tebbit).[36] He did not reply.

2 July 1990 - Project Office letter to SM47(RAF). This exchange of correspondence illustrates the antagonism DM87 was causing, and relates to the Sea Harrier Fire Control Radar. Turn Round Times were continuing to increase along with costs, and SM47 were under constant pressure to meet Service demands for LRUs and repairable sub-assemblies. However, instead of advising their superiors that the root cause was DM87, they demanded that PE lodge formal complaints with industry.

On this occasion, SM47 insisted on the company, Ferranti, be chastised for taking too long to repair and return a radar display, quoting a repair report from the company. (Does the RAF really need to employ Wing Commanders to worry about individual radar displays?). The project manager's reply notes the display had been declared Beyond Economic Repair, and scrapped on his instructions. Not only that, it had already been replaced and delivered to the Squadron. He notes that MoD would be ridiculed for complaining about such a matter.

Very shortly Kuwait would be invaded, which would precipitate the first large scale deployment of War Reserves in many a year. But these had already been committed to sustaining routine peacetime deployments.

1 March 1991 - Project Office letter to SS51(RAF) at Harrogate. An

---

34 It is acknowledged not all PE staff challenged this waste. Many decided not to rock the boat and implemented AMSO's policy; but in doing so compromised themselves in a legal sense by making false Requirement Scrutiny declarations.

35 Letter DPA/C175/JF/62/02, 18 September 2002.

36 Letter DCC2C/pf, 10 June 2002.

Equipment Accounting Centre (EAC) audit report had been received in MoD(PE), asking questions only AMSO could answer; as it was their implementation of DM87 causing the problems.

A previous EAC letter to the project offices, dated 19 February 1991, listed nine problematic contracts at one small contractor (Air Transport Charter, Ltd). The equipments affected included Cloud and Collision Warning Radar, ADF, VOR/ILS and VHF Radios - the lack of which would severely impact Operational Effectiveness. EAC noted MoD's position was becoming *'untenable'* through unnecessary waste; and equipment that had previously been easily and economically repaired was now being declared Beyond Economical Repair (BER) because the cost of buying small quantities of spares was prohibitive. The BER rate is set by the LERC, but general advice is that it should not exceed 40% of the cost of a new LRU, based on a production run of 10. Thus, the doubling of the cost of some major spares, allied to the Firm Pricing of repairs, meant many arisings were automatically BER, effectively changing the class of store from Repairable to Consumable. No funding existed to replace them, and any request would fail Scrutiny).

The MoD(PE) letter to SS51(RAF) notes it is now three years since PE first highlighted the problems, cites unanswered References from 28 December 1989 and 1 August 1990, and reiterates the increased cost of repair and extended Turn Round Times DM87 is causing.

March 1991- Project Office letter to EAC replying to that of 19 February 1991. It reflects on the meeting of 12 April 1988 at which MoD(PE) first highlighted the problem, their advice being DM87 cannot be applied retrospectively without first addressing the disposal/use of assets which DM87 does not permit anyone else to use. It refers to exemptions being sought so that waste may be avoided - and being turned down. The letter is copied to Contracts Branch Policy section, illustrating the need for a policy-level resolution. No reply was received.

21 February 1992 - Letter from SS51(RAF) to SMS81(RAF) recommending removal of the *'across the board embargo, to allow sensible management of our older systems'*. This missed the point that it was not older systems, but those with no Third Line capability, which included some very new equipments. Nevertheless, it was a step forward, and he copied the letter to the project manager who had led the MoD(PE) objections. MoD(PE) were not copied with any replies.

<u>24 June 1993</u> - Project Office letter to SM(AV)46a (RAF), who managed main equipment (LRUs and other repairables). Effectiveness relied entirely on contactors meeting Turn Round Times, in turn relying on SS51 buying spares. A new postholder had asked the project office why no spares were being bought, as RAF Lyneham were complaining about inabilities on Hercules. The reply is a summary of DM87. This illustrates that, despite SS51's admission of 16 months previously that DM87 was causing problems, little had been done and corrective action would take years. The implication is that, in the same way Squadron Leaders has taken years to convince Wing Commanders, SS51 (a Wing Commander) was having problems convincing his Group Captain.

This failure to convince 'senior' staff was clearly related to events of seven months before, when Director General Support Management threatened to dismiss civilian staff who persisted in complaining about this waste, and its effect on airworthiness and Operational Effectiveness.

Summary

In his Nimrod Review, Mr Haddon-Cave criticised the implementation of a *'huge process of stock reduction'*, tying it to the Strategic Defence Review of 1998.[37] In fact, it can be seen that the effect of SDR98 paled into insignificance compared to that of 1987's DM87.

He also criticised 20% cuts implemented by the Chief of Defence Logistics (CDL), spread over five years, only part of which directly affected airworthiness. That is, given the rundown of several aircraft fleets, and huge over-staffing in Air Member Logistics - formerly AMSO - a proportionate reduction in general support costs could be achieved without compromising Operational Effectiveness or safety. By comparison, the fallout from DM87 resulted in 25-28% cuts per year, for at least three years, directly targeting airworthiness.

His criticism of CDL, General Sir Sam Cowan, was misdirected and lacked context. It can be seen that the true context was provided in evidence. It is not known why Mr Haddon-Cave ignored it, but doing so allowed him to blame the wrong person, while protecting the guilty.

---

37 Nimrod Review, paragraph 13.58.

Appendix 6 - Why would MoD dissemble over the existence of a Release to Service?

Executive Summary

On 11 May 2010 MoD misled Dr Susan Phoenix, whose husband Detective Superintendent Ian Phoenix perished onboard ZD576; naming Sir Donald Spiers, Controller Aircraft, as the only person who approved the release of the Chinook HC Mk2. MoD stated Releases to Service did not exist prior to 1995/96.[38] Said Release to Service was issued by the Assistant Chief of the Air Staff (ACAS), Air Vice Marshal Anthony Bagnall, on 22 November 1993.

Dr Phoenix has kindly given her permission for this to be discussed.

Background

The regulations and instructions of the day (JSP553 and Controller Aircraft Instructions) required a Controller Aircraft Release (CAR) signed by Controller Aircraft, which would form Part 1 of a Release to Service signed by ACAS. To recap, the CAR is Controller Aircraft's statement that the aircraft is airworthy, at the build standard presented for Controller Aircraft Release trials. It is <u>mandated</u> upon ACAS.

Freedom of Information Requests and Parliamentary Correspondence

On 10 November 2005, in reply to a question from Steve Webb MP, Adam Ingram, Minister for the Armed Forces wrote:

> 'The Controller Aircraft Release and RAF Release to Service had been signed off in November 2003, and a single amendment list had been produced in March 2004, only 3 months before the crash.' [39]

On 8 March 2010 the RAF Release to Service Authority (RTSA) supplied the Cover Sheet of the Release to Service issued by ACAS, dated November 1993, to the author.

On 11 May 2010, in reply to the same questions asked of the RTSA by the author, Dr Phoenix received a reply from the Assistant Private Secretary to the Minister for the Armed Forces:

> 'The Initial Release document took the form, as was standard at the time, of the CA

---

38 Letter MSU/04/07/03/01/cc, 11 May 2010, signed by Mr Rod Latham, Assistant Private Secretary to Minister for the Armed Forces.
39 Letter D/Min(AF)/AI 4573/05/C/LN, 10 November 2005.

Release signed by the Controller Aircraft, Donald Spiers.[40] *Releases signed by ACAS did not come in until 1995/96, <u>when the post of Controller Aircraft had been disestablished</u>. I enclose a copy of the Release to Service issued by ACAS in January 1996, effectively superseding the CA Release'.* [B36]

In April 1994 Sir Donald was replaced as Controller Aircraft by Air Marshal Roger Austin, and he by Air Marshal Peter Norriss in 1997.

Upon querying these errors and contradictions (by letter dated 7 July 2010) Dr Phoenix received a reply, this time from Min(AF) himself, Nick Harvey MP, dated 28 September 2010:

'I can only reiterate that prior to 1995/96, the Release to Service took the form of a "Controller Aircraft" release, accompanied as necessary by Service Deviations; and the original document would be signed off by the Controller Aircraft, not by ACAS. The original Release for the Chinook Mk2 was signed off by Sir Donald Spiers'.[41]

It can be seen this reply is muddled, although nearer the truth, but the crucial deceit remains - the firm statement that ACAS was not involved in November 1993. MoD makes the extraordinary *faux pas* of naming Donald Spiers, but not ACAS, when Spiers had no authority to approve Service regulated flying.

Conclusions

The effect was to deceive Dr Phoenix, diverting her at a time she was preparing her submission to the Review; the intent seemingly to distance ACAS from the act of releasing an unairworthy aircraft.

It is likely this deceit stems from recent (2009/10) revelations regarding the failure to implement the airworthiness regulations in the lead up to INTERIM Controller Aircraft Release and Release to Service. For example, the Technical Addendum to the Macdonald Report (2000) dated January 2010, and submission to Secretary of State for Defence dated 11 November 2000 by the Macdonald Report authors. Also, the emergence of the complete 1992 Chinook Airworthiness Review Team (CHART) report, hitherto concealed from every Inquiry. Only by interviewing those concerned, and studying the relevant correspondence, can this issue be fully explained.

---

40 Sir Donald Spiers was knighted in July 1993, shortly before his retirement.
41 Letter MSU/4/7/3/2/is, 28 September 2010.

Appendix 7 - What does 'INTERIM' mean in the context of Controller Aircraft Release and Release to Service, and why did MoD dissemble over its meaning?

Executive Summary

Boscombe Down, correctly, reminded DHP that 'INTERIM' and 'Switch-On Only clearance' were the same thing. Their advice, that Controller Aircraft Release (CAR) should not be granted, had not changed by 2 June 1994. In fact, matters had deteriorated and the MoD(PE) Fleet aircraft at Boscombe had ceased flying on airworthiness grounds. In 1996 MoD sought to explain this:

'In the period (20 April - 2 June 1994) there were a number of incidents involving airborne HC Mk2 of which approximately five were due to FADEC malfunction whilst operating in normal mode. There had also been incidents on the ground. The MoD(PE) project office sought explanations of the various incidents from the aircraft and engine manufacturers but in the absence of satisfactory explanations Boscombe Down suspended trials flying. (This) was an expediency within the proper exercise of airworthiness considerations by Boscombe Down and was not seen as a refusal by individual test pilots to fly the Chinook HC Mk2.'[42]

MoD's Director of Legal Services was seriously misled, tainting MoD's evidence to subsequent Inquiries.

Background

The current issue of JSP553 (Military Airworthiness Regulations) defines 'Switch-On Only' as follows:

'Switch-On only means that it is understood that operation of the equipment does not interfere with the proper operation of any other equipment or system fitted to the aircraft. The equipment may be fitted and may be operated in flight within the Limitations defined (which may therefore restrict such operation to specific phases of flight and parts of the flight envelope) but cannot be relied upon to function correctly (which may include incorrect functioning of any failure indications). The aircraft must not be operated in any way that places any reliance whatsoever on the proper functioning of this equipment'.

Boscombe Down Letter AMS 8H/05, and report AMS 107/93 dated 15 October 1993 (Chinook HC Mk2 - INTERIM CA Release Recommendations - Navigation Systems) [B23] explains this, adding:

---

42 Fax 18:46:29, 15 September 1996.

'In order to carry out crew conversion and training an INTERIM (Switch-On) clearance was <u>requested by the Sponsor</u>. This report covers the results of the initial trials to provide INTERIM CA Release recommendations'.

That is, it was a progress report, not a final report.

Boscombe Down Letter Report NR 108/93, AMS 8H/05 dated 19 October 1993 (INTERIM CAR Recommendations for Communication Systems of the Chinook HC Mk2) [B26] fulfils a similar function. It states the <u>tests</u> reported therein took place in October 1993, with <u>trials</u> due to continue until April 1994. This indicates immaturity of process (see Appendix 2) as far as installed performance during flight is concerned.

Switch-On Only clearance could only be replaced by 'Limited' or 'Full' after planned trials. However, these were subsequently delayed and still ongoing in <u>1995</u>; not least because the FADEC safety critical software had not been validated and verified.

Given the definition of 'INTERIM' reiterated four days earlier, the meaning of 'INTERIM CAR Recommendations' provided in Letter Report PE/Chinook/41, APF/247/Annex dated 22 October 1993 (Chinook HC Mk2 - INTERIM CA Release Recommendations) is clear. [B27] And to make sure, Boscombe stated that their 'INTERIM' report should be read in conjunction with these previous reports. They were stating, categorically, that RAF aircraft should <u>not</u> fly operationally. In fact, it is difficult to envisage what useful flying, even training and familiarisation, could take place on an aircraft.

Discussion

Controller Aircraft signed his INTERIM CAR on 9 November 1993. Did trials take place in that 2-week period (22 October 1993 to 9 November 1993) to change Boscombe's advice? The answer must be no, because Boscombe were predicting a start date of April 1994 for the Navigation and Communications systems trials, never mind all the others. And that plan had dependencies which were not satisfied, such as 'Essential' modifications. More fundamentally, they awaited delivery of a Chinook at the Mk2 build standard.

Similarly, what occurred between 9 and 22 November 1993 (ACAS signing his Release to Service) to persuade him that a blanket Switch-On Only clearance could be changed and represented as a Full clearance to the RAF? The only answer is - nothing.

Boscombe's reiteration that 'INTERIM' and 'Switch-On Only' were the same thing unmistakably indicates both were common terms (which I can confirm), and ACAS and his staff would understand them. Notably, Controller Aircraft did not remove the 'INTERIM' prefix from the INTERIM CAR he forwarded to ACAS on 9 November.

Controller Aircraft's letter of promulgation says: *'The Chinook HC Mk2 post Mid-Life Update is issued for Service use subject to the limitations stated in this CA Release'*. Several questions arise:

1. In using the term 'INTERIM' throughout, Switch-On Only clearance unambiguously applies to the whole aircraft. If this was not intended, then why not remove 'INTERIM'?

2. When saying 'for Service use', what *was* that intended Use? The answer lies in the Boscombe letter of 15 October 1993 (above): *'In order to carry out <u>crew conversion and training</u> an INTERIM (Switch-On) clearance was requested by the Sponsor'.*

3. What are the 'limitations' he mentions? The single biggest limitation is that of Switch-On Only clearance. In fact, it was a show-stopping prohibition.

In other words, Controller Aircraft is saying to ACAS:

'You asked for Switch-On Only clearance, and here it is. I will advise you in due course when I consider it airworthy, at which point you may fly it in-service'.

In offering a report *'<u>in the form of</u> INTERIM Recommendations'*, Boscombe were merely reiterating that their task was incomplete, and the aircraft status so immature that CAR could not be recommended. They were consistent in this advice, the meaning unequivocal. They explained the meaning of 'INTERIM', and annotated every page of their report with *'INTERIM Recommendations'*. Controller Aircraft agreed.

Similarly, ACAS did not remove the term. By issuing his Release to Service, he was making a binding legal declaration that the regulations had been satisfied and the aircraft was safe. They were not. Aircrew were misled by omission, by their own senior officers. Both they and the passengers unwittingly boarded an unairworthy aircraft.

Why did MoD(PE) dissemble when MoD PL (Legal Services) sought an explanation?

On 20 September 1995 MoD(PE)'s Director Helicopter Projects (DHP) was advised by PL(Legal Services) that a Fatal Accident Inquiry was to be held, and that families had sought information about the 'clearance certificate' for the Chinook HC Mk2. On 25 October 1995 DHP's Assistant Director Helicopter Projects 1 (AD/HP1) replied on behalf of his line manager, DHP, making various statements:[43] [B38]

1. *'The CAR for the Chinook HC Mk2 was issued in accordance with the regulations and signed by Controller Aircraft'.* It was not a CAR, it was an INTERIM CAR; and its content was non-compliant. (See Section 2).

2. *'I have had access to the Board of Inquiry proceedings and as far as I am able to determine from the evidence ZD576 was operating within the constraints of the CAR'.* How could ZD576 be *'operating within the constraints of the CAR'* when that CAR mandated upon the RAF that it should not be flown? (This is not a criticism of the aircrew, as they had not been made aware of this). And why is an Army procurement officer being asked to comment on RAF operational flying? Was the same question asked of the Air Staff? Moreover, was use of 'constraint' deliberate? A 'Constraint' is very different to a 'Limitation', the latter being something that can be worked around. The main purpose of (any) Mid-Life Upgrade is to remove Operational Constraints.

3. *'When the results of all the trials and demonstrations indicate the aircraft has achieved a suitable standard of airworthiness, Controller Aircraft will issue the initial CA Release'.* This merely quotes the extant regulations, but does not say they were *not* implemented properly. The use of *'initial'* is correct, but omits that Controller Aircraft issued an INTERIM CAR.

4. *'A&AEE (Boscombe Down) provide recommendations for a CAR'.* While this statement is true, it is omitted that Boscombe refused to recommend CAR. In fact, they stated that implementation of safety critical software was *'positively dangerous'.* Nor does it say Controller Aircraft wholly agreed with Boscombe, and endorsed their recommendations without amendment.

5. *'The (Boscombe) trials are extensive, comprehensive and cover all aspects of safety for flight operations'.* Again, while true this omits that Boscombe refused to recommend CAR due to immaturity of this process. That, they had ceased flying their aircraft on airworthiness grounds.

6. *'The (Boscombe) use of the word 'INTERIM' to describe these initial recommendations has led to some common misconceptions. In the covering letter (Boscombe) refer to an 'INTERIM CA Release' when, given the definition of CAR, no such document could exist'.* This gets to the nub of the issue - an admission that the INTERIM CAR sent to the RAF is not a statement that the aircraft is airworthy. By omitting mention of Boscombe's associated correspondence, which was to be read in

43 (Letter D/DHP/HP1/4/1/4/1 dated 25 October 1995, to PL(LS) Legal Services and Sec(AS), copied to ACAS, Boscombe Down and others.

conjunction with the INTERIM CAR, a reader might infer criticism of Boscombe. But as the author's own staff and superiors (ultimately Controller Aircraft) continued to use the term, it can be seen it is actually criticism of *their* actions (although neither Legal Services nor the families would have the detailed knowledge to appreciate this). Effectively, this is the author's 'get out'.

Boscombe issued formal reports recommending Switch-On clearance Only for the entire Navigation and Communications systems, precluding operational flight. What were they meant to say when it came to recommendations for the whole aircraft? It would be illogical, confusing, and a breach of their legal obligations, to contradict themselves by recommending operational flight. So, they simply used the same terminology, and firmly linked the 'INTERIM' recommendations to the reports explaining the reasons for this status - the effect being to establish a verifiable audit trail. It was disingenuous and misleading for MoD to omit this.

Nor does the letter reveal that, on 25 May 1994, the author's predecessor (Captain Mike Brougham RN) chaired a meeting at Boscombe to discuss FADEC software, concluding:

> '(Captain Brougham) said that Director Helicopter Projects was aiming to review the position of the ACAS request to a further INTERIM CAR within the next 2 weeks. He added that this will require a consensus view and that a further meeting would be required. The 10 June 1994 was declared as an end date for this decision making process'.[44] [B46]

That is:

- The predecessor of the author of the letter to Legal Services was on record as using the term 'INTERIM CAR', and undoubtedly understood its meaning.

- ACAS also used the term in his Release to Service, so one assumes he understood the meaning.

- The notes of the 25 May 1994 meeting [B46] make it clear FADEC had <u>not</u> been accepted by MoD, contrary to a claim made by Textron.[45] This is discussed elsewhere, but it is worth repeating that no valid Certificate of Design could exist, rendering it a serious breach of regulations to fit FADEC to a service aircraft.

---

44 D/DHP/57/4/1, 31 May 1994. Notes of a T55-L-712F Engine FADEC meeting held at A&AEE Boscombe Down on 25 May 1994.

45 D/DHP/57/4/1, 31 May 1994. Notes of a T55-L-712F Engine FADEC meeting held at A&AEE Boscombe Down on 25 May 1994, paragraph 3.

Finally, MoD seeks to explain why it chose to ignore Boscombe's advice regarding the need for a FADEC software rewrite, saying advice was taken from other sources. The impression given is that this was the sole issue that prevented Boscombe recommending CAR. This is wrong. As explained, Boscombe withheld full recommendation on various other grounds, which can be summarised as immaturity of the development process. In any case, even if advice was sought from others, ultimately Controller Aircraft chose to issue Boscombe's words, not anyone else's.

Conclusions

MoD's letter is misleading, both by omission and commission. Its purpose is (seemingly) to give Legal Services (and families) the impression the regulations were followed to the letter, and the Chinook HC Mk2 was compliant. Boscombe did not expect their INTERIM report to be misrepresented as a CAR, in any form. Thus, MoD's evidence to the Fatal Accident Inquiry was irredeemably tainted.

The letter was signed by Colonel Barry Hodgkiss, AD/HP1, to whom I reported directly from August 1997 (upon the death of my Assistant Director, Kevin Thomas) to March 1999, when he retired. At the time he was new in post and the letter was drafted for him. It would be wise to interview him to establish the facts.

Appendix 8 - Technical Discussion 1 - Trimble TNL8000 Global Positioning System

Executive Summary

In 1993/4 GPS was an immature technology and, as stated in the Release to Service, the US Department of Defense (who operated the system) had not declared Initial Operating Capability. The Chinook HC Mk2 installation differed in an undefined way from the Mk1, the crucial difference being *'meaningless'* GPS failure warnings which constituted a distraction to the aircrew. That no complementary amendment was made to the Chinook HC Mk1 Release to Service constitutes a Human Factors hazard and confirms immaturity of process.

The GPS unit recovered from ZD576 had several faults.

Introduction

It is not clearly explained in the Inquiry papers that this GPS system is a stand-alone unit. GPS is an accurate timing signal. Other systems put its product to various uses. One important function is to provide Time of Day to synchronise clocks in, for example, cryptographic equipment and frequency hopping (HaveQuick) radios. The Air Accidents Investigation Branch report covering GPS, Annex Z to the Board of Inquiry report [B4], notes two faults:

'The HaveQuick output was not functioning. The reason for this fault was not explored. The facility for switching the main DC power supply for the unit by utilising a low current/voltage line from the aircraft to a FET (Field Effect Transistor) within the unit did not function in that it was not possible to switch off the power supply using this facility. Examination of the component showed the FET had been damaged at some time, it was not possible to say when, by having a high voltage applied to it from the main DC power supply input to the unit (from SuperTANS)'.

There were GPS faults reported on ZD576 on 2, 5 and 9 May 1994.

Discussion

It is disconcerting that the HaveQuick output fault was not investigated further. If the Time of Day was not being presented to the HaveQuick radios, or other equipments, then this introduced (at least) an additional workload for the aircrew to synchronise their radios by other means (over the ether). If they expect the synchronisation to be (semi) automatic, via

GPS, then the failure to do so (or subsequent failure) would be a distraction.

It is not known if the crew were using or attempting to use their HaveQuick radio during the final moments - there were no Accident or Cockpit Voice Recorders fitted. However, it was found in TEST mode, and both pilots had selected UHF, indicating a suspected failure.

The following year it emerged that:

'Due to an ambiguity in the wording of the specification for the HaveQuick Time of Day output in ICD-GPS-060-A published by the Joint Program Office, there exists the possibility that some commercially available GPS receivers may not function as required when transferring Time of Day to a HaveQuick radio'.[46]

In technical terms, the problem was Bit Period Error Requirements, meaning cumulative errors built up over time (during a single flight) causing radios to lose synchronisation, compromising the ability to communicate in the 225-400 MHz a.m. band until re-synchronised. An indication of this loss of sync would be lack of replies to transmissions.

Furthermore, in 1996 it was discovered that a typical GPS unit was only specified to provide Time of Day to two loads (e.g. two HQ radios, or a radio and crypto). More than two (and often only two) overloaded the circuitry, causing failure. (Noting the Field Effect Transistor failure). Ironically, it was another aircraft project (Sea King ASaC Mk7), managed within the same MoD(PE) Directorate, that first encountered this problem. MoD will not say what configuration ZD576 was in, but several equipments would require integration with GPS Time of Day.

The above does not provide an explanation for the accident, nor is it intended to. It is intended to further illustrate the immaturity and lack of understanding of some of the systems in the Chinook HC Mk2. The Release to Service, current at time of accident, warned:

'GPS has not yet been declared operational by the US Department of Defense and <u>accuracy is therefore not guaranteed to any level</u>. Even when GPS is declared operational by the US, accuracy of the TNL 8000 SPS GPS could degrade substantially without any indications to the crew. For this reason, Standard Positioning Service GPS should not be used as the sole navigation aid'.[47]

('SPS' - Standard Positioning Service - refers to Coarse Acquisition code,

---

46 Extract from the notification by Magnavox, HQ radio manufacturers, to their engineers, 27 June 1995.
47 Release to Service, Section O, paragraph 2.2.

not the more precise P (Military) code).

Also, the Chinook HC Mk1 Release contained a warning not present in the Mk2 Release:

'The ALERT light on the RNS252 (SuperTANS) is difficult to see because it is very dim. Operators are to conduct regular checks of the navigation status system.'

There is no indication in the Mk2 Release that this problem had been corrected.

Furthermore, the SuperTANS section warned:

'The GPS is highly susceptible to jamming of which the only crew indication is loss of GPS. The "Err" figure displayed, which has conventionally been taken as a measure of GPS performance, is meaningless and so no indication of the accuracy of the GPS is available to the user. The RNS252 suffers from an average two second processing delay on the displayed GPS position. In "Ext" position, Doppler reversion should be selected to minimise navigational errors during GPS outages.'[48]

It is wholly unsatisfactory to just tell aircrew that an 'Error' message is meaningless. It must mean something, even if that is the design is poor (in which case, what remedial action was taken?). What were they trained to do if the 'Error' message appeared? Reboot the SuperTANS? Switch it off (bearing in mind the Air Accidents Investigation Board opined it was switched off at impact, not by impact)? Revert to 'dead reckoning'? This constitutes yet another Human Factors hazard, as the unexplained differences between the same system, in two different aircraft (Mk1 and Mk2), both in service at the same time, would cause an extended 'thinking time'. The Board of Inquiry stated:

'In the circumstances of the aircraft's approach to the Mull of Kintyre, even a small delay in decision making could have had serious consequences, and the Board concluded that human factors could have been a contributory factor in the accident.'[49]

Having stated the message was meaningless, what retrospective action was taken on the Chinook HC Mk1, which carried the same system, but embodied under Service Engineered Modification? Examination of the Mk1 Release to Service shows no such amendment, indicating a lack of co-ordination of configuration control. On 3 March 1999, the Chief of Defence Procurement (CDP) admitted to the Public Accounts Committee (PAC) that Chinook still suffered from poor configuration control. The

48 Release to Service, Section O, paragraph 2.3.
49 Board of Inquiry, Part 2, paragraph 29.

PAC failed to appreciate this rendered the Safety Case/Argument and INTERIM Release to Service even more invalid. And, hence, the case against the pilots even more unsound.

Following publication of the PAC report, a paper was submitted to CDP's deputy, Mr David Gould, on 11 January 2000, explaining what action was necessary.[50] He did not reply. This paper formed the basis of submissions to the Nimrod Review (see Appendix 1). This systemic failing was also noted in the CHART report.

These unexplained errors and failures would have been confusing to aircrew, especially Flight Lieutenants Tapper and Cook, who had flown the Mk1 exclusively in the three months since their 'Differences' course, which passed as a conversion course. In fact, Tapper was on record as wholly distrusting the SuperTANS/GPS system, even taking the extraordinary step (for aircrew) of visiting Racal to attempt to fill the gaps in the information available to him in official documentation. Regulations require such visits/meetings to be recorded, and proposed actions notified to the Technical Agency; who in turn is required to record his decisions. As is the Design Authority's Post Design Services Officer, an MoD-approved appointment. The purpose and outcome of these visits should be established.

Quite apart from 'not to be relied upon', the general status of the few navigation equipments listed in the Release to Service was *'no guarantee of equipment performance can be given'*. None had the requisite statement of clearance for use. The trials process, intended to establish and advise aircrew of the installed performance, and give warnings of Limitations, had barely started at the time of the accident. Boscombe would regard these as an unresolved conflicts, to be investigated, understood and, if necessary, corrected (through modification action or more precise advice in the Flight Reference Cards, Aircrew Manual and training documentation) before recommending Controller Aircraft Release.

What engineering investigation(s) took place to ascertain the underlying cause of the faults reported by the Air Accidents Investigation Branch (AAIB)? Were Trimble so tasked? The CHART report of August 1992 confirms requests for Fault Investigations were routinely delayed, often for years; and a directive had been issued by AMSO in January 1993 that

50 Submission D/DHP/SK12apf, and Annex 'Modifying Defence Equipment', 11 January 2000 to Mr David Gould, Deputy Chief Executive, Defence Procurement Agency.

they were to cease altogether. It is notable that Racal were tasked to compile and issue the report on their SuperTANS, but it was the AAIB who issued the GPS report. Was the latter underwritten by the Navigation System Co-ordinating Design Authority (if one even existed; and if not, why not)? If not, the GPS report has no place in the Board of Inquiry report (and nor does the Racal report, as it was not independently verified).

When asked on 17 September 2005 by Steve Webb MP about such fault investigations, on 17 May 2007 Minister for the Armed Forces Adam Ingram MP, replied that a decision to cut funding at Design Authorities was irrelevant, as the Maintenance Analysis and Computing Division (MACD) at RAF Swanton Morley would do the work.[51] [B17] He rejected the author's statement that the airworthiness regulations are not implemented properly - a fact later reaffirmed by Mr Haddon-Cave QC.

Both were blatant lies. MACD's job was to analyse maintenance data, not conduct technical investigations. That requires access to Sample/Reference Rigs and design information, held by Design Authorities/Custodians. From 1991-on these rigs were systematically dismantled, compromising *the* basic component of airworthiness, maintaining the build standard. By 1994 it would be unusual for them to exist. If they did, they would likely be unserviceable and unmaintained; and the necessary contracts would not be in place. Not least because the MoD Department responsible for controlling these build standards, ALS/PD, had been disbanded in April 1992; and the overarching HQ Radio Modifications Committee in June 1991.

Note: The dismantling of PDS Rigs came to a head (as far as Director Helicopter Projects was concerned) in 1996, when the RAF's actions compromised several programmes. An example of the debate is recorded in the minutes of a meeting dated 30 May 1996, which state:

'GEC have never had AD3400 or AD3500 (V/UHF Radios, the latter HaveQuick II capable) PDS Sample or Reference equipment or Rigs, and the SK6 and Lx2/3 WBSS (Secure Intercom) Rigs have always been incomplete and consist of B Models, with the exception of the UA6095/1Fs (Secure Intercom Station Boxes) which were provided through MoD(PE) ARad12 for a separate reason. Therefore, they have no complete Rigs to maintain, calibrate, or use for the primary PDS function of maintaining the build standard, have no knowledge of the build standard fitted to Sea King HAS Mk6 or Lynx HAS Mk8, and no means of maintaining configuration control. Hence the subject Airborne Radio Installations are on

---

51 Letter D/Min(AF)/AI MC06559/2006, 17 May 2007.

"limited" PDS.[52]

Summary

Given this information, much of it unavailable at the time, the Racal (SuperTANS) and Air Accidents Investigation Branch (GPS) reports should be validated and independently verified. However, in the context of a *beyond any doubt whatsoever* legal test, the immaturity issue alone introduces a significant degree of doubt. It constitutes clear evidence that MoD knowingly exposed unwitting aircrew to flight safety critical hazards.

Furthermore, the ability to investigate and resolve these problems was compromised by the decision to reduce the necessary funding in the previous three financial years (see Appendix 4 and CHART). While this Submission asks if engineering investigations were carried out, I have explained that instructions were issued in 1992 that investigations were to be curtailed, and in 1993 that they were to cease, as a savings measure to compensate for the waste incurred under the AP830 DM87 policy.

Despite numerous official warnings about GPS (and SuperTANS) immaturity, unreliability, lack of Initial Operational Clearance, erroneous status warnings and, crucially, a directive not to place any reliance on the system in-flight, MoD's entire case is built on the supposed infallibility of this system. Despite warnings that it was <u>not</u> to be used as the sole navigation aid, in fact not to be relied upon in any way whatsoever, MoD used it to justify its findings against the pilots.

In conclusion, the RAF was itself negligent:

1. It authorise Service regulated flying before an acceptable installed performance of these systems could be established.
2. It failed to advise and suitably train the aircrew as to how to manage this immaturity.
3. It failed to maintain the build standard of these, and other, equipments; in turn compromising the Safety Cases.

---

52 D/DHP/24/4/93/25. Notes of a meeting held in Room 313 St Giles Court, London on 30 May 1996. (GFE surpluses).

Appendix 9 - Technical Discussion 2 - RNS252 SuperTANS

Executive Summary

SuperTANS had been installed in the Chinook HC Mkl under Special Trials Fit/Chinook/124 on 1 November 1990. However, the conversion to Mk2 changed the installed performance of the system, as warnings and Limitations were introduced that were not retrospectively applied to Mkl. This constitutes a Human Factors Hazard, especially as the crew of ZD576 had been flying the Mkl exclusively since their conversion course to the Mk2, some months earlier.

Introduction

As outlined in Appendix 8, the Release to Service warned aircrew of the gross immaturity of the Navigation System. MoD asserted the aircraft was serviceable. How did it know, and how were the pilots to know? How was it demonstrated? It didn't, and it wasn't.

It matters not that with hindsight the 'system' in ZD576 turned out to be reasonably accurate - evidence shows that this was something of a hit and miss affair, with other aircraft experiencing errors of up to 2nm over a similar route. What is vitally important here is the lack of confidence the crew had in the system - the human factors component of airworthiness.

Racal, the SuperTANS Design Authority, were tasked to prepare a report on the unit recovered from ZD576. The Board of Inquiry withheld most of the report, only publishing the first six pages.[53] [B4] However, a more complete version has since emerged. [B39] It is a feature of MoD's position that it claims the report is evidence the _entire_ Navigation System was both accurate and serviceable. This is palpable nonsense. SuperTANS is a very simple computer. Racal only claimed the device (not the system) was carrying out calculations accurately - even then caveating their conclusions. They did not comment at all on the Air Accidents Investigation Branch finding that the device was switched off before impact. Notably, cycling SuperTANS on/off was an accepted way of managing Electro-Magnetic Interference - akin to re-booting a personal computer. The Release to Service notes many examples. In particular, interference when using VHF Air Traffic Control frequencies. This aspect remains to be investigated.

There is no evidence whatsoever that SuperTANS was providing accurate

---

53 Annex Y to Board of Inquiry report.

indications to the crew. It is a common feature of the ZD576 investigations that MoD ignores one simple concept - a sensor might be working correctly, but the associated indicator may not be. Throughout, MoD has implied, and even claimed, that if the former works so does the latter. One analogy is again that of a PC. The processor, memory, hard drive, motherboard and power supply may be working perfectly, but if the display is broken, too dim or even disconnected, the system is useless. In the case of SuperTANS, there is no evidence the unit was indicating properly after Waypoint A acceptance; only a suggestion the internal electronics were processing (but not recording) instantaneous input data, which was discarded and updated every second.

At no time was any attempt made to simulate or reconstruct the environmental conditions in the aircraft, especially in Electro-Magnetic Compatibility terms. Racal's testing was conducted in a benign environment, whereas the system operated in a confused and complicated environment of multiple electronic emissions that exists in the aircraft during actual use - known as 'RF Soup'. The Racal report is but one small piece in the jigsaw puzzle that is the Navigation System. MoD has invented or imagined the remaining pieces.

Lack of confidence in SuperTANS/GPS contributed to the pilots asking for a Chinook HC Mk1. This line of investigation was not pursued.

The evidence of Witness 20 to the Board of Inquiry

The witness stated crews could be *'complacent'* about, and *'over reliant'* on, SuperTANS/GPS. Yet elsewhere the Board of Inquiry heard that Flight Lieutenant Tapper did not trust the system. Perhaps this is an indication of Tapper's experience, dedication and attention to detail - that he suspected problems and, lacking official information or explanation, sought to find the answers himself by visiting Racal the previous month. The Board did not pursue this contradiction. If they had, the failure to implement the airworthiness regulations, by not mitigating a series of flight safety critical hazards, would have been exposed. This should not be construed as criticism of the aircrew. Rather, it highlights the maladministration which led to an immature aircraft being misrepresented as a mature one.

This is not trivia. MoD's case is built on the claim that negligence took place before Waypoint A. Its 'proof' is largely based on the assumption that, because the Navigation inputs to SuperTANS were present, they were accurate, uncorrupted, properly displayed and intelligible for the entire flight.

Finally, a brief mention of the unanswered Air Traffic Control radio call. The crew would only know it got through upon acknowledgement, which wasn't forthcoming. Why was there no follow-up call? Normally three attempts would be made. There are many such indications of avionics problems and <u>distractions</u> occurring in ZD576. Perhaps the biggest was caused by the SuperTANS/GPS, a system described by the Release to Service as *'not yet declared operational'*, *'accuracy not guaranteed'* and *'meaningless'*.

Appendix 10 - Technical Discussion 3 - FADEC/DECU connector issues

Executive Summary

This section concentrates on an issue which further illustrates how immature the design was. The Digital Electronic Control Unit (DECU, part of FADEC) electrical connector installation design was so poor that aircrew had to check its security, every 15 minutes, in-flight.

The systemic failures reflect precisely those noted in the CHART report of 1992, demonstrating they had not been corrected.

Introduction and Background

The following is from House of Lords Select Committee:

'Evidence of Squadron Leader Robert Burke

Squadron Leader Burke had extensive experience in flying helicopters including Chinooks Mks 1 and 2 and was described by his unit commander in April 1993 as having air-testing skills on the Puma and Chinook which were unique. He was able to provide us with useful information about the problems which he had experienced when testing Chinooks. At the outset of the investigation in to the accident he was contacted by Mr Cable and had two or three telephone discussions with him in relation to control positions. Thereafter he had nothing further to do with the Board of Inquiry.

After Squadron Leader Burke gave evidence, Group Captain Pulford submitted a statement to us (p 68 of HL Paper 25(ii)) in which he sought to explain why Squadron Leader Burke had not been asked to give evidence to the investigating board. He stated that as the Chinook maintenance test pilot his 'flying was conducted in accordance with limited and pre-determined flight test schedules and he therefore lacked the operational currency to provide relevant evidence to the Inquiry'. This reasoning seems to assume that problems which Squadron Leader Burke might have encountered on test would not or could not occur in operational flying - an assumption whose justification we feel to be in doubt.

Squadron Leader Burke spoke to having experienced two engine run ups on the ground at the Boeing factory in Philadelphia while flying with an American Army test pilot and similar run ups when testing the overspeed limiter on the ground at Odiham. He also spoke to problems with the multi-point connectors which went from the engines in to the DECU. These were of bad design and liable to be displaced by vibration which then produced a power interruption. Although there was a back-up system this did not always work and on two or three occasions pilots had lost control of the engine condition lever. As a result squadrons introduced a procedure whereby crewmen every quarter of an hour checked that the connections had not been displaced in flight. At the time of the accident DECUs still presented recurring problems. They were removed from the aircraft when something had gone wrong and returned to the makers who on many occasions could find no fault'.

Assessment of Servicing Instruction SI/Chinook/57 (based on Squadron Leader Burke's evidence)

A Servicing Instruction (SI):

'Details repetitive work to be carried out within a specified time or other limit, to seek to repair, or prevent, a potential fault'.[54]

That is, it is recurring, while a Special Technical Instruction (STI) is non-recurring. Also, an SI:

'Acts as a temporary alteration to existing servicing methods, and is not used if the appropriate servicing schedules can be amended in an acceptable time'.[55]

STI/Chinook/57 begins:

'A case has occurred where a DECU connector worked loose in-flight. The connector loosened sufficiently to affect the functioning of the FADEC system. This Instruction details the application of a witness mark, and specifies a routine inspection to determine if this is an isolated fault, or a fleet wide problem'.

It is to be applied at Turn Round Servicing and Before Flight Servicing.

Unlike most other such Special Instructions (Technical), SIs are issued by MoD(PE), not the Service Engineering Authorities or Units.[56] However, the RAF Engineering Authority, SM(Hels)29(RAF) at RAF Harrogate, issued this SI on 19 November 1993. That is, it had no official status.

This date is significant, as it is three days <u>before</u> Service regulated flying was authorised by the Assistant Chief of the Air Staff in his (illegal) Release to Service.

The Engineering Authority's role is to assess the SI for *'effect on Operation and/or Handling'.* If an effect is likely to be of concern to aircrew, they are to refer the draft instruction to RAF Handling Squadron at Boscombe Down.[57] This makes the delineation clear - aircrew do not apply SIs. The

---

54 Defence Standard 05-123, chapter 406, 2.2.1.
55 Defence Standard 05-125/2, chapter 7.13.3.
56 Defence Standard 05/125/2, chapter 7.13.3.
57 Defence Standard 05-123, chapter 406, Appendix 3, Annex A, 9a.

SI relates to pre/post-flight ground checks of the suspect connectors. It should tell the maintainer what to do if it is found to be loose/damaged, etc. The maintainer, not aircrew.

The Design Authority may be asked to draft SIs and approve their content, as it is generally tasked with maintaining the Safety Case, which must be revalidated against the proposed SI. The entire process is managed by the Post Design Services Authority (PDSA) in MoD(PE) - in practice the Technical Agency, the named MoD civilian engineer responsible for maintaining the build standard. This was the Directorate of Helicopter Project's role.

Here, the issue is slightly clouded as it is unclear if the Chinook HC Mk2 design was Under Ministry Control (or 'Formal Control') or Under Contractor Control at the time of issue. If the latter, one would substitute Boeing Helicopters for PDSA and Technical Agency. Regardless, the MoD Project Manager is required to consider the possible effect on the Controller Aircraft Release.[58] The crucial issues here are:

- The root problem is one of design quality. It is a defect, not a fault.

- The wrong part of MoD issued the SI.

Having identified the cause and effect (poor installation design, leading to loss of FADEC control), the regulations require this to be notified through the appropriate channels via the Fault Reporting process. In this case, a Serious Fault Signal would be expected. As it relates to a Safety Critical system, it is reasonable to expect an immediate decision would be required on grounding. Given the known history (the associated software implementation was *positively dangerous*, and there being no Controller Aircraft Release), it is highly unlikely the RAF Handling Squadron would agree to this proposed SI without referring to safety criticality. Modification action was required, yet the regulations state:

'SIs are not to be used to circumvent modification procedures.'[59]

This is further evidence of the cavalier attitude within the RAF, and its general dismissal of mandated regulations, that permeate this case.

Turning to the application of SI/CHK/57, nowhere do the regulations or procedures address the concept of *in-flight* SIs. A MF731 Equipment Label must be attached to a rejected item.[60] This is not an action one takes in-

---

58 Defence Standard 05-123, chapter 406, 5.2.2.
59 Defence Standard 05-123, chapter 406, 7.4.
60 Defence Standard 05-123, chapter 406, Appendix 3, Annex A, 7a.

flight. The SI required pre- and post-flight checks but, according to Squadron Leader Burke's evidence, the applicability was 'extended' by Odiham to have a more periodic check in-flight (every 15 minutes). The implication is that Odiham were not convinced the SI addressed the scale or scope of the problem, or that the necessary follow-up action (Fault Investigation) was proceeding in a timely manner. OC Engineering at RAF Odiham, at the time, should be interviewed. (In fact, he was a witness to the Board of Inquiry). Obvious questions include:

1. Did a suitable contract exist to investigate the problem?
2. Who (illegally) approved Odiham issuing/amending an SI, and where is the reasoning recorded?
3. Was the test visual or physical, and was training was provided?
4. What recording action took place?
5. What was the impact of the FADEC malfunction?
6. The Safety Case must reflect the current In-Use build standard. Therefore, what safety and risk related documentation exists to support the SI, and was there an impact or risk assessment?
7. By definition, the SI accepts the connectors can become detached or loose. Is the system design (not just the male and female connectors, but FADEC/DECU/Engines) able to cope with 'hot-swapping'? That is, does it facilitate safe removal/insertion when powered up, by means of, for example, offset contacts which ensure certain pins mate before others? Getting this wrong tends to trip circuit breakers, interrupt power and force system resets. These constitute Human Factors, Engineering, Handling and, hence, Flight Safety hazards.

Someone at Odiham, perhaps recognising many of the above issues, apparently disagreed with the probability of occurrence and, doubtless, impact. Hence, the extension to *in-flight* servicing and increased periodicity. Did Odiham notify this concern to the Issuing Authority? A pre-flight check may be temporary risk mitigation in exceptional operational circumstances, but it is not the engineering solution.

In this case, the impact and probability of occurrence combine to create a Class A risk - in other words, unacceptable and to be tolerated only under exceptional circumstances. A transit flight to Fort George is not exceptional circumstances. Even viewed in isolation, the very existence of this SI should have been sufficient to preclude any flight.

A crucial conflict

The Release to Service requires that the Transmission Debris Screens be checked *'at least'* every five minutes. Which check was conducted first when this coincided, every 15 minutes, with the connector check? (Noting the first clash would occur as they approached the Mull). One assumes the periodicity of the Transmission Debris check indicates it was more important, but would the aircrew think otherwise, as the DECU is Safety Critical? This indicates the SI was not assessed against the Release to Service.

Modification action

What modification, if any, superseded the SI to replace/improve the design? What do Fields 6 and 7 of the MF714 modification proposal say? ('Title and Description' and 'Origin' respectively). This is a key question, because the regulations demand a multitude of answers before approval can be granted, including in Field 7 two definitive statements selected from mandated lists. [61] This would reveal prior knowledge and understanding (or otherwise) of the problems.

The SI was only later issued correctly, by MoD(PE), on 2 August 1994. On 20 October 1994, the Defence Helicopter Support Authority issued an amendment, adding technical ground staff who were authorised to conduct the check. A year had passed - more than sufficient to develop and issue a proper engineering solution.

Comments, in the author's capacity as Deputy Chair of the Radio Modifications Committee (RMC) - (post disbanded in June 1991)

The HQ committee that decided the classification of engine modifications would have been the Engines, Propellers and Accessories (EPA) Modification Committee, operating in accordance with AvP115. I always found it strange that an electronic 'accessory' like FADEC's DECU was overseen by EPA, as it increased the likelihood of error through not understanding failure modes and effects. It should have been under the Radio Modifications Committee (RMC, overseeing all Electronics) or, at least, the RMC Chairman should have been consulted. I know he was not, because I was his Deputy.

A Deputy Chair was required because the Chair was a Technical Agency in his own right, so not allowed to approve his own submissions. This independent scrutiny was abandoned (but the mandated policy requiring

---

61 Defence Standard 05-125/2, chapter 8, Page 59, paragraph 7, Columns 1 and 2.

it remains extant) when the HQ Modification Committees were disbanded in June 1991, and all decisions delegated to the Engineering Authorities (who, hitherto, had merely sponsored the modifications). The predicted outcome, which immediately came to pass, was they would rush through their own 'nice to have' ideas, without careful and independent thought given to other 'minor' things, like system integration, interoperability, functional safety, affordability, and so on. Put another way, they incorrectly used the modification process to enhance the build standard, when it is for maintaining it.

This single issue (DECU) could form the basis of an entire submission, as it explains the otherwise throwaway 'systemic failings' line (by MoD staff throughout the 1990s, and more recently Mr Haddon-Cave), exposing the true scale of the problems.

Such a defect should not have been managed by a Servicing Instruction. There are some parts of an aircraft design you just don't mess with, and fuel computers are one. For example, you can accept an Electro-Magnetic Compatibility problem almost anywhere, but if the fuel system is affected, the aircraft doesn't fly. Users and maintainers tend not to see such problems in-service - precisely because they MUST be designed out. Even the basic information screams Class A modification *('essential for safety, to be embodied irrespective of delay, scrap or downtime involved')*. A Class A does not necessarily mean grounding, but in this case it required serious consideration, especially given Boscombe's concern with the associated software. Moreover, if the problem was known about before CA Release was granted, a Class AA modification should have been issued, meaning:

'Essential for initial approval, for Service Use or a new type of equipment. To be embodied prior to delivery, irrespective of cost, scrap or delay involved.'[62]

---

[62] Defence Standard 05-125/2, chapter 7.4.

Appendix 11 - Technical Discussion 4 - The possibility of Undemanded Flight Control Movements (UFCM)

Executive Summary

The RAF's most senior Chinook Test Pilot of the day has consistently stated that the most likely cause of the accident was an Undemanded Flight Control Movement (UFCM). This section presents evidence of UFCMs prior to the accident, withheld from previous Inquiries; concluding that an UFCM cannot be positively discounted and casting further doubt on MoD's claim that the aircraft was under full control between acceptance of Waypoint A and impact.

UFCMs are an unexplained change of aircraft in-flight attitude without a legitimate flying control input, or any movement of flying control input controls when there should be none, or any movement of flying control surfaces or systems without a corresponding legitimate input.

Evidence of Squadron Leader Robert Burke, RAF Test Pilot

Squadron Leader Burke, in a written statement of 14 September 2002:

'UFCMs were relatively common at the time of the accident and were occurring for years afterwards, and if caused by the Automatic Flight Control System leave no trace and are completely random in nature. From the first, a UFCM has been a primary possible cause of this accident, and if it occurred in roll or yaw could well explain some of the still unexplained aspects of the crash. (It) would leave no clues in the wreckage'.

And in a 13 October 2002 critique of the second Boeing simulation:

'It has been a bedrock of the MoD position that the Chinook was under full control of the pilots before the crash. Boeing were not asked to look at the effects of control malfunctions in the second simulation. However, in a remarkably frank and detailed paragraph (E4, P13, 3.3 last paragraph) Boeing admit concern that the bank angle they postulate for the last instant of flight is not consistent with the evidence from the wreckage. Boeing are not able to explain a slight turn to the right, and draw attention to the highly unusual position of the left rudder pedal. To me, as a helicopter test pilot with probably as much experience as anyone of control malfunctions in helicopters, this paragraph shouts out "possible control malfunction". The first Boeing simulation mentions nothing like this'.

Special Flying Instruction (RAF)/Chinook/12

On 28 February 1994, three months before the accident, the RAF issued

Special Flying Instruction - SFI (RAF)/Chinook/12. This warned:

'SFI(RAF)/Chinook/12, Issue 1 (Restrictive) - Chinook HC Mk2. Undemanded Flight Control Movement.

There have been a number of incidents of yaw kicks on Chinook HC Mk2 ZA718 during recent flight trials at Boscombe Down. The characteristic is manifested by very sharp uncommanded inputs to the yaw axis which result in a <u>rapid 3-4 degree change in aircraft heading</u>, in both the hover and when in forward flight when the aircraft is subject to high levels of vibration.

Any aircraft exhibiting these characteristics is to be treated as having an Undemanded Flight Control Movement (UFCM). The heading hold is to be disengaged and the aircraft is to be landed as soon as practicable.

Engineering modification action is in hand to cure the cause of the problem and this SFI will be cancelled once the modifications have been carried out'.

The Boeing report dated 18 June 2002, by Mr J. Mitchell, stated:

'It was also right of its original course from the Air Traffic Control fix to Waypoint A. The bearing from Waypoint Change to Last Steering Command is 22.22 degrees True, which indicates that the route of the aircraft is <u>~3 degrees right of the initial route</u>'.

Discussion

These statements raise several issues and questions:

- There have been a <u>number</u> of incidents.

- ZA718 was the trials aircraft allotted to Boscombe Down. Any assumption that only this aircraft suffered from UFCMs would be wrong. It is Boscombe's job to report such events on their PE Fleet aircraft, or any aircraft allotted them. It is the RAF's to advise Boscombe of events in the operational fleet.

- The sharp movement of 3-4 degrees aligns closely with the Boeing conclusion of a slight right turn shortly before impact. It is unclear if Boeing were advised of the Instruction, but it is not mentioned in their reports. It also describes <u>exactly</u> what Squadron Leader Robert Burke stated in his evidence had happened to him, at the end of a straight run (such as the approach to the Mull).

- The instruction to land as soon as practicable is a slightly less urgent than 'as soon as possible'; but an event such as an UFCM, and the necessity to determine alternate landing sites, would be a distraction at a critical time, when the aircraft might not be under control.

- The need to disengage Heading Hold would be a distraction.

- The statement that engineering *modifications* (plural) are in hand indicates the problem has been investigated and an engineering solution agreed. However, there is no record of any such modifications in the subsequent amendment to the Release to Service, dated March 1994; or indeed up to Amendment 6 (10 January 1996). The precise history of these modifications, from initial discovery, through reporting, tasking, development, testing, trialling and production, should be ascertained.

- The fact there have been multiple occurrences, an investigation (apparently) conducted, and modification action proposed, indicates this Instruction is not the initial reaction to the first, or a single, event. Therefore, what previous notification was given, between issuing the Release to Service on 22 November 1993 and this Instruction of 28 February 1994? Were changes made to the training regime for Mk2? Were these events, and how to deal with them, included in the Mk2 'Differences' course attended by the ZD576 pilots?

When this Instruction came to light in 2010, Squadron Leader Burke was asked if he knew of it at the time of issue, or at all. He replied:

'No. I did not know of this SFI. I suspect that very few people did, either aircrew or groundcrew, as when another pilot (by coincidence Witness A to the House of Lords) had this problem quite severely in Northern Ireland, and I was called over there to fly the aircraft sometime <u>after</u> the Mull accident, we were not aware that this was a known problem. Often, SFIs took a long time to reach the actual front line operators, getting bogged down in the various layers of admin and command. However, the following points may be of interest:

1. The AFCS (Automatic Flight Control System) section of the control closet (broom cupboard) of the Mk2 Chinook was completely different to that of the Mk1. I stress that this was a complete redesign which hardly even resembled that of the Mk1 physically, let alone in its internal workings.

2. The ability of the simulator to reproduce a number of the AFCS faults that I had experienced in those early Mk2 days was very limited; not only due to the limited abilities of the equipment, but also to the inexperience of the operators, who, just like the aircrew, were new to the Mk2. The aircrew, as well as the groundcrew and the simulator instructors, were in no way helped in those early days by the appalling lack of proper, up-to-date, paperwork. For the pilots this was made even worse by the flying restrictions placed on the circumstances in which they could practice AFCS failures in the air. Basically these were that the AFCS could only be taken out in Visual Meteorological

Conditions with the aircraft straight and level. When one got a real AFCS malfunction, of which I suffered a fairly large number, they invariably showed themselves during manoeuvre. These could be quite random and of dramatically different intensities.

3. *The continued refusal of MoD to consider the likelihood of an AFCS malfunction causing, or largely contributing, to this accident is either puzzling or tellingly significant; perhaps because it completely destroys the repeated assertions of the MoD Establishment that the pilots were in full control of the aircraft as it flew in to high ground. This assertion is fundamental to their case that the pilots were grossly negligent.* [63]

Conclusion

Taking an aircraft to extremes, or dealing with it at extremes, is a skill that only comes with direct experience. Despite the acknowledged experience and skill of the deceased pilots on Mk1, it is fair to ask if this was adequate on Mk2. ZD576 was the first Mk2 in Northern Ireland and, in the months since their conversion, the pilots had flown exclusively the Mk1. They had not been afforded the opportunity to train and gain experience of the Limitations and, especially, these alarming UFCMs. Squadron Leader Burke was only able to work out the problem and recover his aircraft each time due to his experience and because he had sufficient time and height. This may have been denied the ZD576 pilots. The Mk2 Limitations, and perhaps more importantly the almost complete lack of equipment clearances, meant they were not permitted to be at the altitudes that enabled Squadron Leader Burke to recover.

Dr Lewis Moonie (now Lord Moonie), when Minister for the Armed Forces and in reply to a Parliamentary Question by Mr Martin Bell MP on 27 June 2000, stated that a UFCM *'could easily have been dealt with'.* While recognising Dr Moonie's vast experience, the Review may prefer the evidence of a Chinook pilot. And reflect on the crassness of such a statement given, for example, the seven deaths in February 1987 due to such a UFCM in a Mk1. Squadron Leader Burke's evidence reveals that instances of UFCM increased rapidly with the introduction of the Mk2. The limited data released by MoD suggests this was due to the new design features of the Mk2.

---

63 E-mail to author, 13 September 2010, 15:10.

Appendix 12 - Air Accidents Investigation Branch (AAIB) recommendations

Executive Summary

The AAIB report made nine recommendations. [64] All relate to airworthiness/safety and repeat long-known failings; some systemic, others specific to Chinook. That no action had been taken over a period of some years is an organisational failure.

Discussion of recommendations

1. *Fit a Cockpit Voice Recorder.*

2. *Fit an Accident Data Recorder.*

Previous Boards of Inquiry had made the same recommendations (e.g. following Chinook HC Mk1 ZA721 on 27 February 1987, seven killed). It is reported both recorders were in the original Chinook HC Mk2 requirement specification, but cancelled. It should be established why, and whether this falls into the 'savings at the expense of safety' confirmed by Mr Haddon-Cave. Failure to fit them prevents one learning lessons, a fundamental requirement of any Safety Management System.

3. *Measures to reliably verify the attachment integrity of the flight control pallet inserts used to mount flight control components (such as bell-cranks).*

The poor design of these inserts was well known. It involved bonding peg type inserts into blind drilled holes. Unfortunately, the honeycomb structure of the pallet was not structurally robust enough to retain them with any strength. The only bond that was possible was between the peg and the extremely thin metal skin of the pallet itself. The AAIB stated:

'As an insert could apparently pull out of the pallet without appreciable distress to the components necessarily resulting, the possibility that insert(s) had detached prior to the accident could not be dismissed. Little evidence was available to eliminate the possibility of pre-impact detachment of any of the pallet components'.[65]

Mr Cable (AAIB) reiterated this to the House of Lords in 2002.

Upon ZD576's arrival at RAF Aldergrove it was discovered the pallet

---

64 AAIB report EW/D94/6/1, 5 January 1995.
65 AAIB report, paragraphs 7.4.2 and 7.4.9.

had detached, with squadron staff were invited to view it. It was raised a good 1.5 inches from the floor at the rear. The delaminated pallet was re-fixed that day. There is no indication in any subsequent Inquiry that the bonding material used to effect the repair was of the correct type and fit for purpose. Nor has it been established if the curing time and environmental conditions (temperature, humidity) were correct in the hangar overnight. And how was the repair verified? A ground run with control inputs being made, or an air test? In short, ZD576 was far from serviceable when it arrived at Aldergrove, and it was still not serviceable for the final flight.

4. *Measures to monitor flight control system control actuator wear and hydraulic system debris.*

The 1987 ZA721 Board of Inquiry also commented on this, recommending an urgent and comprehensive hazard analysis be produced with special emphasis on quality control at Boeing and hydraulic return line blockages.[66] It noted that costs were being sought by MoD(PE) for the analysis, and MoD(PE) would make appropriate financial provision in LTC89. This apparently positive statement hides a multitude of sins and systemic failings, not least that MoD(PE) did not make financial provision - that was a Service HQ job.

Most importantly, any Safety Management System requires continuous assessment of hazards - which should be contracted as a through-life task under Post Design Services (PDS). It is clear there was inadequate PDS tasking. If such a breakdown occurs, then one cannot validate the Safety Case, and hence the Release to Service. One must ask serious questions of, particularly, the RAF's resident staff at Boeing, whose job it was to manage this aspect.

5. *Differential Air Speed Hold actuators to be tested under load during acceptance testing.*

6. *Longitudinal Cyclic Trim Actuators (LCTA) to be tested under load during acceptance testing.*

Again, it is considered these two recommendations stem from the above ZA721 crash, when the same investigator (Mr Cable) reported:

'The aft LCTA was incapable of extending against a load of approximately 900lb or more, due to clutch slippage'.[67]

In fact, almost the entire ZA721 AAIB report concentrates on critical

---

66 Chinook HC Mk1 ZA721 Board of Inquiry report, Annex A, paragraph 1.
67 Chinook HC Mk1 ZA721 AAIB report, paragraph 3.5.

and systemic failures of the aircraft flight control system and Quality Control during manufacture/repair. The report ends by stating:

'Little in-depth knowledge of the actuators was apparent in the responsible Design Groups of Boeing-Vertol.'[68]

This last is an indictment of the way the design was controlled, and aligns closely with the CHART criticism five years later, in which the RAF Director of Flight Safety voiced concern over the difficulties caused by Boeing having never been an MoD-appointed Design Authority. That is, the procedures for selecting and appointing Design Authorities had broken down. (In simple terms, if a proposed Design Authority is deemed unsuitable, one appoints a Design Custodian; as required by Defence Standard 05-125/2).

7. *Frequent downloading and logging of the conditioning monitoring and fault information from the DECU non-volatile memories.*

This is a serious programmatic failing. If one specifies a safety-critical device must hold such maintenance and analysis data in memory, it follows that it should be put to use. This would have been a conscious decision not to use the data, rather than an omission.

8. *Measures to confirm wide pulse output from the radar altimeter transmitter/receiver above 800 feet during bay testing.*

9. *Measures to confirm correct adjustment of the sensitivity range control potentiometer of the radar altimeter transmitter/receiver.*

These were long-known and well understood problems; reported by the author in 1983 when employed as a supervisor responsible for training technical staff. Contemporaneous notes indicate that a meeting had been convened at Smiths Industries on 22 February 1985 to discuss the issues.

MoD Third Line workshops were expected to carry out Depth C repairs using the same Second Line / Depth B Test Sets. That is, even if one knew the parameters to be set, there was inadequate test equipment and information to verify repairs. Correct setting at Third Line was entirely dependent on using locally determined values. A typical example was the critical setting for retaining track and indicating correct range in maximum attenuation conditions (i.e. poor quality signal returns). The setting of 52dB was based on the say so of a (very good) diagnostician from RNARW Copenacre. Ensuring such a device can regain track after loss is fundamental to the safe operation of the

---

68 Chinook HC Mk1 ZA721 AAIB report, paragraph 3.12.

aircraft, yet the setting up procedure amounted to a few personal notes in a jotter, which were not traceable to formal design documentation. This situation is indicative of a complete breakdown of the MF765 (Unsatisfactory Feature Report) reporting and feedback loop.

While the Transmitter/Receiver could 'pass' the Standard Serviceability Test (SST), it was in fact unserviceable and unfit for purpose, and carried design defects. Therefore, the SST was not fit for purpose.

Summary

It is startling how closely aligned these recommendations are with the ZA721 crash of 1987, the recommendations of the CHART report of 1992, and various internal MoD reports and audits from 1988-2003. It should be ascertained why the recommendations in these reports were not implemented.

In general terms, the process whereby recommendations are 'pulled through', and implementation managed, should be formalised. Many of the points made in these reports concerning build standards, Safety Cases and, hence, airworthiness, were formally notified to the Defence Procurement Agency's Deputy Chief Executive in January 2000.[69] He did not reply, and none of the recommendations were implemented. While perhaps not within the remit of the Review, it is clear this was a significant and gross negligence, resulting in many deaths.

---

69 Report D/DHP/SK12apf, 11 January 2000 'Modifying Defence Equipment'.

ADDENDA

Addendum A - Comparison of the Chinook HC Mk1 and Mk2 Releases to Service, and further evidence as to the immaturity of the Mk2

Executive Summary

It is only by comparing the Mk1 and Mk2 Releases that the true scale of the Mk2 immaturity can be appreciated. This Addendum details the major differences and omissions, concluding that the failure to reconcile and align the two Aircraft Document Sets resulted in a series of Human Factors hazards or risks.

It also expands upon Appendix 2, providing an example of Technical Immaturity with respect to FADEC and its safety critical software.

Two Annexes to the Addendum are presented, discussing Parts 1 and 2 of the Release to Service.

Training - The Chinook HC Mk1 >> Mk2 'Differences Course'

The introduction of the Mk2, and the time taken to convert the Mk1 fleet, created a period during which operation of a mixed fleet was necessary. This was unavoidable, so the task required careful planning, management and implementation. (The planning of such programmes is well understood in MoD, but the practical problem is that responsibility rests with the wrong people. At the time, policy was that this was the responsibility of Service HQ Modifications Sections, but they had been disbanded with no compensatory provision. It fell to whoever had the knowledge, experience and capacity - a poor starting point).

Unexplained differences, especially additional or new Limitations and restrictions, constitute Human Factors hazards and risks, as the 'thinking time' necessary to mentally switch between aircraft can be considerable; noting the primary reference during flight, the Flight Reference Cards were, according to MoD witnesses, unfit for purpose.

The pilots of ZD576 attended their Differences Courses in February 1994 (Tapper) and March 1994 (Cook), and immediately returned to flying the Mk1. They only encountered the Mk2 again the day before the accident. The inherent risks are obvious, and there are certain basic principles to be observed, including:

- The content of conversion (or Differences) courses for multi-Mark operations of the same basic aircraft type depend on the complexity of the aircraft, number of differences, and any new equipment introduced; all of which must be fully explored and explained.

- The Instructors should be fully conversant with the subject being taught; in turn requiring a maturity of Testing and Trials process.
- The Aircraft Document Set needs to be carefully prepared, without blank pages or 'To be Issued/Advised' annotations. While minor compromises may be necessary to commence initial Training and Familiarisation, it is not acceptable to omit vital detail on an entirely new concept (e.g. FADEC, containing safety critical software).
- It is advisable that the Release to Service presents Limitations, restrictions, warnings, etc. in adjacent columns, system by system, with limits (e.g. temperature, icing, etc.) that differ between aircraft shown in a different colour, for contrast (immediate attention getter).
- Similarly, the Flight Reference Cards, with colour-coded response actions highlighting differences between Marks, although not necessarily as dual Mk1/Mk2 Cards.

MoD failed to mitigate these risks. The Differences Course comprised a one-day course, followed by two simulator 'trips' and one flight. No course notes were provided and, at this remove, the overall impression (gleaned from attendees) is of the differences being presented as minor. Notably, the courses attended by ZD576 crew took place before Amendment 1 to the Release to Service, Service Deviations and, importantly, SFI(RAF)/Chinook/12 (Undemanded Flight Control Movements) were promulgated. (Noting Squadron Leader Burke's confirmation this Instruction was not promulgated before the accident).

The effect on the Safety Case

The criticality of the above demands the Safety Case Reports between November 1993 and June 1994 be assessed. The respective Issues must be different, if only because two Service Deviations were introduced in March 1994, requiring an up-issue. One obvious example is that the Safety Case cannot take account of *'positively dangerous'* software implementation (given a valid Certificate of Design cannot exist).

If the build standard, Safety Case and Release to Service cannot be reconciled, that is further proof the Chinook Airworthiness Review Team report of 1992 applies to ZD576; because that is precisely the major failing it cites as being solely responsible for previous fatal Chinook crashes.

Conclusions

Serious deficiencies were not conveyed to aircrew during the Differences Course or in the Release to Service. Yet, it is clear the RAF rumour mill was acutely aware that Boscombe Down and their own test pilot (at Odiham) had reservations. This is a Human Factors hazard, as the doubt created in the mind can be a major distraction and sub-consciously influence thinking and actions.

Annex 1 to Addendum A - Primary differences between the Chinook HC Mk1 and Mk2 Releases to Service

The following is a factual list, and illustrated fully at [B41]. It is not exhaustive, and no attempt is made to assess the precise impact. It simply offers a flavour of the scale of Mk2 immaturity, illustrating how much work was still outstanding in June 1994.

General

The Chinook HC Mk2 Release to Service does not convey, in any way, the concerns held by both Boscombe Down and MoD(PE) over immaturity and safety. It is not an exaggeration to say that concealing this information from aircrew was maladministration and negligence; and *prima facie* evidence of gross negligence manslaughter. Major omissions include:

- Various Special Flying Instructions, notably that relating to Undemanded Flight Control Movements (see Appendix 11).
- Status of safety critical software.
- The aircraft had Switch-On Only clearance.
- Essential modifications had not been embodied.

Icing

Icing warranted two pages of restrictions in the Mk1. As explained in Section 7, the Icing Limitations were removed in March 1994, and only reinserted in July 1994.

Navigation and Communication Systems

Boscombe Down had barely commenced trialling the Navigation and Communications systems at the time of the accident. The Mk1 Release to Service has a full list of avionics, is generally compliant with regulations, and notes Limitations and restrictions arising from comprehensive installed performance testing. However, the Mk2 Release is almost completely devoid of such information. (See Section 2).

Of the few systems noted in the Mk2 Release, most have not had their installed performance assessed. Some, such as SuperTANS and GPS, carry warnings so restrictive that aircrew would automatically regard them as suspect. Regulations demand that Releases contain *no undue*

195

restrictions. Prohibiting aircrew from relying on their Navigation System and fuel computers is perhaps the ultimate *undue* restriction.

The Mk2 Release removes warnings about compass errors due to vibration, implying either (a) the vibration has been reduced to an acceptable level, or (b) the performance has not yet been confirmed in the Mk2. Given Boscombe's statements of 22 October 1993 that vibration levels have <u>not</u> improved in the Mk2, the latter is more likely.

The restriction in the Mk1 Release that Instrument approaches using VOR/ILS are not permitted due to the system's poor performance is omitted from the Mk2 Release, as is all reference to VOR/ILS.

This immaturity of Mk2 progress is reflected in Controller Aircraft's mandate placed upon the Assistant Chief of the Air Staff that the aircraft must not be flown.

Operating temperatures

In addition to the Mk2 Icing clearance being only +4°C, there are numerous examples of differences in operating temperatures between the Releases. For example:

- The Mk1 as a whole is cleared to -20°C, but the Mk2 to -10°C.
- The Mk2 system performance *'cannot be guaranteed'* below 0°C; a severe restriction on any aircraft.
- The starting minimum for all transmissions/Auxiliary Power Unit is -20°C for Mk1, but only -10°C for Mk2.

The Board did not mention the differences between the Mk1 and Mk2 operating temperature limits, or the possibility of this being a significant distraction given the extended thinking time and the crew's relative unfamiliarity with the Mk2.

Flight Control Systems (Hydraulic Systems)

The Board of Inquiry (Part 2, paragraphs 35a & d) noted faults with the Utility Hydraulic System installation, considering it:

'Possible that an abnormal Utility Hydraulic temperature indication could have been a distraction to the crew'.

'Given the large number of unexplained technical occurrences on the Chinook HC2 since its introduction, the Board considered it possible that a technical malfunction or indication could have provided a distraction to the crew'.

In the event of a single system failure the Mk1 Release instructs the pilot to land as soon as practicable. However, the Mk2 Release requires the pilot to determine the cause of the failure; which determines whether the Power Transfer Unit is to be turned off; in turn dictating the urgency with which the aircraft has to be landed. But it does not state how, or where this information is presented.

Rotor Brake / Fire Hazard

The specific warning in the Mk1 Release that *'Operation of the Rotor Brake could present a fire hazard'* is omitted from the Mk2 Release, yet the remaining text (relating to use of a fire extinguisher) is the same.

Electromagnetic Interference

There are numerous examples where the wording of the Mk1 Release is merely replicated in that of the Mk2, but a warning added that the system under discussion could be affected by external electromagnetic fields. This indicates that the necessary Electro-Magnetic Compatibility testing, at the appropriate build standard, has not yet been conducted. This is confirmed in Boscombe correspondence.

Landing on sloping ground

The limits differ between Mk1 and Mk2, the latter being more restrictive).

Additional Aircrewman workload in Chinook HC Mk2

- To inspect Transmission Debris Screen Magnetic Indicators at least every five minutes.
- To inspect FADEC/DECU electrical connectors every 15 minutes. This (illegal) Servicing Instruction is not mentioned in the Release.
- To check Flight Control Hydraulic pressure gauge every five minutes.

These additional duties would have increased the normal workload of the crewmen - especially when troops or passengers were aboard - making communication, co-operation, lookout and situational awareness much more difficult, and human error more likely.

Electrical Systems

The Mk1 Release has no restrictions. The Mk2 Release has two, one being to shed all non-essential loads when the Auxiliary Power Unit is brought on line following a double generator failure. However, there is no indication in the Flight Reference Cards of the Load Shedding convention (the creation of which is often a major task).

Engines - General

The Mk2 introduced new type engines with a FADEC, so differences between the Releases are to be expected.

On Mk2 spurious Engine Fail Caption warnings are noted, requiring the crew to wait 12 seconds before determining if the 'Engine Fail' caption is false. An interminable time if faced with such a warning. One cannot emphasise enough the importance of this as a major human-factor distraction and area for likely error and/or confusion - it is a significant mental bear trap. While the Mk2 Release includes a reduced All Up Mass limit to cater for the single-engine case, it is prudent to note that successful autorotation is not always possible at low-level (and in the Mk2 at low masses) and the risk assessment of this Limitation would be balanced on a knife edge. The excessive failure rate of the engines/FADEC/DECU experienced by the Mk2 made over-reliance on autorotation dubious, at best.

Lack of Instructor knowledge

Given the above, were the instructors on the Differences Courses adequately trained or briefed? As Boscombe had barely commenced testing and trials, and had not validated and verified safety critical software (and hence, could not have established the installed performance of most avionics or the engines), it is highly unlikely the Instructors had anything to work on except crewroom rumour and the basic details of major changes between Mk1 and Mk2.

FADEC is known to have caused concern among crews. The complexity of the Procurement Strategy meant Boeing knew little about the system. Witness, when the RAF's Training Development Group visited Boeing in 1992 to learn about FADEC (to facilitate 'teaching the teachers'), they ended up passing on to Boeing what little they knew. It was at this point that the poor state of Boeing's drawings covering FADEC was discovered. This is not necessarily a criticism of Boeing. It was incumbent upon MoD to ensure the Aircraft Design Authority (Boeing) was provided with sufficient Government Furnished Information to enable them to carry out their duties (noting the CHART concern they had never actually been an approved and appointed MoD Design Authority). This is a fundamental component of airworthiness. The key questions are (a) what dialogue took place between Boeing and MoD regarding this failure, and (b) what contractual relationship existed between Textron, HSDE, Boeing and MoD? That is, were there directed sub-contracts to avoid MoD having to act as a 'Post Office'?

Summary

Chinook HC Mk2 did not meet the Chief Scientific Advisor's requirements for Technical or System Integration maturity, and the Release to Service was non-compliant with extant regulations. However, it is only when the Mk1 and Mk2 Releases are directly compared that the sheer scale of Mk2 immaturity is revealed.

No reasonable person would claim the Differences Course was adequate, especially as vital safety related information was withheld from aircrew. The instructors <u>must</u> have recognised the paucity of information available to them, so why proceed with the courses? The CHART report (Addendum C) provides a clue at paragraph 18, discussing the oft-postulated view that Army pressure was being brought to bear on the RAF. Somewhat incongruous in an airworthiness report, where the primary aim must be to ensure safety, not air inter-Service rivalry. Unless, of course, this rivalry and uncertainty caused an organisational fault or breakdown - which it did.

Nor were major components of the Aircraft Document Set fit for purpose. It remains a serious failing that the Board noted numerous airworthiness failings, but not once mentioned 'airworthiness'. Yet it must have been patently clear that much of the evidence related to airworthiness failings. This can only have been directed.

Similarly, the RAF Chief Engineer (Air Chief Marshal Alcock) and Assistant Chief of the Air Staff (Air Vice Marshal Bagnall) would recognise the issues from, at least, CHART. Did either admit to superiors '*I knew this, but withheld the report*'? In Scotland, failure to do so is termed 'defeating the ends of justice'. It is also an offence under the Air Force Act 1956 (the relevant section is known as the Board of Inquiry (Air Force) Rules). Neither were called to any Inquiry.

On 2 June 1994 much of Boscombe's testing and trials had yet to commence. The reason for recommending Switch-On Only clearance becomes startlingly clear.

Annex 2 to Addendum A - A discussion of the status of the Chinook HC Mk1 and Mk2 Service Deviations

Executive Summary

Service Deviations (SDs) are promulgated by the Assistant Chief of the Air Staff in Part 2 to the Release to Service (RTS), and set out permitted deviations from Part 1. They remain in force until subsumed in changes to the Controller Aircraft Release (CAR).

The Chinook HC Mk1 had 48 extant SDs at the time of the ZD576 accident; Chinook HC Mk2 two. It is unclear from the Release what the status of these 48 was in the Mk2. Many were introduced under Operation GRANBY ('Gulf War 1'), but given they were retained in the Mk1 one could reasonably infer the RAF intended them to be retained, subsumed or superseded in Mk2. The introduction of FADEC, especially, would require that Mk2 testing and trialling be conducted at the intended In-Use build standard, to ensure the fuel computers were not adversely affected. It is therefore vital to ascertain what the precise build standard of the Aircraft Under Test at Boscombe was, given Boscombe's statement, only a few weeks before the Release to Service was issued, that it was <u>not</u> a representative Mk2, merely a *'prototype'*.

Differences between Chinook HC Mk1 and Mk2

Possible explanations for the differences in SDs between Marks are:

1. Mk1 SDs not listed for Mk2 had been subsumed into the Mk2 build standard (i.e. Design Incorporated) by Cover Modification (whereby MoD remains responsible for the design), or Superseding Cover Modification (whereby Boeing assumed responsibility).

2. The failure to mention them in the Mk2 Release was a result of immaturity of process. That is, the Release was issued before Boscombe assessed them; so, they could not be cleared for, or 'read across' to, the Mk2.

3. The SDs were not intended for the Mk2, in which case the Mk2 capability would be severely restricted and safety compromised.

It is thought (3) is unlikely in the case of most SDs. It is probable that (1) was intended, and (2) the most likely explanation. This is simply an extension of the logic applied by Boscombe when recommending Switch-On Only clearance. The Mk2 design and clearance process was so immature, it would be nugatory effort to conduct performance trials on electronic equipment before the FADEC safety critical software was validated and verified. Had Boscombe commenced this testing and trialling only for (a) MoD to implement the recommendation to re-write the FADEC software, or (b) supply a Mk2 at a representative build standard, then the work would have to be repeated.

Given the immature status of the programme reflected in the INTERIM CAR, one could not reasonably expect Boscombe to have cleared these SDs or associated equipment. To illustrate this point, it can be seen below that the majority of Mk1 equipment mentioned in SDs is not mentioned at all in the Mk2 Release. This would be confusing to aircrew and maintainers. It constitutes a major risk and hazard, because if an equipment is not listed in Part 1, there is no authority for it to be in the aircraft. Authority to use cannot be inferred from the presence of equipment. There must be a positive statement of level of clearance.

Chinook HC Mk1 Service Deviations extant on 2 June 1994

Key:

SEM - Service Engineered Modification

STF - Special Trials Fit

Items in **bold** do not have a clearance statement in the Chinook HC Mk2 Release to Service, therefore there was no authority to fit or use them. The use of the term 'No guarantee of performance' implies installed performance testing and trailing has not yet taken place, it was unsatisfactory, or not yet deemed safe.

Service Deviation number/Description

7   Ship Operations.

8   Use of 718U/4A HF Radio. (Automatic Flight Control System disturbances causing multi-channel runaway, and Actuator movements when using HF. Effects differ between aircraft).

13   Extended Range Fuel System. (STF 028B (double tank) and 034A (centre tank). **Mk2 RTS, Section T/5 - Different from SD**).

15   Use of NVG. (Requires SEM/Chinook/064/DD. **Mk2 RTS W/3 - Not Cleared**).

18   Operations in High Ambient Temperature. Alters temperature limits.

19   Operations in NBC Equipment. **Mk2 RTS W/4 - Not Cleared**.

21	Operations with Skis Fitted. Max IAS 130Kts. But see SD 9/92.

21   Operations with Skis Fitted. Max IAS 130Kts. But see SD 9/92.

23   Use of Chaff and Flare Dispenser. SRIM 4084.

24   Use of High Intensity Strobe Light. SEM/Chinook/105.

27   Mine Dispensing equipment. STF/Chinook/DDAE2/5/3/101.

1/91   RNS252 / Trimble 80000 (sic) GPS Navigation System. STF/Chinook/124 RNS252 ALERT light dim. **Mk2 RTS O/2.2/2.3 - GPS not cleared by US Department of Defense**.

2/91   PTR1751 WWH HQII UHF radio. STF/Chinook/126 EMC incompatibilities. **Mk2 RTS L/1.3 notes no guarantee of performance**. Subject to Boscombe comment I Mk2.

3/91   Avionics Crate. STF/Chinook/115.

4/91   Centre Console Extension. STF/Chinook/113 Removes Co-Pilot Auto Chart Display remote connection.

5/91   No1 and No 2 Power Distribution Point (PDP) Extensions. STF/Chinook/114.

6/91   Intro of Busbar Assembly in to No 2 PDP. STF/Chinook/147.

8/91   Cossor 4760 Mk12 IFF. STF/Chinook/109A. **Mk2 RTS M/2 - No guarantee of performance**.

9/91   Intro Twin Filter Modification to UHF AM System. STF/Chinook/123.

10/91   Robertson Extended Range Fuel System. STF/Chinook/139, 149 & 145. **(Mk2 AUM limit would preclude use)**.

11/91   NVG Anti-Collision Light.   STF/Chinook/129

12/91   Dual Mode Landing Light. STF/Chinook/137.

13/91   NVG Formation Lights. STF/Chinook/128.

14/91   Internal Cargo Handling System. STF/Chinook/152 & 153. **Mk2 RTS T/2.2 - Not cleared**.

16/91   Fast Roping. STF/Chinook/125.

17/91   Lighting Balance Unit. STF/Chinook/125.

18/91   OMEGA Grid Mode Selector. STF/Chinook/143.

19/91   NVG Compatible Dome Lights. STF/Chinook/142.

20/91   NVG Anti-Collision Light post-SEM 105. STF/Chinook/141.

21/91   NVG Compatible Glass for PV1754AA or 1754AAH UHF Control Units. STF/Chinook/141.

22/91   NVG Compatible M130 Arm Light. STF/Chinook/144.

23/91 SATCOM Aerial. STF/Chinook/135. Superseded by SD 10/93.

24/91 Breeze Dash 58 Rescue Hoist. STF/Chinook/108.

26/9 Cougarnet/Keystone Secure Radio Installation. STF/Chinook/119.

27/91 Delco Carousel IVA Inertial Navigation System. SEM/Chinook(RE)/067 & Chinook/074. STF/Chinook/118

28/91 OMEGA Navigation System. SEM/Chinook/044 & 072. STF/Chinook/136

30/91 Use of GE M134 7.62mm Minigun. STF/Chinook/138A & 150.

1/92 Sky Guardian (ARI) 18228/13PD RWR. STF/Chinook/54A & 54B.

7/92 Loral AN/AAR 47 Missile Approach Warning System. STF/Chinook/148A & 148B.

8/92 ALQ 156 with M130 Interface. STF/Chinook/134 SF Only.

9/92 Engine Air Particle Separator (EAPS) System. STF/Chinook/121, 122A & 146. Limits IAS to 120Kts.

10/92 M130 Parallel Firing. STF/Chinook/155.

12/92 NVG (Nite-op) Counter-Weights. ODI/LEI/257/91 (RAF Odiham Local Engineering Instruction?) To be removed before crashing if time and circumstances permit.

13/92 M60D Armament System. STF/Chinook/158 & 159. SEM/ARM/108 & 109/SM(Wpns) 13.

1/93 Improved Integration of AN/AAR 47 and AN/ALQ 156 MAWS. STF/Chinook/177.

3/93 Clearance of Dowty Armour Shield Restrictive Entry Vest (REV) Body Armour. To be removed before crashing if time and circumstances permit. **Mk2 RTS W/2 - Not approved.**

7/93 Use of Dragonlight T12 Hand Held IR Searchlight.   Approved for Mk2 by SD 19/94, 23 September 1994.

8/93 Fast Roping Insertion and Extraction System. STF/Chinook/189.

9/93 GOTEC RDL4 Rubber Kneepad Protection for Crewmen.

10/93 Improved UHF SATCOM Installation (SF Only). STF/Chinook/135A. LTC94 measure running for DA Modification.

1/94 ARI 18228/19 Sky Guardian RWR. Note Only: Cancelled 6 May 1994.

Chinook HC Mk2 Service Deviations extant on 2 June 1994

The two Service Deviations promulgated in the Chinook HC Mk2 Release to Service at the time of the accident were:

1/94   Installation and Operation of Secure HF Role Radio. STF/Chinook/205.

2/94   Repositioned ALQ 157 Transmitters. STF/Chinook/204. ALQ157 is ARI 23469 Infra-Red Jammer (not stated in SD).

SD 1/94 assumes pre-fit of ARI 23257 Collins 718U/4A HF radio. Authority to fit it was only granted the following month, but pending trials no guarantee of performance can be given. In any case, Switch-On Only applies. It is therefore difficult to understand how SD 1/94 could have been cleared, given prerequisite equipment (Intercom and HF Radio) was not permitted in the aircraft. (The HF Radio was later cleared, but without the Intercom it is useless). Such contradictions are confusing to maintainers and aircrew.

SD 2/94 assumes pre-fit of ARI 23469 Infra-Red Jammer. Part 1 (Section T, Role Equipment) of the Release notes it is fitted, but pending trials no guarantee of performance is given. The repositioning of the IRJ Transmitters might imply performance trials have taken place and repositioning found necessary. Equally, it could mean the Transmitters have been moved to negate an obstruction, snagging or chaffing hazard, make room for other equipment or, more likely, to mitigate an Electro-Magnetic Compatibility issue. The Board of Inquiry (Part 2, paragraph 33) notes the *'realistic'* threat of Surface to Air Missiles (SAM). The aircrew would be aware the Mk2 Release contained no clearance for the self-protection equipment they were used to on the Mk1.

Conclusion

In time, some risks would naturally reduce as the effects became better understood. But on 2 June 1994 many remained in the *Not Yet Understood* category (for example, Caption Warnings and aircraft behaviour).

It is not a case of these risks being unrecognised - Boscombe understood their potential effect, if not cause, prompting them to withhold CAR recommendations. As ever, it is the cumulative effect that must be assessed, not just the effect of an isolated hazard/risk.

The Review may wish to ask pilots whether they would consider the Release to Service Mk2 build standard, at this time, a retrograde step.

Addendum B - Miscellaneous observations

Servicing Instructions and Special Technical Instructions

Annex B to the Board of Inquiry report ('Details of Aircraft') states at paragraphs 3 (Airframe) and 6 (Engines):

'Serial Nos and classes of relevant modifications embodied and of SIs and STIs complied with; NONE.'

This cannot be reconciled with, for example, SI/Chinook/57 - a check of DECU electrical connectors (see Appendix 10). The Board is making a clear statement that this pre-flight check was not carried out. That might point to cause. And how would it know it was not carried out *in-flight*, as per the illegal Servicing Instruction and its amendment?

Purpose of final flight

The Board did not explore the reasons for the final flight. An extraordinary omission given it removed the only Chinook HC Mk2 from an operational theatre at precisely the time (April - June 1994) when the Chinook availability low point was planned (12 aircraft). [B43, paragraph 118] At Part 2, paragraph 2, the Board stated:

'Whilst in Northern Ireland, the crews were attached to No 230 Squadron and tasked by the Joint Air Tasking Operations Centre (JATOC) at HQNI. The detachment aircraft provided the NI Security Forces with a medium lift capability in accordance with a HQ 1 Group Operation Order.'

The Review may wish to ask:

1. Was the purpose of the flight within the terms of the HQ 1 Group Operational Order?

2. Why did the original Puma tasking change to Chinook?

3. Did JATOC have the necessary authority, within the Operational Order, to remove ZD576 from theatre? If not, who did? Did HQ 1 Group need to approve a deviation from the Order?

4. Given the passenger list, who else would need to be consulted? 39 Brigade HQ, Lisburn? The Chief of Defence Intelligence, or his staff?

5. Were the authorisers aware of the nature of the duty at Fort George?

6. What was that duty? A meeting followed by rest and recreation? Other?

7. Was this intelligent and/or proper use of a scarce asset?

Evidence of previous behaviour in similar circumstances

The Review may wish to consider events in the Falkland Islands in 1989, when Flight Lieutenant Cook was Handling Pilot on a Chinook HC Mk1, with his (78 Squadron Mount Pleasant) commander in the Left Hand Seat. It is understood Flight Lieutenant Cook was faced with similar circumstances and refused to fly into cloud covering a hill, clear indication of a behavioural trend conducive to safe operations.

Serviceability of the Control Pallets

The Board of Inquiry (Part 2, paragraph 35c (3)) noted previous problems with the Control Pallets causing Undemanded Flight Control Movements, stating a Pallet was replaced.

The Board does not link this to Special Flying Instruction (RAF)/Chinook/12 (UFCMs) (see Appendix 11). It is unclear if the Board even knew of the SFI, given it was not promulgated in the Release to Service, and the Odiham Unit Test Pilot (Squadron Leader Burke) has stated he had not seen it.

The Board implies the replacement/repair of the Control Pallets was carried out satisfactorily, but does not dismiss the possibility of pre-impact detachment of control springs or inserts. The Review may wish to revisit this area. In particular, seek the expert opinion of the AAIB investigator and those at Aldergrove who viewed the detached Pallet the previous day.

Author's note (2024) After further investigation I was able to ascertain the answers to some of my questions, and published them in 'The Inconvenient Truth'. The Review's report did not address them.

Addendum C - A discussion of the 1992 Chinook Airworthiness Review Team (CHART) report

Executive Summary

The Review was initiated two years after the Chinook Mid-Life Upgrade contract was let. It reported after the Trials Installation aircraft had flown, but before the first Mk2 was delivered.

The subject report [B43] was submitted by the RAF Director of Flight Safety (Air Commodore Martin Abbott) to the RAF Chief Engineer (Air Chief Marshal Michael Alcock) on 14 August 1992; copied to the Assistant Chief of the Air Staff (ACAS) Air Vice Marshal Anthony Bagnall (who, 15 months later, signed the Chinook HC Mk2 Release to Service). As CHART was published on the latter's first day in post, it is considered highly unlikely he did not discuss it with his immediate superior, Chief of the Air Staff Air Chief Marshal Sir Peter Harding.[70]

The author obtained the main body (52 pages) in October 2010. On 15 January 2011 Mr Steve Webb MP retrieved the same 52 pages from the House of Commons library. The complete 373 pages, plus a covering Loose Minute from the Director of Flight Safety, were provided under Freedom of Information on 13 April and 10 May 2011 respectively. The report had been concealed from all previous Inquiries. Of its 46 recommendations, 26 are mandated policy.

It reveals:

- CHART notified the Chief Engineer and ACAS of systemic airworthiness failings, repeating and citing notifications to (e.g.) HQ Strike Command by RAF Odiham in June 1985.

- The Review was deemed necessary because: *'Since entering RAF service in 1980, the Chinook HC Mk1 has been dogged by configuration control problems, inadequate publications and system unreliability'.* (Opening sentence of CHART report). This confirms the specific area of airworthiness concern, which is directly linked to the Safety Case and Release to Service.

- Chinook accidents, some fatal, had been attributed to airworthiness failings. Therefore, the Nimrod Review baseline of 1998 can be pushed further back to the mid-1980s, and is applicable to Mull of Kintyre (and other accidents).

---

70 CHART report covering letter, D/IFS(RAF)/125/30/2/1, 7 August 1992.

A Cross Reference Index is presented here, mapping the 17 Core components of maintaining the build standard to the CHART Report, illustrating (a) the build standard was already compromised on Chinook HC Mk1 before the Mk2 entered Service, and (b) the solutions to the failings noted by CHART were readily known, but not implemented.

CHART is not a revelation. It is corroborating evidence supporting previous similar reports and audits. During discussions between the author, Minister for the Armed Forces, and senior RAF staff (including the immediate past Chinook Integrated Project Team Leader) on 17 January 2011, it became clear the latter were unaware of this report.

Recommendations

It is strongly recommended that:

The former Controller Aircraft (Donald Spiers) is interviewed by the Review. He is on record stating he knew nothing of CHART, so should be asked if, with hindsight, he would have signed his INTERIM CAR knowing of the systemic and ongoing airworthiness failings reported by the Director of Flight Safety.

The former RAF Chief Engineer (Air Chief Marshal Michael Alcock) is interviewed to ascertain:

1. What directives he issued upon receiving CHART on 14 August 1992. (Noting the evidence contained in this submission, confirmed by various senior staff and Ministers, and recorded in numerous reports/audits, that no significant action was taken and systemic airworthiness failings remain the norm).

2. What discussions regarding CHART took place between himself, Air Member Supply and Organisation, the Assistant Chief of the Air Staff, and the Chief of the Air Staff.

3. If the impact on the Chinook HC Mk2 programme was assessed.

The former Assistant Chief of the Air Staff (Air Chief Marshal Anthony Bagnall) is interviewed to ascertain:

1. What advice he sought and received from the Director of Flight Safety, RAF Chief Engineer, and Chief of the Air Staff following receipt of CHART.

2. What direction (if any) he received from his superiors as to how he should proceed with the Chinook HC Mk2 Release to Service in the light of evidence of systemic airworthiness failings.

The former Chiefs of the Air Staff (Air Chief Marshals Peter Harding and

Michael Graydon) are interviewed to ascertain:

1. If they were consulted about CHART, or had its contents reported to them.

2. What action (if any) they directed.

The Director of Flight Safety (Air Commodore Martin Abbott) is interviewed to ascertain:

1. If he was asked to brief any senior staff and, if so, what did he advise.

2. If he was tasked to conduct further airworthiness reviews and investigations.

Background

To recap, the Controller Aircraft Release and Release to Service are tied to a specific Issue of the Safety Case; in turn reflecting the In-Use build standard; meaning at all times this build standard must be maintained.

A letter from RAF Odiham to HQ Strike Command dated June 1985 [B45] reveals serious configuration control problems, citing:

'A fully documented case of a new-build aircraft being inadvertently de-modified due to there being "no reference in the air publications". RAF Odiham states the problem is "serious, posing a flight safety hazard".'

That is, since the In Service Date the build standard of Chinook HC Mk1 had not been maintained in accordance with Military Airworthiness Regulations. It follows that the Safety Case and the Mk1 Release to Service were progressively compromised over that period. CHART details, throughout its 373 pages, the sheer scale of the failings; confirming they applied not only to Chinook, but to Puma and Wessex as all three aircraft were managed by the same RAF Support Authority. As many of the failings were centralised functions within MoD during this period, other aircraft suffered similarly.

On 3 March 1999 the Chief of Defence Procurement (Sir Robert Walmsley) confirmed to the Public Accounts Committee that configuration control problems remained on Chinook. It can now be seen that the Committee, in all likelihood, were able to refer to the CHART report - but only the 52 pages retrieved by Steve Webb MP.[71] If so, then each member present would be fully aware that the gross negligence findings were unsustainable. Even if the report was not made

---

71 Those of the committee in attendance - Mr David Davis (Chair), Messrs Alan Campbell, Ian Davidson, Richard Page, Gerry Steinberg, Derek Twigg, Charles Wardle and Alan Williams, and Ms Jane Griffiths.

available, Walmsley's admission would be sufficient, although that would require one of the members to understand what he was saying. I note Richard Page MP was a trained engineer.

Applicability to Chinook HC Mk2

It is anticipated MoD will deny any link between CHART and Chinook HC Mk2. The CHART author understood the link, referring to Mk2 and its programme 284 times.

But on 10 November 2005 the Minister for the Armed Forces (Mr Adam Ingram) rejected the notion, stating to Mr Webb:

> *(The author) talks about "configuration control", the problem of the accretion of equipment onto a platform that may interfere with other systems and the associated problem of aircraft documentation being out of date. In the case of Chinook Mk2, we are dealing with an aircraft for which the Controller Aircraft Release and RAF Release to Service had only been signed off in November 2003* [he meant 1993], *and a single amendment list had been produced in March 2004 (sic - 1994), only 3 months before the crash. This is not a situation in which the problems of "configuration control" would have arisen.*[72]

Anyone unfamiliar with Chinook would infer that the Mk2 was new-build in November 1993, and/or nothing that occurred before that date on Mk1 could affect configuration control. Nothing could be further from the truth, and it is deceit and failures such as this that has prevented corrective action over the past two decades, leading directly to the loss of Nimrod XV230 and the Nimrod Review.

In other words, Walmsley and Ingram can't both be right.

Chinook HC Mk2 was a modification to the Mk1. It is a basic requirement of such programmes that the Induction Build Standard be agreed between MoD, the RAF and the contractor. It is the baseline for engineering design, safety and cost. The build standard and Safety Case must be stable when the contract is let, and maintained throughout. It may change during the life of the contract for good reason (in this case, the onset of Gulf War 1), but those changes must be tracked and, importantly, understood in the safety context. CHART confirms this was not the case; and remained so throughout the Mid-Life Upgrade programme.

The ZD576 Board of Inquiry did not see CHART. Had they done so, it

---

72 Letter D/Min(AF)/AI 4573/05/C/LN), 10 November 2005.

would have explained much of the evidence they took regarding poor standards, documentation, configuration control, Quality Assurance, etc. However, this does not excuse the Board's failure to investigate and report on these issues.

Key questions arise, which the Review may wish to ask:

1. Given the distribution of the report (RAF Chief Engineer and the Assistant Chief of the Air Staff), all those in the RAF's airworthiness senior chain of command were fully aware of these systemic failings. Why was the content, and its implications, not advised to the ZD576 Board of Inquiry or taken into account by the Reviewing Officers?

2. Who was responsible for actioning the recommendations of the report? Is there commonality between these staff and those involved in the decision to (a) prematurely release the Mk2, and (b) blame the pilots?

3. What corrective action was taken by, for example, the RAF Chief Engineer?

4. Most importantly for current purposes, CHART is exculpatory evidence; even more so when viewed alongside Controller Aircraft's mandate that the aircraft must not be flown.

While this submission does not suggest Mr Haddon-Cave should be asked to reconsider his position and revise the list of those he named (the facts speak for themselves), in the light of the CHART report it is vital both the Review and MoD understands and accepts the scale of the problem. As matters stand (the Haddon-Cave baseline), the new Military Aviation Authority must regress to 1998 to, for example, fill gaps in audit trails. That Nimrod Review baseline has now been pushed back a further 10, or even 18 years, and the financial and timescale implications are significant. This was put to Min(AF) Nick Harvey MP on 17 January 2011. He did not demur.

The CHART Report - Discussion

While purporting to be an Airworthiness Review, the team's Terms of Reference are very restrictive, only permitting them to study 'internal' RAF responsibilities; mainly First and Second Line activities, plus the Support Authority. They are <u>directed</u> not to comment on MoD(PE), where MoD's practical airworthiness experiences lies; or the Naval Aircraft Repair Organisation (NARO), who carried out Second/Third Line, Depth B, C and D maintenance on the aircraft and their equipment. Air Member Supply and Organisation's own airworthiness staff were not interviewed. Nor does the report penetrate the higher echelons of the airworthiness chain.

Nevertheless, it is clear the team realised they were not getting to the root of the problems being encountered, because they conducted a visit to RNAY Fleetlands (who, in this context, prepared the aircraft for induction into Boeing). Fleetlands was classified as both a Second and Third Line unit, being scaled to be able to replicate all rotary wing activities carried out by Second Line workshops at front line Air Stations.

Key points from the Terms of Reference:

- Conduct a wide-ranging independent review under direction of an Inspectorate of Flight Safety Steering Group.
- Determine the effectiveness of Logistic Support Management ensuring airworthiness of the Chinook fleet.
- Recognising other RAF helicopters have similar maintenance procedures, note and highlight any issues which may apply to those other aircraft.
- Examine the effectiveness and support provided by Group and Command HQ.
- Aspects outwith the control of the RAF are excluded.
- Examine the balance between operational tasking and resources.
- Specifically, the Review is to determine:
  a. The adequacy of Statements of Unit Policy in respect of tasking and compliance.
  b. Standards of maintenance both at Main Operating Bases and deployed Squadrons (e.g. RAF Aldergrove).
  c. The effectiveness of the remedial action process.
  d. The adequacy of Aircraft Technical Publications and aircraft documentation.
  e. The effectiveness of zonal maintenance.
  f. The adequacy of configuration control both before and after the Chinook Mid-Life Upgrade.
  g. The airworthiness implications of Service Engineered Modifications, Special Radio Installation Modifications, Special Trials Fits and Service Deviations.
  h. The adequacy of Support Authority manpower resources to discharge the authority delegated by Chief of Logistic Support (RAF).

The review was set up in April 1992, and directed to report by 1 July 1992. In this period the three members were instructed to visit some 40 individual postholders (and their staff) at 10 units, ranging from the UK, to Germany and the Falkland Islands - but to be in London every fortnight to present an update to a Steering Group. This was an onerous and demanding task, and the tight timescales would permit only a quick assessment. Their realisation and concern can be gleaned from the main report and recommendations, including the requirement for follow-up studies.

What follow-up occurred is not clear, but the embarrassing impact of the report would have been obvious to recipients (Alcock and Bagnall). In particular, it would be immediately clear Alcock himself was culpable. What is known for certain is the immediate reaction was to make further #28% cuts in direct airworthiness funding, which led to similar reports over the following 10 years. For example, the Nimrod Airworthiness Review Team (NART) in 1998 reported *'neglect'* during the early-90s, culminating in low manning levels, declining experience, failing moral, overstretched tasking and reduced resources; calling for *'highly attentive management'* which needs to be *'closely attuned'.* In short, CHART and NART reported the same problems; which were systemic and the responsibility of the RAF Chief Engineer to address.

Yet, the Nimrod Review referred to this as *'the golden period for airworthiness'* (paragraph 13.124). In the same way CHART was constrained to assessing only front line and Support Authorities, Mr Haddon-Cave seemed under the impression, or was led to believe, that *'visiting Multi-Disciplinary Groups (MDG) and auditing their airworthiness processes'* (paragraph 13.125) was sufficient to ensure airworthiness. Implementation was ignored.

A simple example. An MDG may, indeed, follow the regulations and seek a Fault Investigation. But the system collapses if there is no resource to conduct an investigation or, as explained previously, non-engineering staff can overrule the Engineering Authority and cancel the request. Mr Haddon-Cave confirmed that savings were made at the expense of safety, but did not follow through and link this critical failure to policies of the day; or explain these policies (as this Submission does). Instead, he named and praised those directly responsible for the policies, practices and failures.[73] While perhaps not within the remit of the Mull of Kintyre Review, it is clear the very personal criticism of General Sir Sam Cowan

---

73 Nimrod Review, paragraph 13.124.

and Air Chief Marshal Sir Malcolm Pledger by Mr Haddon-Cave is completely unfounded. Both officers, especially General Cowan, inherited decades of neglect - evidenced by CHART. It is a practical impossibility to resurrect upwards of 12 years of neglect during a 2-3 year posting, especially at a time when further cuts have been ordered at a political level.

Much of CHART concentrates on operational and organisational matters. ('Organisational Fault' was a contributory factor available to, but not considered by, the Board of Inquiry). Confusion and duplication of effort is revealed. It complains that vital tasks are not carried out due to lack of understanding and clear direction as to boundaries of responsibility. The image of a 'stove-piped' organisation in disarray emerges.

The report takes a 'top down' approach. The problem with such an approach, by a team headed by a Wing Commander, is that the 'top' (i.e. Group Captain and above) is unlikely to react well to criticism. Yet it is their management and leadership that sets the tone. It should be established if the CHART leader, at least, was asked to brief the RAF Chief Engineer or the Assistant Chief of the Air Staff.

The Devil is in the detail, but the team's Terms of Reference and short deadline prevented them from digging too deep. The report presents a long list of problems, but lacks deeper analysis to identify where the breakdown of airworthiness occurred, or where responsibility lay to (a) prevent further breakdown, and (b) fill the gaps in the audit trail. What corrective action was taken? This Submission reveals the answer - none.

This is the truly astonishing aspect of the report - the specialist staff who would know how to resolve every technical problem it lists had, by April 1992, been transferred to AMSO and were part of the organisation the team was directed to assess. The associated procedures had been updated in July 1992, recognising the organisational changes. For example, Director Support Management (PDS) letter SM(AV)PDS/18/3/1 dated 1 July 1992, promulgating updated PDS Specifications 1-20. Interviewing these staff first would have prevented nugatory work later, and facilitated a report which included practical solutions. The CHART team was seemingly unaware their colleagues had been making the same representations (all rejected) to the same senior staff in AMSO, since 1988. In turn, these specialist airworthiness staff were kept unaware of CHART. Had they known about each other, the report would almost certainly have been better directed. Consequently, the report takes a narrow and shallow view of airworthiness; consistent with an organisation facing front line Users. Even so, it articulates many valid and well-known problems, expressing them well.

The CHART team were unaware that the (RAF) organisation responsible for many of the airworthiness components that had failed had, by August 1992, slashed Post Design Services funding and deemed solving the problems a waste of money. (The primary criticism reiterated by the Nimrod Review, 17 years later - making *savings at the expense of safety*). This prior negligence almost certainly set the tone for what was to follow - a distinct lack of action. It is highly unlikely the recipients would agree to publish such a report containing, effectively, criticisms of themselves. The Independence pillar of airworthiness had fallen.

It is inconceivable the team was not advised of this when visiting the Support Authorities and RAF Harrogate. One must ask why these staff would, seemingly, withhold such vital information. The answer lies in AMSO's immediate reaction to CHART - the implementation of further draconian cuts to airworthiness funding, preventing the implementation of JSP553 Chapter 5 (Maintaining Airworthiness). Staff would be aware any criticism would reflect directly upon, at least, Director General Support Management (DGSM), whose organisation was responsible for many of the airworthiness failings noted. To accept and implement CHART's recommendations would have left senior staff open to ridicule. To implement CHART required these staff to accept they were wrong and order an about turn. They did not.

To further illustrate this ethos and systemic failure, at paragraph 29 the report confirms DSM2 (AMSO's Director Support Management 2 - an engineer) correctly required his staff, in their letters of delegation, to report airworthiness issues. Yet, within four months (December 1992), DSM2's immediate superior (DGSM, Air Vice Marshal Christopher Baker) was in London threatening to dismiss civilian staff who insisted on implementing this mandatory requirement. (See Appendices 4 & 5). This conflict, whereby the airworthiness management chain had non-engineers with no delegation, but authority to overrule, is a cornerstone of the CHART report. It is abundantly clear that these two events, CHART and Baker's threats, are linked.

It is striking that the report praises certain aspects of airworthiness as being implemented well, but does not seem to appreciate that at the same time the RN could only dream of this work being carried out on their aircraft, as their funding had been cut to bolster the RAF's.

Rather than dissect every paragraph, it is believed the following Cross Reference Index will best illustrate and explain the problem.

Cross Reference Index mapping the 17 core components of maintaining a build standard against the CHART report of 7 August 1992

The core components set out Defence Standard 05-125/2, mandated in all aviation contracts, are listed, followed by the CHART Reference and comments. Note: Updating Safety Cases is a common thread running through each core item.

1. Appointment of an Aircraft, Equipment or System Design Authority - and Co-ordinating Design Authorities / Design Custodian

CHART, Paragraph 10. *'Boeing Helicopters had not acted as an offshore Design Authority before'*. If MoD was not confident the relevant PDS specifications could be complied with (by Boeing), on what basis was the contract let? Did MoD explore the possibility of, for example, a competent Aircraft Design Authority such as Westland acting as Co-ordinating Design Authority, or Design Custodian, with a directed sub-contract on Boeing?

Reference - PDS Specification 5.

2. Investigation of Faults

Paragraphs 64, 68. *'Not all faults recorded in MF700'*. It follows that a MF760 (Narrative Fault Report) for the same fault would not be raised.

Yet at Paragraph 80 - *'Number of incidents arising from technical faults remains unacceptably high'*. And paragraphs 81, 82 - action by Boeing on fault reports has been awaited for more than two years.

To state the obvious, one should not complain about faults not being investigated if one does not use the fault reporting system.

The report merely states the Support Authority *'follows up'* unresolved reports, but does not explain why it lacks resources to do so.

Were Boeing tasked correctly through the PDS contract, and why have the investigations been delayed? At the time of the report, Engineering Authorities were under instruction to limit requests. The team seems unaware of this policy.

Also, the immediate oversight committees, the HQ Modification Committees, had been disbanded by AMSO in June 1991, with periodicity of Local Technical Committees reduced to 6-monthly; if held at all. Also, the scope for Extraordinary Local Technical Committees and Local Equipment Repair Committees was reduced by further funding cuts, a reduction in Quality Assurance staff, and the policy to let only Limited PDS contracts and/or delay renewal.

The report omits that, if Boeing (or any other Design Authority) were contracted in accordance with PDS Specifications, then they had the authority to self-task to initiate urgent investigations. This delegated authority to commit MoD funding is unique, and aimed at getting safety related tasking under way as soon as possible. Was this process available to, or used by, Boeing?

Reference - PDS Specification 5, paragraph 4.2.2.

3. Design of modifications

Paragraph 88. *'Technical Publications do not reflect all modifications'.* Adhering to Defence Standard 05-125/2, including HQ Modifications Committee oversight, would ensure the task is complete and publications amended. In 1992 AMSO had directed this work cease; and ensured it by withholding funding.

Reference - PDS Specification 5, paragraph 4.4.

4. Submission of modification proposals

Paragraph 88 (see above). The Design Authority's proposal must include amending Air Publications. If it does not, the proposal should be deferred by the HQ Modification Committee.

Linked to cuts in PDS funding and shortcuts taken by Support Authorities on Service Modifications, as they have no direct link to Air Publication tasking initiation, which is conducted via PDS.

Reference - PDS Specification 5, paragraph 4.6.

5. Design incorporation of approved modifications and changes, and maintaining configuration control

Systemic failure to maintain configuration control was the basic reason for the CHART Review. It is cited by the report as the primary cause of recent Chinook accidents. If configuration control has not been maintained, then PDS has not been conducted properly. Linked to cuts in PDS funding, culminating in the January 1993 directive that even safety critical tasks should not be carried out. At that point, PDS became a minor task for many, instead of a specialist discipline.

Paragraph 37 reports that post cuts implemented by AMSO re-organisation adversely affected configuration control. This corroborates submissions to the Nimrod Review; and confirms predictions by MoD staff and auditors from January 1988-on.

Paragraph 38. Similar to paragraph 37, stating the Support Authorities are overworked following re-organisation; and have less time for their primary task, airworthiness. If the Support Authority has insufficient time to conduct its primary role, then the RAF must look to itself to resolve root problems instead of accepting this deficiency and expecting others to compensate. For example, was there a compensatory bid to increase PDS funding? No, it was cut (again) by ~28% that year.

Paragraph 39. Similarly, outstanding Aircraft Engineering Development and Investigation Team tasks are noted, including configuration control, Technical Publications Review, Maintenance Procedures Review, Missile Approach Warner Integration, and Preliminary Warning Instructions. These are all airworthiness issues, the impact on safety self-evident.

Paragraph 40. *'Engineering Change Proposals difficult to manage due to staff shortages in US'*. This is a simple failure to fund and contract PDS, and manage activities. Reference - PDS Specification 18.

Paragraph 44. *'Design Authority modifications, Special Technical Instructions and Special Trials Fits (STFs) not reflected in Aircraft Maintenance Manual'*. The first two are failure to implement regulations, however STFs are a separate matter. They have no status under PDS, being purely an In-Service RAF device. Failure to appreciate this subtlety is a major contributory factor to this and other accidents.

Paragraph 88. *'Failure to maintain Maintenance Procedures following modifications'*. The content of Air Publications is entirely linked to the Maintenance Policy Statement. If it is invalid, then the ability to validate and verify publications is entirely compromised; in turn rendering it impossible to have a valid Safety Case. Reference - PDS Specification 5.

6. Holding and maintaining master drawings

Paragraph 71. Systemic *failure to maintain accurate drawings*. Equipment PDS was a centralised function - as Chinook aircraft and equipment were affected, then so too were other aircraft.

References - PDS Specification 5, paragraph 4.5 & 5, and PDS Agency 1.

7. Management of component replacement / unavailability

(Often, wrongly, called obsolescence, which is merely one reason why a component can be unavailable. Failure to understand this explains many supply problems).

Paragraph 66. *'Poor availability of critical spares'*. The Aircraft and Equipment Design Authorities have a key role in solving general unavailability. They are employed by MoD to provide continuity. Most Design Authorities know more about the running of MoD than MoD itself. If they do not, it could be argued they are unsuited to the task - the clear implication, given the comments about Boeing.

The report emphasises lack of gearboxes. It is too simplistic to imply, as the report does, that Third Line is to blame. They (RNAW Almondbank) were not asked what caused delays, which was AMSO's refusal to provide spares on time. (Source - RNAW Production Controller). Moreover, the report mentions poor quality of Foreign Military Sales sourced spares.

A key dependency is Design Authority support for transmission test rigs - yet the report does not ask if such contracts have been in place, continuously. (They had not).

Paragraph 124. Discusses spares provisioning for the Mk2, expressing concern that spares may not be available after the 2-year Initial Provisioning phase. This is a function of the Service HQ.

Paragraph 69. Fly Away Packs can only be completed by robbery. Permanent Long Term Costings instructions specifically address this point, requiring a satisfactory plan before funding is committed. In short, DefCon 82, SNAEC 118 (Special Notice to Aircraft and Engine Contractors) and ESPAN (Electronic Spares Provisioning Amendment Notice) procedures must be implemented.

All the above requires correct Materiel and Financial Provisioning, and the report details numerous examples of this not being conducted properly. This is no surprise - the RN stopped meeting this mandatory requirement in 1988 (post Hallifax Savings), by which time it was evident (to RN staff managing equipment also used by the RAF) that the RAF had ceased also. Almost every support problem can be traced to the demise of these HQ sections, exacerbated by it having been their role to act as 'trouble shooters' and solve major problems as special tasks.

Reference - PDS Specification 5, paragraph 4.8.2.

8. Responsibility for complete systems

Paragraph 10. Boeing criticised, but no other Design Authority mentioned. In discussing the role of Industry in airworthiness, the report addresses Boeing's input, but not the plethora of equipment Design Authorities, especially on avionics.

In this context the aircraft is the 'system' and Boeing is responsible. However, they have dependencies and rely on MoD continuously contracting all other Design Authorities, and appointing System Co-ordinating Design Authorities e.g. for the Navigation or Communications sub-systems. This was the area most affected by the financial cuts of the early 1990s, and has never been resurrected.

Reference - PDS Specification 5, paragraph 4.9.

9. Provision of Technical advice to MoD and their agencies

The report implies Users and the Support Authority did not know they should have had direct access to specialist advice from (e.g.) Boeing. Yet this is part of the continuous feedback, review and improvement mandate.

PDS Specification 5, paragraph 4.10 requires the Design Authority to provide advice to Government Departments, Service Units and other contractors.

Mandatory assessment of Service Engineered Modifications is covered by PDS Specification 8.

10.   Visits to User units

(Primarily to discuss system performance with users in the light of Service experience, again part of the reporting and feedback obligation).

Paragraphs 47, 49 & 136 note numerous visits to Air Stations, but clearly Boeing were not present. As a minimum, annual visits are mandated, to conduct separate Operator and Maintainer conferences to facilitate an exchange of views, ideas, problems - and agree contractually binding actions. In turn, this informs the Capability Working Groups and, ultimately, prioritisation of funding.

If the Support Authority undertakes such a visit alone, then there is no User confidence that any observations will be actioned, because the Support Authority does not have the authority to do so. For example, in 1992 the Chinook Support Authority had no control or influence over the build standard of any avionics or engines - and the report does not mention those who did.

Similarly, CHART reports the Support Authority is not necessarily staffed by Chinook or equipment experts; so there can be no confidence that a given issue or the means to resolve it are understood. The restrictive Terms of Reference prevented detailed exploration of this.

Reference - PDS Specification 5, paragraph 4.11.

11.   Packaging and Handling

CHART makes no reference to this component. It is an inordinately expensive component of Aircraft Support. If not managed closely, the drain on resources and effect on Availability and Maintainability is immense. An uninspiring aspect of PDS, but of vital import.

Reference - PDS Specification 5, paragraph 4.14.

12.   Maintenance and Supply of documents (to Project Teams and agencies).

Paragraph 10. This component of PDS is crucial to the success of modification programmes, as PDS is the vehicle by which the contractor is assured that Government Furnished Information is maintained throughout the programme. Failure to provide this service absolves the contractor of many contractual liabilities, transferring risk to MoD.

Reference - PDS Specification 5, paragraph 6, and PDS Specification 20 - Form 500/778 Procedures.

13.   Management of sub-contractors, and monitoring their capability

Paragraph 1. Due to the policy requirement to use Foreign Military Sales, the quality of products compromised safety. The example provided is poorly manufactured Droop Stop Blocks allowing rotor blades to strike the fuselage. The report addresses this issue intelligently, recommending greater authority for MoD staff in the US (an RAF engineer in St Louis).

However, it does not address the role of the resident RAF staff at Boeing, or the contractual requirement to manage (e.g.) FMS sub-contractors.

Reference - PDS Specification 5, paragraph 4.9.

14.   Preparation of amendments to Aircraft Technical Publications

Paragraph 88. Linked to 224 Maintenance Procedures being out of date.

At Annex C CHART notes front line units resorted to using Argentinian Chinook publications, as they were more accurate than the RAF's. In doing so, the airworthiness audit trail was broken. See above - 3/4/5.

The report states this process was not the subject of continuous review, a fundamental safety management requirement. How many of these 224 procedures applied to the Mk2 build standard? Were they all corrected? At what point does one say *We no longer have confidence the Safety Case and Release to Service are sufficiently up-to-date to ensure airworthiness*?

Paragraph 44. Most difficulties occur because changes arising from Design Authority modifications, Special Technical Instructions, Special Trials Fits, etc. have not been reflected in the Aircraft Maintenance Manual. See above - 3/4/5. With the exception of STFs, this is a failure to implement Defence Standard 05-125/2.

Reference - PDS Specification 5, paragraph 7.

15.   Conduct of Trial Installations (when a modification or product is first installed, and proven at a pre-production build standard).

Related to 3/4/5/14 above. If the requirement to conduct a Trial Installation is implemented, it is at this time one checks the proposed amendments to Air Publications (and thereafter, during the Proof Installation). If the publications subsequently found to be incorrect, then the procedures have not been implemented correctly. This would be clear from the mandated Trial Installation report.

Reference - PDS Specifications 5, 10 and 13.

16.   Holding and maintaining the Sample and Reference systems

Related to 15. The Trial Installation is conducted on the Sample, the Proof Installation on the Reference. If either does not exist (and AMSO ordered rigs to be dismantled as a savings measure throughout the 1990s), then the ability to validate and verify any changes to the build standard is compromised; in turn compromising the Safety Case.

Reference - PDS Specification 13.

17.   Dealing with day-to-day correspondence from MoD, their agencies and suppliers

Paragraph 48. *'The Support Authority has to rely on advice from Boeing, but it is common for such advice to be incomplete. Follow-up actions are delayed, caused by Boeing's misunderstanding of their responsibilities, non-standard methods of spares procurement, and diminishing expertise'.* It is again clear that Boeing and other Design Authorities are not being used properly, and their PDS contracts inadequately funded. The problem stems from PDS no longer being a centralised MoD function, and ceasing to employ specialist Technical Agencies (the named individuals in MoD responsible for maintaining the build standard).

See Item 1. If, in 1992, Boeing do not understand their role (after 12 years), then this indicates a very serious hazard and systemic failure. It points to a degree of resistance on the part of Boeing to adopt MoD procedures, yet they have been contracted to do so and willingly accept payment.

This raises the associated question of Requirement Scrutiny. Who signed to say the cost was fair and reasonable, and for acceptance, if the Customer (the RAF) was unhappy with the deliverable?

It also indicates a systemic failing on the part of MoD (Controller Aircraft in this case) to ensure the Chinook HC Mk1 Procurement Strategy invoked the MoD policy requirement for (usually) 15 years guaranteed support.

It follows the Mk2 strategy was similarly tainted - a contract was let to create the Mk2, despite MoD knowing Boeing had failed to meet their Mk1 obligations, and that this had led directly to accidents.

Reference - PDS Specification 5, Paragraph 4.11.

Additional points reported by CHART (in report order)

For brevity, this section only addresses the 52-page main body. The complete report comprises many Annexes and Enclosures, totalling 373 pages, plus a Loose Minute in the form of an Executive Summary.

Paragraph 1

A fatal accident (seven killed) on the Falkland Islands on 27 February 1987 is cited (Chinook ZA721):

'ZA721 while on an air test, after Minor maintenance and following a series of grounds runs and hover checks, pitched nose down from about 300 feet and impacted the ground, killing the occupants. The cause was never fully determined'.

The *'Minor maintenance'* included structural repair (Military Aircraft Accident Summary, paragraph 1 [B44]).

The CHART report addresses airworthiness, so the obvious question is - why mention ZA721 when the cause was, allegedly, *'never fully determined'*? It is clear the reader is meant to draw inference that it *was* airworthiness-related. The ZA721 Board of Inquiry actually stated:

'The true cause was not positively determined but the Board of Inquiry revealed a possible defective longitudinal cyclic trim actuator, errors and omissions in F700 and SNCOs not properly trained, etc...'

In fact, the AAIB report revealed numerous examples of defects and faulty workmanship (by suppliers), including ruptured seals, and seals fitted the wrong way round.

This accident was brought up again at the Chinook ZD576 Fatal Accident Inquiry (March 1996), when Flight Lieutenant (later Air Commodore) Carl Scott stated:

'Boeing Vertol have a vested interest in deterring any report which leaves them liable. This company is well funded and has shown a determination in the past to influence the outcome of inquiries. When Wing Commander Malcolm Pledger took command of 78 Squadron in the Falkland Islands in Feb 88 I asked him to brief the Chinook Flight on the findings of the BOI for the fatal crash which killed Flight Lieutenants Moffat, Newman, Sgt Johns and a number of engineering personnel, as this had not then been published. As Chairman of the Board of Inquiry he briefed 2 findings: the first his own most probable cause (failure of a hydraulic jack due to poor quality control at Boeing Vertol) and then that which would actually be published due to the failure of MOD to face pressure brought to bear by Boeing Vertol (cause unknown)'.

The Review may wish to ask:

1. Were Scott's claims regarding Boeing, and the implication that pressure was brought to bear on the Board of Inquiry, investigated?
2. Was the issue of adequate training raised and investigated?
3. Was there a breakdown of Quality Assurance (MoD) and Quality Control (Boeing), what caused this, and what corrective action was taken (for example, by the RAF Chief Engineer)?

Moreover, the Review may wish to interview Squadron Leader Robert Burke (retired), whose work was crucial in identifying the cause of this accident (notwithstanding the claim that it was not determined).

It would be a failure of duty of care by the Board and Reviewing Officers not to investigate such an obvious flight safety issue. Scott's evidence reveals aircrew concerns and suspicions which, as noted before, breed Human Factors hazards/risks. The CHART report, listing previous accidents caused by airworthiness failings, serves to support such suspicions, and the Review may wish to establish how widely the CHART report was circulated (given it was unsighted by the Board, Fatal Accident Inquiry and Houses of Commons/Lords, in addition to current MoD staff). In fact, this one report would serve well as a case study for MoD Engineering Authorities, Support Authorities, Requirements Managers and the like, before being promoted into procurement.

The ZA721 Military Aircraft Accident Summary (MAAS) was issued on 17 March 1989, over two years after the accident. It is fair to ask if the Chinook Mid-Life Upgrade specification intended correcting the rapidly accumulating Mk1 safety related problems. The MAAS describes various process and procedural failings. Taken with other comments in paragraph 1 of the CHART report, it is clear the RAF, at this time (August 1992), was fully aware of systemic failings in the application of basic airworthiness regulations and procedures. This corroborates a central point of this Submission, that the failings confirmed by the Nimrod Review apply equally to Chinook ZD576, and before.

Paragraph 13: States there is no Chinook Statement of Operating Intent and Usage (SOIU). Lacking a SOIU, Board Submissions to obtain funding are difficult to validate, leading to many of the support/funding problems outlined in the report (and this submission). Crucially, lacking a SOIU the Aircraft Document Set is incomplete, an omission which would render the Release to Service and Safety Case invalid. Not least because the Aircraft Specification and Safety Case are based on the Concept of Use stated in the SOIU. Also, regulations mandate that aircrew be familiar with the SOIU.

Paragraph 15: Full Training quotas are not met.

Paragraph 27: Insufficient Line Replaceable Units (LRU) for Special Trials Fits (STFs). This is caused by the STF procedures being 'quick and cheap' at the expense of proper Materiel and Financial Provisioning, it being rare to adequately range and scale STFs, or have a viable maintenance policy (both mandated prerequisites to approval, illustrating the breakdown of the Requirement Scrutiny process that had occurred in recent years). If Provisioning is not carried out properly, then the primary impact is insufficient funding. Director Internal Audit highlighted this in his report 'Requirement Scrutiny' in June 1996; initiated in 1993 as a direct result of the savings being implemented at the expense of safety. It is clear that STF 'requirements' were not scrutinised for accuracy.

Allied to this, the report cites poor asset tracking. The report is dated seven years after Air Member Supply and Organisation abandoned a planned asset tracking programme. This was a source of great frustration to the RN. Hitherto, when in control of its own airborne equipment, the RN supply computer at the Royal Naval Stores Depot (RNSD) Copenacre facilitated, for example, an Historical Transaction Record. However, the Naval Air Radio Stores Integration (NARSI) programme, whereby all control was transferred to AMSO at RAF Harrogate (final phase 4 - 1986), was a backward step as the RAF supply computer was not so advanced. The immediate effect was that the RN lost track of valuable assets, compounded by the RAF system not recognising the concept of support at sea; whereby aircraft and equipment, notionally based at a land station, are deployed for long periods. Numerous assets were lost and, as discussed elsewhere, supposedly 'surplus' assets were scrapped. Most were not 'surplus'; they were awaiting issue as part of the ships' storing process, whose aircraft were now depleted of vital equipment.

Paragraph 28: Recommends LRU holdings be controlled by a single authority. This is already mandated.

Paragraph 42: Chinook Support Authority under-resourced. While probably true, this observation would be unlikely to garner sympathy from their RN equivalents; who had the trained staff but were refused funding by AMSO supply staff, who had diverted RN funding to the RAF.

Paragraph 46: Refers to 'low priority' Class B/2 modifications not being embodied. There is no such thing as a 'low priority' B/2 - a Class B/2 modification is defined as 'high priority' and 'to be embodied forthwith'. That is, it is a classification just below that which would ground the aircraft. If the RAF was treating B/2s as low priority, then it indeed had very serious problems, and an approvals system that 'waived through' proposals without proper scrutiny or prioritisation.

It appears the Support Authorities had to further prioritise high priority mods, when the regulations demanded equal status and, in fact, serious re-consideration of the Aircraft Release if not embodied in the correct timescale. This is indicative of inaccurate Cost and Brief Sheets to the HQ Modification Committees (disbanded in June 1991), and not at all thereafter, because the process requires them to confirm resources are available to embody and support the modifications. If the Support Authority cannot reassure the Chairman of this, then he will defer approval and force escalation. If there is no committee, the problem will be invisible to those charged with oversight.

Paragraph 49: Complains MoD(PE) (implying the Directorate of Helicopter Projects) are not actioning airworthiness recommendations. But elsewhere the report states nobody is making materiel or financial provision, so where was DHP to get the funding from if their Customer (the RAF) has neither stated a requirement nor made complementary provision?

Paragraph 50: Link to Nimrod, via the Chinook Role Office and Nimrod both being under the functional control of the same Wing Commander. What became acceptable and the norm on one aircraft, quickly became the norm on others, with both defaulting to the cheapest option. The key issue is oversight and having the necessary authority to direct conflict resolution; when it is career-limiting to delegate upwards.

Paragraph 52: Unclear responsibilities for planning modification programmes. It would appear this was a case of these responsible being under-resourced due to cutbacks and, perhaps, making a conscious decision not to carry out this task. Responsibilities for modification programmes are (were) laid down, and Service HQs had specialist sections. However, the RN's equivalent section (DGA(N) HQ Mods Section) was disbanded, with no replacement, as part of the 1988 Hallifax Savings. As staff were posted elsewhere to unrelated jobs, the work defaulted to MoD(PE) project offices, who did not necessarily have staff with appropriate expertise. Immediately, there was no longer a natural recruitment ground or logical career progression which would ensure MoD(PE) acquired suitable staff. This situation remains today.

While the RAF suffered similar but less draconian cutbacks - the only difference being the inevitable effect on airworthiness taking slightly longer to manifest itself - the effect was easily predictable, and was.

Author's note: In the late 1990s the Health and Usage Monitoring System (HUMS) programme manager in Director Helicopter Projects (a Commander RN) was faced with this situation. The RAF would not plan and manage the Chinook modification programme, so he was forced to recruit, on promotion, a civilian technical officer from RNAY Fleetlands whose current role was planning aircraft modification programmes. The officer did a fine job (as one would expect), but the wider effect was to lower the standards expected of MoD(PE) Project Officers.

Summary

Most of the failings reported by CHART would have been prevented, and could be resolved, by implementing regulations. Especially Defence Standard 05-125/2 and JSP553, Chapter 5 (Maintaining Airworthiness).

Crucial information was withheld from the CHART team. The inevitable result, the Nimrod Review, was avoidable. CHART, along with other similar reports, reviews and audits is the detailed evidence of systemic failings Mr Haddon-Cave chose not to report.

SUPPLEMENTARY SUBMISSIONS

Supplementary Submission #1

8 February 2011
Mr Alex Passa,
Mull of Kintyre Review,
1, Melville Crescent,
Edinburgh EH3 7HW
(For the attention of The Right Honourable the Lord Philip)

Dear Mr Passa,

Mull of Kintyre Review

On 10 November 2010 I submitted a report for consideration, adding three Addenda on 25 January 2011. The latter were presented in such a way Issue 1 remained valid in its own right.

I beg your indulgence, but feel I need to draw together two important strands from the main body and Addendum C, which will make the Review's task a little easier. In this supplementary submission I address what are known as 'trend failures'. In considering this submission, I ask the Review to bear in mind that what I say applies equally to the Chinook HC Mk1 and Mk2. That is, the advent of the Mk2 did not wipe the slate clean on Mk1, as implied by MoD. (Letter D/Min(AF)/AI 4573/05/C/LN, dated 10 November 2005).

The possibility of a trend is considered upon two identical technical failures, although the MoD Technical Agency (TA, the named individual responsible for maintaining the build standard, a prerequisite to airworthiness) is expected to apply engineering judgment. If the failure is related to a safety critical component, where failure can be catastrophic, in theory an immediate investigation commences. Complex statistical analysis can be brought to bear, but the nature of Defence aircraft equipment (low volume, high risk, high impact) requires, above all else, the application of engineering judgment and sound decision making, born of practical experience. This must be allied to the ability to take immediate action; facilitated through continuous, adequate Post Design Services tasking. These attributes and requirements are no longer available in MoD to a satisfactory level. My main submission addresses this in detail.

However, the term can also be applied to failures of process or procedure. In this context the systemic airworthiness failings confirmed by Mr Haddon-Cave QC, and first reported on Chinook in 1985 (see Addendum C). Again, in practice, identification of such trends often falls to Technical Agencies - it is they who deal with higher level airworthiness problems on a daily basis.

The purpose of this supplementary submission is to draw the Review's attention to these trends and, by means of Ministerial correspondence, demonstrate they have been consistently denied by MoD, to the detriment of aviation safety; ultimately contributing to loss of life.

Submission

In 2005 I entered into correspondence with my MP (Mr Steve Webb) regarding Early Day Motion 651:

'MULL OF KINTYRE CHINOOK HELICOPTER CRASH

20 July 2005

Bellingham, Henry

That this House urges the Government to ensure that the Ministry of Defence revisits the issue of the Chinook helicopter crash on the Mull of Kintyre on 2 June 1994; notes that the General Assembly noted the findings of the Fatal Accident Inquiry held in Paisley, the Public Accounts Committee of the House of Commons and the House of Lords Select Committee, all of which rejected the findings of gross negligence by the RAF Board of Inquiry against flight lieutenants Jonathan Tapper and Richard Cook, and of the House of Commons Defence Select Committee; supports the General Assembly's pastoral concern for all the families affected by the accident; recognises that the RAF's rules on fatal accidents have subsequently been changed, such that the Chinook pilots would not have been blamed after their deaths; and calls on the Government to overturn the verdict of gross negligence ascribed to the deceased pilots in the 11th year following the accident'.

I cited several verifiable incidents which indicated both systemic airworthiness failings and trend failures that had not been addressed.

In his initial response (D/Min(AF)/AI 4573/05/C/LN, dated 10 November 2005), Min(AF) Mr Adam Ingram stated my evidence could only be used to challenge the Reviewing Officers' ruling if it *'related to the aircraft concerned'* (ZD576). This contradicted MoD's own policy regarding trend failures, fault reporting, investigation and corrective action. In adopting this line, Mr Ingram/MoD disregarded historical evidence gleaned from 14 years of Chinook operations.

An analogy here is car manufacturers issuing recall notices. If a trend is identified, and it adversely affects safety, a recall notice is issued to have vehicles checked. They expect some cars, but not all, to have developed the problem; but the primary aim is to prevent occurrence or recurrence across the fleet. Evidence of absence in a given vehicle is not absence of evidence of a trend failure. Users must still be warned. Similarly, if a failing cannot be proven on ZD576 due, mainly, to the physical evidence being destroyed by impact and fire, that does not mean there was no such failure.

This was pointed out to Mr Ingram in a letter dated 25 November 2005. He replied on 21 June 2006 (D/Min(AF)/AI 5909/05/L/is):

> 'Mr Hill claims that his earlier letter indicated trend faults and that these demand investigation. He will be aware the MoD had, and continues to have, a robust airworthiness regulatory framework that mandates the need to regularly review faults for trends, which are highlighted by a variety of reports, and takes necessary investigative and corrective action. The accident investigation at the time and subsequent reviews will have examined the fleet fault trends evidence pertinent to ZD576; it is a routine activity for any accident investigation. Furthermore, it will certainly have examined the recent history of the aircraft for faults that might indicate a broader or more involved problem that may have contributed to the accident. However, the issues Mr Hill has raised do not in themselves demonstrate a trend, rather they are a catalogue of individual unrelated incidents, which each would need to be further examined to understand if they were part of a trend.'

The main body of my report discusses this in the context of MoD cutting the funding for this activity, conducted under Post Design Services. However, at time of writing no new or independent evidence (i.e. from sources other than myself) was available to add to what MoD had rejected, despite the 'old' evidence being compelling. The revelation that is the 1992 Chinook Airworthiness Review Team (CHART) report (see my Addendum C) changes this position entirely. In effect, it lists a raft of trend failures, primarily related to Undemanded Flight Control Movements (UFCM), Flight Control components and Quality Control, and provides evidence of systemic airworthiness failings.

Mr Ingram's claims were later proven to be without foundation - as reported by Mr Haddon-Cave QC. While the Secretary of State and MoD accepted the Nimrod Review report *in toto*, no action was taken to ascertain why MoD staff were permitted to consistently mislead successive Ministers - actions that demonstrably cost lives. Nor is it clear if these staff remain in post. This casual acceptance, by both MoD and Ministers, that one can continue to mislead the other without fear of censure is itself a serious breach of any Safety Management System, and an abrogation of duty of care; breeding a culture where the inevitable consequence is preventable deaths of Servicemen. My view is this - MoD has been found so terribly wrong on the overarching subject (airworthiness) that this must cast doubt on the validity of its claims regarding ZD576.

Mr Ingram makes a further claim, that the ZD576 Board of Inquiry and all subsequent Inquiries examined Chinook fault trends. May I respectfully suggest the Mull of Kintyre Review verify this claim, as it would appear the Board did not see what would have been primary evidence of both systemic airworthiness failings and trend failures - the CHART report.

Furthermore, Mr Ingram claims MoD *'takes necessary investigative and corrective action'* on any trend failures. This cannot be reconciled with the fact that, in 1990, trend analysis tasks at PDS Contractors were cancelled as a 'savings measure'. My report cites one example - smoke in Lynx cockpits, whereby three incidents occurred and the Air Station was forced to make direct contact with the MoD Technical Agency (myself), as their normal route (through their Engineering Authority) was compromised; the latter having been advised to curtail submitting Requests for Fault Investigation. This was a typical example of what Mr Haddon-Cave referred to as sacrificing safety to save money.

Nor can Mr Ingram's claims be reconciled with the CHART report. He was misled by omission. Perhaps the Review would care to ask Mr Ingram, and other Ministers who have been similarly misled, if they would have maintained the same stance on ZD576 had they known of CHART.

What remains wholly unsatisfactory from this exchange of correspondence is this. Following my reply of 20 July 2006, refuting Mr Ingram's claims, he replied to my MP on 25 August 2006, stating:

'Mr Hill has raised a number of difficult technical issues and it will therefore take some time to research and answer the points he made'.

Mr Ingram eventually replied on 17 May 2007, merely repeating the previous claims, and stating that the MoD's airworthiness regulations were:

'Applied robustly and I have no reason to believe that these principles were not applied with similar vigour during the period immediately preceding the (ZD576) accident'. And, 'There is no direct evidence that the application of airworthiness procedures in respect of Chinook Mk2 were not adhered to'.

The Review will note:

1. The inordinate time taken to reply to the raising of very serious safety issues. In the interim, on September 2006 Nimrod XV230 had crashed. But nine months after the crash, when it was clear airworthiness failings had contributed, Mr Ingram denied there was a problem.

2. The implication MoD no longer had staff who could answer the simple questions I posed. That is, there was a loss of corporate knowledge, a fundamental component of airworthiness. Yet MoD insists it remains undiminished.

3. In direct contradiction of Mr Ingram's final claim, the evidence of extensive and serious airworthiness failings was noted by the ZD576 Board of Inquiry. While they did not use the term 'airworthiness', it was clear to all concerned that this was what was being discussed.

If the ZD576 Board of Inquiry was unaware of the CHART report, then it may be it dismissed the evidence of airworthiness failings as minor or isolated (despite obviously being systemic). However, if it sighted the CHART report and ignored its detail, then one might view that as negligence, as any reasonable person would immediately see the significance of past Chinook accidents having been attributed to airworthiness failings.

Most importantly, in the light of subsequent events (fatal accidents), if the Board did not see the CHART report, who decided to withhold this key evidence? MoD cannot claim it was in the past and irrelevant, as Mr Ingram states (this time correctly) that Boards are <u>required</u> to assess such evidence.

Moreover, since the accident, and in attempts to justify the Reviewing Officers' decision, MoD has consistently adopted the line that evidence of no subsequent failures is evidence of no prior failures. (Noting there *is* evidence of subsequent failures; in fact, an Aldergrove Chinook experienced an Undemanded Flight Control Movement shortly after the accident). Again, this is illogical, in addition to being contrary to MoD's own safety regulations. Yet, this reactive approach to safety and risk management is precisely what has become the norm in MoD - again through financial 'savings' being made at the expense of safety. In effect, MoD policy became: *Ignore the risk/hazard, let's wait to see if a problem occurs*. I would respectfully ask the Review to disregard such a line of argument; instead asking why a proactive approach was not taken, and why evidence (e.g. the CHART report) of prior accidents being attributed to systemic airworthiness failings and trend failures was not taken into account by the Board and Reviewing Officers; and MoD hierarchy as a whole.

I believe the CHART report fatally undermines MoD's entire case.

In summary, there exists clear evidence of trend failures which, given normal levels of funding and the application of mandated procedures, would have identified serious shortcomings in flight safety critical Chinook components - years before the accident. As funding was denied, implementation failed, meaning the aims of the Safety Management System could not be met.

What is perhaps worse is that, over many years, MoD staff have consistently misled Ministers on this subject. One cannot ignore the fact that, had the truth been told, systemic failings would have been identified, corrective action initiated and lives saved. The Nimrod Review would have been unnecessary. This failure is inexcusable and, recently, the new Min(AF) has been invited to consider whether the system whereby MoD staff advise him is sufficiently independent and honest. That is for Ministers to address. I merely note that misleading Ministers is a serious breach of the Civil Service Code.

Supplementary Submission #2

30 April 2011

Mr Alex Passa,

Secretary, Mull of Kintyre Review,

1 Melville Crescent,

Edinburgh EH3 7HW

(For the attention of The Right Honourable the Lord Philip)

Dear Mr Passa,

<u>Mull of Kintyre Review</u>

You will be aware I submitted an Addendum C to my report in January this year, analysing the main body of the Chinook Airworthiness Review Team (CHART) report of August 1992, which confirmed systemic airworthiness failings in the RAF. Along with the Chief of Defence Procurement's admission to the Public Accounts Committee in March 1999 that the failings remained extant, this constitutes vital evidence covering the years before and after the loss of ZD576, and encompasses other fatal losses. Thus, refuting MoD's claim that the Chinook had an impeccable safety record - a cornerstone of its 'defence'.

I have now been supplied, under Freedom of Information, the complete report, including Annexes A-O and Enclosures 1-9; but not the Distribution List.

This last is of vital import. The RAF Chief Engineer's letters of airworthiness delegation to his engineering staff did not delegate organisational or management issues. (I have already supplied you with a sample letter, signed in January 1992). This is normal. The intent is to force a system whereby such serious failings are delegated upwards. A single officer with delegation may notice a problem with his aircraft or equipment (and may even be able to correct it), but have no visibility of, or control over, others. Thus, the problem may be isolated to his aircraft, or may be systemic. In matters affecting aviation safety, one must assume the worst case until proven otherwise, so upward delegation is the means of initiating corrective action at the appropriate level.

As the RAF Chief Engineer was a member of the Air Force Board, and ultimately responsible for RAF engineering procedures and standards of the time, Lord Philip will no doubt wish to ascertain whether or not the systemic failings recorded in the CHART report were correctly delegated (upwards), assessed, what rectification action was ordered, and when. His first port of call should be the CHART Distribution List. You will be aware my Addendum C includes a Cross Reference Index of the primary failings noted by CHART, mapping them to the mandated regulations. I also noted that the RAF's immediate reaction to CHART was to further slash airworthiness funding, actively preventing any corrective action. I believe this, and other vital information, to have been withheld from the CHART leader. I ask the Review to consider these facts and read the CHART report. The Annexes are even more disturbing than the main body.

Should you require further details or written evidence of the above, please do not hesitate to contact me.

Supplementary e-mail 3 May 2011

Dear Mr Passa,

Forgive this further e-mail, but I should have included this point in the letter I sent on 30 April (attached again for your convenience). This note raises serious questions regarding fundamental airworthiness principles.

The 1992 CHART report notes, at Annex C, that the <u>RAF were forced to use ex-Argentinian Aircraft Technical Publications (ATPs), because they contained more accurate detail than our UK versions</u>, facilitating vital repairs at Second Line. Given the importance of these Publications, warranting their own Chapter (6) in JSP553 (Military Airworthiness Regulations), this raises several points:

- Who authorised their use?
- What nature did this authorisation take? A Quality Assurance concession? For how long? Was it periodically reviewed? Were complementary MF765s (Unsatisfactory Feature Reports) raised and were they actioned?
- Was the Aircraft Design Authority's advice sought (Boeing Helicopters)? Or that of our own ATP specialists?
- Were they validated and verified in accordance with our own MoD regulations? That is, was it confirmed that these Argentinian ATPs reflected our UK build standard? If not, then there would be no traceability to the Safety Case, and hence the Release to Service, which must include a list of approved aircraft publications.
- What follow-up action was taken, post-CHART, to ascertain how widespread this practice was in the RAF? This is important, because the CHART was under severe time constraint and directed to interview only certain staffs at each Station. That is, it is only by chance they spotted this Argentinian factor.

Please note, MoD will again try to claim CHART applies only to Chinook HC Mk1. It does not. CHART's terms of reference specifically address Mk2. That being so, the question is - *Was the Mk2 suite of publications accurate and valid at time of Release to Service?* The answer is an emphatic <u>NO</u>, evidenced by witnesses at both the Board of Inquiry and Fatal Accident Inquiry. Again, this raises a question mark over what information was withheld from these Inquiries, and what their reaction would have been had they known.

I submit that the above questions are crucial to understanding the organisational faults extant in the MoD and, particularly, the RAF at the time. As you know, I can answer some of the questions from the perspective of my responsibilities at the time. The RAF's immediate response to CHART was to further cut airworthiness funding. At the time of issue (August 1992) Technical Agencies (named individuals having airworthiness delegation) were under instructions <u>not</u> to progress MF765 Unsatisfactory Feature Reports. Funding was withheld to stop us disobeying, which we did whenever we could (in order to meet our higher airworthiness obligation to the Secretary of State, and our duty of care). That a system can place staffs in such a position is the key evidence highlighting organisational fault.

Supplementary Submission #3

14 May 2011
Mr Alex Passa,
Mull of Kintyre Review,
1, Melville Crescent,
Edinburgh EH3 7HW
(For the attention of The Right Honourable the Lord Philip)

Dear Mr Passa,

<u>Mull of Kintyre Review - Chinook Airworthiness Review Team report</u>

On 10 November 2010 I submitted a report for consideration, adding three Addenda on 25 January 2011 and Supplementary Submissions on 8 February 2011 and 30 April. All were presented in such a way each remained valid in its own right.

I have now been able to review the complete Chinook Airworthiness Review Team (CHART) report of August 1992, including the covering Loose Minute written by the Director of Flight Safety (RAF). I am informed this Loose Minute, in the form of an Executive Summary, was not prepared by the report's author (Wing Commander D C Denham) but by Director Flight Safety himself (Air Commodore M J Abbott). I enclose the report on CD-R. For your convenience, each part is a separate .pdf file, numbered sequentially.

This Loose Minute ends speculation as to who initially saw CHART when Director Flight Safety issued it on 14 August 1992. It was sent to the RAF Chief Engineer, Air Chief Marshal Sir Michael Alcock, and the Assistant Chief of the Air Staff (ACAS), Air Vice Marshal Anthony Bagnall. ACAS received CHART on his first day in post. Once and for all, this demonstrates his prior knowledge of (a) ongoing airworthiness failings in the Chinook fleet, and (b) wider systemic failings. Yet, demonstrably, he issued a non-compliant Release to Service. It is central to this case that the reasoning be established.

If I may, a few brief points:

1. In anticipation that MoD and/or retired senior staff claim CHART applies only to Chinook HC Mk1, may I draw your attention to the Terms of Reference which specifically call for a wide-ranging report,

not necessarily exclusive to Chinook. Also, they do not differentiate between Mk1 and Mk2, referring to the 'Chinook Programme'. Any confusion as to applicability would have been allayed by Director Flight Safety's final sentence:

'The current organisational structure for tasking and fleet management, and the lack of resources, are not a healthy recipe for the future sound airworthiness of the Chinook'.

2. The Terms of Reference make clear the need to address configuration control issues for Mk2. This is crucial to your deliberations given the accident history of RAF Chinooks in 1993. If an aircraft or equipment is not under configuration control, then the Safety Cases become progressively invalid. CHART opens with the statement that previous Chinook crashes (some fatal) were caused solely by airworthiness failings, specifically configuration control. You are already aware MoD and Ministers have constantly denied any configuration control problems on Chinook. (Letter D/Min(AF)/AI 4573/05/C/LN dated 10 November 2005 from Mr Adam Ingram). CHART exposes this deceit.

3. At the time of the original ZD576 Inquiries, Chinook had an appalling history. It is highly disingenuous to claim, as MoD has consistently done, that the Mk1 and Mk2 aircraft are completely different. The Mk2 retains much of the Mk1 design. Importantly, the MoD and Industrial organisations responsible for safety, airworthiness and support remained the same, except their activities had been curtailed by financial savings made at the expense of safety - as confirmed by Mr Haddon-Cave.

Should MoD claim these failings were corrected in time for Mk2, then I respectfully suggest the Review considers this:

- The Chief of Defence Procurement confirmed the headline problem was extant on Chinook, when giving evidence to the Public Accounts Committee on 3 March 1999.

- The overarching control mechanisms in MoD (primarily HQ Modification Committees and Technical Agency posts) were progressively disbanded in the early 1990s, concurrent with successive cuts exceeding 25% per year to associated funding. (As reported to Mr Haddon-Cave and confirmed by CHART).

- The immediate reaction to CHART, in late 1992, was to order further cuts to the centralised function in MoD (i.e. Post Design Services) whose sole role was to maintain build standards.

- Even if a decision was made to resurrect the build standards and provide the necessary resources recommended by CHART (and the evidence shows it was not, at this time), the way in which the MoD financial planning system operated would have precluded availability of funding until late 1994. In simple terms, August 1992 was too late to run an Alternative Assumption for LTC93. A bid would have to be made in the LTC94 Main Assumptions (Feb/Mar 93) which, if approved, would release funding about 15 months later. Quite apart from this aspect, the 12 years of neglect reported by CHART simply could not be resurrected before November 1993 (when the Release to Service was issued). It would take longer than that to scope the extent of the problem, never mind agree a strategy and costs, negotiate contracts and deliver. My main submission notes the Chief of Defence Logistics' staff were still actively preventing this basic airworthiness work being conducted in the late 1990s. Related to this, it is important to note that Controller Aircraft, Sir Donald Spiers, was never notified of CHART. As the head of the MoD(PE) organisation (Air Systems Controllerate) responsible for delivering many airworthiness components, this is an extraordinary omission.

Notably, other Airworthiness Review Teams were set up, including the NART (Nimrod), which in July 1998 reported precisely the same range of failings as CHART did six years earlier, and made similar recommendations. Revealingly, Mr Haddon-Cave notes:

'These concerns and warnings in the NART report were dismissed at the time as uninformed, crew-room level, emotive comment lacking substantive evidence and focus.' (Nimrod Review, paragraph 13.4)

Such failures do not happen overnight. They accumulate over time. NART is evidence of systemic failings continuing throughout the 1990s. This is the fatal error in the Nimrod Review - the problems are correctly reported but the timescale is entirely wrong, as evidenced by CHART and my submission. Crucially, the evidence that concerns and warnings were dismissed is entirely consistent with what was happening elsewhere in MoD at the same time, and throughout the previous 15 years. Warnings from staff directly involved in practical airworthiness assurance were dismissed out of hand and, ultimately, they were disciplined for persisting. For example: D/DHP/71/1/5/2 dated 4 June 1998, warning that Critical Design Reviews were being waived and paid off, leaving safety critical problems on helicopters. (Note - same Directorate as Chinook). Also, the SR(S) 6131 Risk Register (Risk #11) notes that DGAS2 (Nimrod,

Chinook 2 Star in MoD(PE)) was notified on 27 January 1998 of the inability of *'over-worked, stressed staff* (with airworthiness delegation) *to undertake even routine tasks'* due to resource cuts and abrogation by other departments.

Now that the Review knows who received a copy of CHART, I believe it imperative their involvement (and that of their superiors) in subsequent events be assessed, especially regarding:

1. Releasing the immature Mk2 to service.

2. Withholding CHART from Controller Aircraft, the Chinook Project Director, the Board of Inquiry and other Inquiries.

3. Advising Ministers, over many years, that the problems highlighted in CHART did not exist.

4. Taking a public stance (e.g. letters to the press) against the pilots.

I believe the Review should establish what action was directed and taken (not necessarily the same thing) post-CHART. In his Nimrod Review (paragraph 13.124), Mr Haddon-Cave describes this as the *'golden period'* of airworthiness. Not according to the RAF's Director of Flight Safety. What action did the Chief Engineer and ACAS take? Was the content of CHART reported to the Chief of the Air Staff, Air Chief Marshal Sir Peter Harding, or his successor, Air Chief Marshal Sir Michael Graydon? From my perspective, as an avionics/aircraft project manager in MoD at the time, holding airworthiness, technical and financial delegation, I cannot answer these questions. But I have already offered irrefutable evidence that the practical impact at my working level was further financial cuts, the disbandment of the very committees responsible for technical and financial oversight, and non-engineering staff being permitted to overrule our engineering design and safety decisions. To such an extent that our work dried up and we were forced to seek other posts. Throughout the period 1988-2001, the systemic failings reported by CHART remained extant. In fact, got progressively worse, culminating in Director General Air Systems 2 and the Chief of Defence Procurement, a mere few months after NART, ruling it a disciplinary offence to disobey an order to ignore the regulations.

Supplementary Submission #4

(Text of e-mail 17 June 2011 12:55)

Dear Alex,

I am aware the Review must be winding down. However, evidence has come to my attention which I believe vital to understanding the sheer immaturity of the Chinook HC Mk2 in June 1994, and which supports issues discussed in my submission.

I attach the notes of a meeting held at Boscombe Down on 25 May 1994, discussing FADEC safety critical software. For convenience, I also enclose the minutes of a previous meeting held in the USA in January 1994. You will see that, at the meeting of 25 May, Colonel Hodgkiss' predecessor (Captain Brougham, RN) used the phrase 'INTERIM CAR'. Also, the Assistant Chief of the Air Staff (ACAS - Air Vice Marshal Bagnall), the signatory of the Release to Service (and recipient of CHART), used the term; and, one assumes, understood its meaning. What is missing is an explanation why ACAS had to seek a further INTERIM CAR. The inference I draw is that the existing one, signed by Controller Aircraft (Sir Donald Spiers) on 9 November 1993, was time-limited and about to expire. Ergo, so too was the Release to Service. This implies a formal process, or at least one agreed between Sir Donald and Air Vice Marshal Bagnall. Again, we return to the issue of the regulations requiring formal correspondence between both. Yet MoD claims none can be found.

Has the Review explored this aspect? I consider is vital because, as you know, 'INTERIM' is defined as Switch-On Only clearance, and aircrew are not permitted to rely on any system in any way whatsoever. The status of the entire Navigation System was 'INTERIM', precluding flight in Instrument Meteorological Conditions; negating the cornerstone of MoD's case. (Most of the Communications System had the same status, but as the intercom was not even permitted in the aircraft, none of the comms could be used). These facts were withheld from Inquiries, and I view the subsequent dissembling as evidence senior staff recognised the weakness of their case.

Tragically, this debate was ongoing only a few days before the accident, with further meetings scheduled after 2 June 1994. This is not a minor modification or routine 'Development Event' being discussed here. The notes of 25 May make it clear FADEC has not been approved, and could never be approved in its current state. Above all else, one must ask how, under these circumstances, a Certificate of Design could exist for the safety critical software. If there is no valid Certificate, then it cannot be released to service. In fact, it would take a major concession on behalf of Boscombe to allow it in their trials aircraft. This reinforces the fact that the Mk2 was not adequately mature at the time, its status being that of an aircraft in development, lacking the Technical or Systems Integration maturity necessary to enter production - never mind Service.

This is not just my opinion, but regulations laid down by Ministers based on the advice of the Chief Scientific Officer; and reinforced (at the time) in Controller Aircraft Instructions, which project managers were required to implement. This entire saga reeks of systemic failure to implement these regulations, all to the detriment of aircrew who rely entirely on staff doing so. This is the detail Mr Haddon-Cave chose not to publish.

In summary, the existence of these critical Safety Risks and Hazards make it impossible to say the pilots were grossly negligent and solely to blame. It is further evidence of serious organisational fault.

I would be grateful if you could acknowledge receipt and confirm this has been placed before the Review.

Bibliography [B#]

Except were annotated *'Available from MoD'*, the following documents were provided on CD-ROM to the Mull of Kintyre Review. It is beyond the scope of this book to include them - they form 482MB of data and thousands of pages. However, many are downloadable and the narrative of the submission includes the relevant extracts.

1. The Nimrod Review.
2. Controller Aircraft Release, at INTERIM Issue & Amendment 1 (March 1994).
3. Release to Service, at INTERIM Issue 1 & Amendment 1 (March 1994) - including Cover Sheet issued by ACAS November 1993.
4. ZD576 Board of Inquiry Report.
5. The Macdonald Report (2000) & Technical Addendum (2009).
6. MoD Airworthiness, Design Requirements and Procedures (ADRP) Course - Application of Technical Procedures (November 1993 / April 1994).
7. JSP553 - Military Airworthiness Regulations. (Available from MoD).
8. Compendium of Guidelines for Project Managers. (Available from MoD).
9. Defence Standard 05-123 - Technical Procedures for the Procurement of Aircraft, Weapons and Electronic Systems. (Available from MoD).
10. Defence Standard 05-124 - Technical Procedures for the Procurement of Aircraft Engines and their Accessories. (Available from MoD).
11. Defence Standard 05-125/2 - Technical Procedures for Post Design Services, incorporating PDS Specifications 1-20. (Available from MoD).
12. Defence Standard 00-970 - Design and Airworthiness Requirements for Service Aircraft. (Available from MoD).
13. Defence Council Instruction GEN 89/1993 - Airworthiness Responsibility for UK Military Aircraft (incorporated in Item 6).
14. DUS(DP)/924/11/2/9 dated 14 December 1989 - Joint MoD(PE) / Industry Computing Policy for Military Operational Systems.
15. D/MAP/12/20B-38 Issue 3 dated November 1993 - Application of

Technical Procedures (incorporated in Item 6).

16. Letter reference RTSA RW/11/5/3 dated 8 March 2010.

17. Letter reference D/Min(AF)/AI MC06559/2006 dated 17 May 2007, from Mr Adam Ingram when Minister for the Armed Forces.

18. Ministerial Correspondence/Brief Ref 2214/2003 dated 23 April 2003.

19. A&AEE PE/Chinook/40 APF/246/011/1 dated July 1993 - Chinook HC Mk1- Assessment of T55-L-712F FADEC.

20. A&AEE AEN/58/119(H) dated 18 August 1993 - Chinook HC Mk2 - Status of Engine FADEC Software.

21. A&AEE AEN/58/119(H) dated 27 August 1993 -Task E1536 - Chinook HC Mk2 - CA Release Trials.

22. A&AEE Letter Report TM 2174, incorporating Letter Report E989 and PE/Chinook/40 dated September 1993 - Chinook HC Mk1 Assessment of T55-L-712F FADEC.

23. A&AEE AEN/58/119(H) dated 30 September 1993 - Chinook Mk2 - T55 Engine FADEC Software.

24. A&AEE AAD/308/04 dated 12 October 1993 - Chinook Mk2 - CAR for T55 FADEC.

25. A&AEE AMS 8H/05, Letter Report AMS 107/93 dated 15 October 1993 - Chinook HC Mk2 - INTERIM CA Release Recommendations - Navigation Systems.

26. A&AEE Letter Report NR 108/93, AMS 8H/05 dated 19 October 1993 - INTERIM CA Release Recommendations for Communication Systems of the Chinook HC Mk2.

27. A&AEE Letter Report PE/Chinook/41, APF/247/Annex dated 22 October 1993 - Chinook HC Mk2 - INTERIM CA Release Recommendations.

28. A&AEE AEN 58/012 dated 26 October 1993 - Engineering Systems Division letter Report E1109 Chinook HC Mk2 - INTERIM CA Release.

29. A&AEE - Annex A to Letter Report TM2210 dated 26 October 1993 - Chinook HC Mk2 - Document in the form of an INTERIM CA Release.

30. Extract from memo from Captain M Brougham RN, AD/HP1.

31. AD/HP1 Textron Visit Report 21 January 1994.

32. MoD reasons why A&AEE stopped flying - Fax dated 15 September

1996.

33. Table of Service Deviations at 2 June 1994, produced after the event.

34. D/DIA/5/295/10 dated 27 June 1996 'Audit Report - Requirement Scrutiny'.

35. National Audit Office (NAO) report 'Accepting Equipment Off-Contract and In to Service' dated 11 February 2000.

36. DM87 - Notification to THESBAC.

37. MoD letter MSU/04/07/03/01/cc dated 11 May 2010 to Dr Susan Phoenix.

38. Letter D/DHP/HP1/4/1/4/1 dated 25 October 1995, to PL(LS) Legal Services and Sec(AS).

39. Racal RNS252 SuperTANS report.

40. Special Flying Instructions, including SFI(RAF)/Chinook/12 (UFCM).

41. Chinook HC Mk1 Release to Service (Part 1), marked up to illustrate differences between it and the Mk2 Release to Service.

42. Chinook HC Mk1 Release to Service (Part 2).

43. Chinook Airworthiness Review Team (CHART) Report D/IFS(RAF)/125/30/2/1 dated 7 August 1992, complete with Annexes and Enclosures.

44. Chinook ZA721 Military Aircraft Accident Summary dated 17 March 1989.

45. RAF Odiham Letter ODI/774/1/Eng dated 25 June 1985 to HQ Strike Command.

46. Notes of a T55-L-712F Engine FADEC Meeting held at A&AEE Boscombe Down on the 25 May 1994.

Glossary of Terms and Abbreviations

AAIB	Air Accidents Investigation Branch, at the time part of the Department of the Environment, Transport and the Regions, and from 1997 the Department for Transport.
A&AEE	Aeroplane and Armament Experimental Establishment (MoD(PE), Boscombe Down)
ACAS	Assistant Chief of the Air Staff (RAF 2 Star post)
AD/HP1	Assistant Director, Helicopter Projects 1, MoD(PE) Project Director for all Chinook and Lynx programmes, and from August 1997 Sea King, Helicopter Health and Usage Monitoring System, and Queen's Flight Replacement (VVIP).
ADA	Aircraft Design Authority. (Now erroneously termed 'Design Organisation' by MoD. This is an *accreditation*, whereas ADA, or the DA of an equipment, is an *appointment*).
ADS	Aircraft Document Set
AEW	Airborne Early Warning
AFCS	Automatic/Advanced Flight Control System
Altitude	Above Mean Sea Level
AM	Aircrew Manual
AML	Air Member Logistics (formed April 1994)
AMSO	Air Member Supply and Organisation (RAF, preceded AML)
AOC	Air Officer Commanding
AOC-in-C	Air Officer Commanding-in-Chief
AP	Air Publication
APM	Aircraft Project Manager
ASaC	Airborne Surveillance and Control
ATP	Air(craft) Technical Publications
CAI	Controller Aircraft Instructions (Replaced AvP 88)
CA(PE)	Controller Aircraft (Procurement Executive) (in the context of Forms such as Certificate of Design CA(PE) 100)

CAR	Controller Aircraft Release.
CDP	Chief of Defence Procurement
CHART	Chinook Airworthiness Review Team (and its report)
DASH	Differential Airspeed Hold
DECU	EMC-32T Digital Engine Control Unit, part of FADEC.
DGAS2	Director General Air Systems 2, in MoD(PE) - 2 Star post.
DHP	Director(ate) of Helicopter Projects, MoD(PE)
EMC	Electro-Magnetic Compatibility
FADEC	Full Authority Digital Engine Control
FRC	Flight Reference Cards
GPS	Global Positioning System
HaveQuick	A frequency hopping anti-jamming system for UHF radios, providing Transmission Security (TRANSEC).
Height	Above Ground Level
HF	Human Factors or High Frequency (2-30MHz HF radio)
IPT	Integrated Project Team
JSP	Joint Service Publication
LRU	Line Replaceable Unit
MALPAS	Malvern Program Analysis Suite, developed at RSRE Malvern
MoD(PE)	Ministry of Defence (Procurement Executive), often just PE.
ODM	Operating Data Manual
PDS	Post Design Services
RAF	Royal Air Force
RNS	Racal Navigation System (as in RNS252)
RTS	Release to Service
RTSA	Release to Service Authority
SATCOM	Satellite Communications
SCDA	System Co-ordinating Design Authority
SD	Service Deviation
SFI	Special Flying Instruction
SI	Servicing Instruction

SOIU	Statement of Operating Intent and Usage
STI	Special Technical Instruction
STF	Special Trials Fit
TANS	Tactical Navigation System
TRT	Turn Round Time
UHF	Ultra High Frequency (225-399.975 MHz in this context).
UFCM	Undemanded Flight Control Movement (sometimes Uncommanded/Flying)
Validation	'Have we built the right system?'
Verification	'Have we built the system right?'
VHF	Very High Frequency (30-173.975 MHz, with some bands receive-only).

END of Submission to the Mull of Kintyre Review

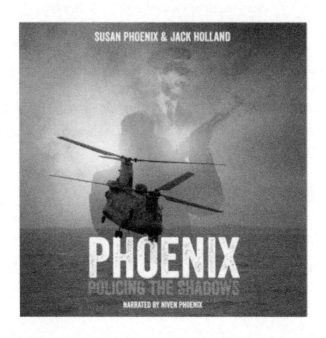

Phoenix is the true story of intrigue, danger and family loyalty centred within the Northern Ireland Troubles. This is the voice of Detective Superintendent Ian Phoenix and his dedicated journey from paratrooper to police officer. IRA assassinations, covert police and SAS operations, with booby-trap bombers and snipers making the rules of the era.

This audio version, narrated by Ian's son, Niven, continues to intrigue and inform listeners about a very different life in Northern Ireland, as it was during the troubles. The family's lives were wrapped in danger too, but cocooned in love and sustained by Irish humour in an outdoor lifestyle, surrounding their wild coastal home.

Hearing his son's voice read his father's words is nostalgic. It has recaptured a richness to those years in spite of the danger under which the family lived. It provides meat to the anonymous bones of normal life during the Irish "Troubles". Phoenix ultimately describes the disastrous killing of 29 good people in a military helicopter crash that has never been adequately investigated or explained.

Printed in Great Britain
by Amazon

37967195R00145